Tony R. Kitchens

CONTENTS

FOREWORD

By Anthony Ricardo Caradine-Kitchens, son

There are a lot of ways I can describe my dad. He loves his family more than anything, he always tries to help others in need, and from what I've seen, he's never let even the most unbearable pain stop him from fulfilling his duty as a business owner, son or father. For the seventeen years that I've known him, even when times seemed tough, I've never felt like any problem was too big for us to handle. I don't know how he does it, but even when I've felt so defeated that I couldn't get up, he somehow helped me look at the big picture and get back on my feet.

Not only have I seen how he's helped me, but I've witnessed him act as the pillar of our family. For as long as I remember, I've viewed Papa as a leader in our family, even when I wasn't old enough to know what a leader truly was. I know he doesn't like to talk about it, but I know he's really made an amazing difference in a lot of people's lives. Sometimes it's like he just gives and gives without worrying about what happens to him after. I don't just mean monetarily, but as a friend and mentor as well.

I can't count the times that I've heard him on the phone giving one of his spontaneous TED Talks to whoever is on the other end. Just when I think I've heard all the wisdom and knowledge that he has to give, he surprises me with even more. There is just so much life experience that he's shared that really makes me wonder how I got such a special dad. I must've been the luckiest child in the world to have a dad who tells me he loves me every day and has made an effort to be there for me my entire life. I really hope that someday, not too long from now, I can find a way to truly thank him for all the things he's done. I also hope that with this book he's poured so much time into, he can help others stand up and learn from their pain.

Anthony Ricardo Caradine-Kitchens

INTRODUCTION: NO PAIN? NO GAIN.

How does an average boy from the South Side of Chicago, whose father only had a third-grade education, grow a business from zero to more than $100 million, all before the age of 50?

Let me start at the beginning before I give you the answer. As children, we had hopes, dreams and even places we escaped to in our minds to ease the pain of our circumstances. As a child, I dreamed of having enough money and freedom to take care of myself and my family. I couldn't wait to be able to buy my parents the house they dreamed of. I fantasized about the cars I wanted but enjoyed only in the pages of magazines. I wanted to buy the gym shoes I saw athletes wearing in Sports Illustrated magazine, not the generic ones my parents bought because those were all they could afford.

At some point, life tends to get in the way of our dreams and plans, and they seem nearly impossible to realize. While dreaming of the good things, we don't know how suddenly the realities of life can extinguish those flames (or at the very least dim them). The difference between childhood and adulthood is simply the passing of time and the experiences we go through during that period. Do our dreams have to die? As adults, why don't we dream like we did as children?

Is it irresponsible to imagine being someplace or someone other than where you are or who you are today?

As we get older, we have experiences that cause us enough pain that we avoid the free-spirited, anything-is-possible dreams we once had. Many times, our dreams are not only for us but for others we hoped to help. None of us chooses the circumstances we were born into. None of us could know how good or bad they were until we were old enough to feel the joy or pain that life would bring. When times were good, we hoped they lasted forever; when they were bad, we did everything we could to escape them.

We have all found ways to avoid pain, to ease its sting, to quickly move past it and to warn others about it. We shy away from risk and gravitate toward the stability of working for others and enjoying life through the glamorous photos and captions others post on social media. We wonder why others seem to be living the life we dreamed about years ago and quickly conclude that they didn't have it as bad as we did. We soothe ourselves thinking that luck and fortune put others in the places we wanted to be. Subconsciously and consciously, we make ourselves comfortable right where we are. We attract, pacify and nurture those inner voices that tell us we cannot achieve more because of race, social status, economics, government and many more things. We relinquish the power we had as children to dare to think past the present to imagine what could be. Seeing others as deserving, we blame ourselves for not taking advantage of the time and opportunities we were presented earlier in life.

We all do it. Be honest: How many times have you

said or thought to yourself, "if I could go back, I would," or "if somebody would have told me then, I would do things differently?"

Be honest: How many times have you said or thought to yourself, *If I could go back, I would, or if somebody would have told me then, I would do things differently?*

You are not alone, and it is not too late. There is a difference between those who advance and those who do not. I don't think we are born with this special trait; I believe it is a skill that is learned and practiced many times over. It's something that we don't want to get comfortable with or used to. Even the strongest among us feel it differently each time we experience it. You can change your life today if you are able to identify, evaluate, and proceed with faith and confidence that you can get to the other side of it, even if you don't know the steps involved to do so.

What am I talking about? My friends, it's PAIN. Pain asks a lot of us. It demands a high price, but on the other side of pain is where you want to go. The question you must answer is this: Will you settle for average to avoid pain, or get familiar with it and develop the skills needed to overcome it?

In every aspect of life, in every venture, success comes when you can recognize the gifts that adversity and pain can bring. Successful people share a few common experiences. They all failed at a certain point and all eventually got back up.

Just look at the struggles faced by businesspeople and celebrities when their pain has been on full display for the world to witness. People love a good comeback story and seem to embrace people even more after hearing what they overcame to achieve a new level of success. Think about people who lose all their worldly possessions and build an even greater life afterward, or beat addiction and become one of the best actors in Hollywood, or recover from a potentially career-ending injury only to reach a new zenith in their athletic careers. What do they have that you don't?

They're all willing to embrace their pain because they have mental toughness. This is a mindset that all of us can develop. You must change yours to believe you can do anything you dream of. You must shut out the negative images and stories that live rent-free in your head. You must have the heart to take risks. You must look past your current circumstances and tell your mind to push through; you must force your body to do uncomfortable things in order to get the results you want.

Mental toughness isn't a secret superpower that only celebrities have. I believe with my entire being that anything another person can do, I can do. You have the power to coordinate the forces of your heart, mind, spirit and body to achieve anything you want. The conviction to tell our minds that we can do so and the courage to speak these goals into existence determine the outcomes of our heart's desires.

Success requires coming to terms with pain.

Success requires coming to terms with pain. We must realize that there is pain associated with most things we do on a daily basis. If you don't show up at work today, you could lose your job, which will lead to pain.

If you start a business, you may have to work long hours, which you may view as pain as well. The question is, what is the best outcome of the two scenarios? Most everyone would agree that pushing through and going to work and even starting that business are the best options. There is a gift associated with the pain you may believe you would endure by working long hours: the pay you receive in exchange.

The pain principle applies here. Pursue your wildest dreams in the same manner. Understand that the best rewards in life come from pushing through difficult times and staying the course. Learn to look at each situation you find yourself in and find the upside, the blessing, the gift. Even in some of life's most painful experiences, like the death of a loved one, you can find life in the aftermath. You can learn lessons, experience positive changes and strengthen your faith and resolve.

I believe finding the gift of pain has been the key to unlocking success in my life. In this book, I share the story of how life knocked me down on many occasions, but each time, I got back up and said thank you for the pain. I found a way to use it as motivation to move forward. Each time I encountered pain, I developed a few more tools in my mind, body and spirit to confront, overcome and thrive in the face of adversity. The challenges you face are not there to destroy you; they are there to make you stronger. There are nearly eight billion people in the world today. You are not the only person in a bad situation or who has faced difficult times. Learn to lean into your pain rather than creating a bubble of protection or attracting sorrow and pity from others.

Henry Wadsworth Longfellow wrote a famous poem, "The Rainy Day", which contains the familiar line "Into every life a little rain must fall." The longer we live, the more likely it is that we will experience serious difficulties. Prepare yourself now to notice that your life is a compilation of past experiences that give you the tools to overcome the next, larger challenge. Be aware of how the challenges we faced in the past, as bad as they were, seem smaller than what we face today. At the same time, recognize that because of those previous challenges, you may have learned patience, compassion and other skills that will prepare you for the future. Learn to say thank you for the times in life when you experienced pain, because in those times, you were forced to learn, to grow, to have faith, to lean on others and to appreciate the simple things in life.

This is the gift of pain.

1: THE AVERAGE BOY NEXT DOOR

Montvale. The foundation, the lessons, the joy—and the place I visit whenever I go to Chicago. My neighborhood was just like every other one I saw through the backseat window of our car, as we passed by throughout my childhood. There may have been gangs, but you didn't see many visible signs of them. The only drug I had heard of was weed, and you knew when you were near it because of the deep outdoor smell, like someone burning leaves.

My family was my dad, my mom, my older sister Francine and me. Even though Fran was two years older than me, it felt so far ahead of where I'd be at that age. She had household responsibilities that I didn't yet and experienced things way before I did. I adored my older sister and remember how talented she was and still is today.

Our parents were regular people. My dad worked at Sears in the data processing department and my mom at Hyde Park Hospital, as an administrative support person for a surgical team. Our house was modest. Aside from the house, we had no other material possessions besides my father's Toyota Corolla and my mom's Chevy Celebrity. Our dog was a beautiful dark German shepherd named Lad. Lad's brother Butch lived at the house next to ours.

My father seemed to work all day, every day. He was either on second or third shift, so during school days, the only time we'd see him was during the five-minute car rides when he'd pick us up from school and drop us off at home before heading to work. My mom worked during the day and usually got home in the evening around 5 P.M.

The latchkey kid life

I'm sure we received the same speech as other kids, that between the time my dad dropped us off and my mom arrived at home, we better not be seen outside, even if the house was on fire. My father had spies lurking around, hiding in the bushes and under cars (at least, that's what it seemed like). Fran and I would hear about it from my mom if we were seen even standing at the front door, looking at our friends play in the streets. We later figured out that the snoopy neighbors were well-positioned, like military snipers with their targets in a triangulated kill zone. Our next-door neighbor named "Pops" was to our left, where Butch the dog lived. Mr. Sutherland was across the screen at the eleven o'clock position and Mr. Keith was across and down the street at the two o'clock position. My dad even set up claymores with tripwires in the back yard. Mr. Cox, across the alley behind us, was there to call in air support.

We were trapped in our own house, while all our friends were outside having fun. What seemed like hell was actually for our own good, but it didn't feel like that at the time. I remember feeling the lack of trust my parents had in us to be outside while they were away. Fran and I didn't know about the potential dangers of two young kids being at home alone. What we did know was that we wanted to go outside.

We wound up causing our parents stress because our only form of available entertainment was talking to friends on the house phone. Running up the phone bill was a bad thing, and we surely heard about it every month. Yep, the old-school house phone, without caller ID but with this long-coiled cord that nearly choked me to death many times while I walked around talking.

I remember when the phone company updated the phone service to include call waiting and three-way calling. Once we had call waiting, I'd answer every call hoping it was my friend. This got us in trouble many times. What we'd learn the hard way was that those calls that we clicked over to answer were bill collectors looking for my dad. I remember dad would tell us to not answer the phone many times, and we didn't understand why. I recall getting in the habit of avoiding incoming calls so much that we developed a skill of predicting which friend it probably was, then calling them a few minutes later to see if it was them who had called. On those occasions when we would answer incoming calls while on another call, and it was a bill collector, we then yelled for my father to pick up the phone. After he finished the call, we would get some verbal heat and a reminder to not do it again.

Time at home with my mom and sister in the evenings was cool. As soon as Mom got home, we would let her know that our homework was complete and that the chores were also done, and then we could race out of the house to find our friends. The street rules were always simple: If we could not see the front door of our house from where we were, then our parents could not see us. If they had to walk out onto the front porch to peek down the street, we'd gone too far. We didn't go into our friends' houses unless we told our parents first. Even then, it seemed like our friends' parents knew we were coming over before we got there. These folks knew how to set up some sophisticated command and control systems long before the Internet came about. There weren't even cell phones or cordless phones in our neighborhood yet, but we were under constant surveillance.

A strong family bond

One of the best parts of being a kid is not having the perspective of rich or poor. We always had what we needed, so it seemed. We slept in a bed at night, had food, water and clothes, and went to school during the day. We didn't really need more than that.

On the weekend, we spent time together. My dad was usually off work. I get my work ethic from him. This man would bust his butt, never complained about work and the long and late shifts, because he was doing what the leader of the family needed to do. I've never seen my father sit around in pajamas, not even on holidays. He would wake up, shower, check the house to make sure all was well, then

start breakfast. I don't remember my
father even wearing house shoes until
later in life.

On the weekends there was always
something planned, day trips to the
places of our dreams, like Sears, or to
the grocery store or even the occasional electric company to
pay the bills. Those were the good old days when we paid
the bills in person and the company gave you free light bulbs
right there at the bill payment counter. It didn't matter where
we went; all that mattered was that we were together.

My dad would also run errands with just me sometimes.
I'd be in the front seat, feeling like a grown man, barely able
to peek over the passenger side door frame. Back then, seat
belts were not required, and I don't even remember if our car
had them or not. What I do remember is when my dad made
a hard-right turn, I would slide across that bench-style front
seat and slam into his right leg. He'd push me back over to
my side of the car, and we'd keep on driving, listening to Al
Green on the 8-track tape.

My dad was a neat freak and seemingly was constantly
making sure things were in order in the house. If he cooked,
all the prep dishes were washed and in the strainer before
the food was ready for the table. This carried over to the
yard. Everybody on the block had lawns that were neatly
manicured and edged, and none of the kids were allowed
to walk on them. If we looked at someone's lawn the wrong
way, we would get a lecture and be asked to stop, back up
and use the same footsteps we came across on to go back

on. Cars were the same. We kids would be in the middle of the street, playing baseball, talking smack and eventually lean against someone's car. We knew which cars we could lean on. If it was Mr. Bailey's, Mr. Keith's or Mr. Vaughn's, we would not go near those. We would lean on our own car, if it was parked on the street instead of in the garage, which was in the alley behind the house. Even when we did this, there was a technique. We would squat down a little so when we leaned on the car, our bodies pushed against that long hard strip on the side that was there to prevent dents from shopping carts and other things.

I also spent many hours in the garage with my dad, when he was doing shade-tree mechanic repairs on the cars. He wasn't a professional mechanic by any means, but he did change the oil, brakes and attend to other minor maintenance items. My job was to hold the flashlight so he could see what he was doing. The flashlight had a long cord on it that plugged into a power outlet. It had a metal cage around the front side, and an enclosed metal cover on the back so the light would be protected if it was dropped. I remember always trying to move the light closer to my dad so he could see better, and accidently burning him with the hot metal cage. That's when he would send me inside the house, to wait for the mailman at nine o'clock at night, or at least that's what he told me to get me out of the garage.

My parents always stressed that education was the best way for us to provide for ourselves and families, later in life. My father never made it beyond third grade. Born in Athens, Georgia, he learned early that hard work would be required if he wanted to provide for his family. My dad's mother, Irene, died when he was 13 years old, eventually prompting him to leave Georgia to move to Chicago and stay with my great-grandma Della.

My mom was born in Puerto Rico and moved with her family to Chicago in the 1950s, after graduating from high school. Mom and Dad met while she was working at the Sears Tower and his job was nearby. This union created an amazing cultural experience for me to appreciate later in life.

Fran and I went to a Catholic school named Holy Name of Mary, which was only a few blocks from our house. Looking back, I know it was a struggle for my parents to pay tuition for both of us, but they sacrificed and did the best they could to afford it. We got our school uniforms from Gateley's department store, just like everyone else in our classes. We had hot lunch at school and learned discipline and abuse from the nuns and teachers. I believe my parents sent us to Catholic school partly for the Catholicism teachings that my mom practiced and partly for the discipline.

Fran has talent. She played the clarinet in band, taught herself to play the piano and was very active both in elementary and high school. She was a Girl Scout and always seemed to be busy with activities. I was the same way: a Boy Scout and altar boy, played basketball in school, baseball at the park district and trumpet in the school band.

Friends surrounded our family. Some of my closest friendships began in elementary school and remain strong today, like those with Tracey, Neva and Ugochi. Our block had some amazing people on it. My best friend Jerry is a few years older than me, and although we didn't hang out during my younger years, he was still a huge inspiration to me then and now. His family is so cool, and his mom had the heart of an angel. Jerry would ride up and down the block on his Yamaha dirt bike doing wheelies. He also could wheelie a regular bicycle up and down the whole block. Carl, aka Spoon, was also on our block and is still my brother. These guys treated us younger kids as little brothers and were the guardians of the neighborhood. They always spoke with us, were respectful to the elders and went on to become police officers to serve the community. I'm not sure how they passed the background checks, but that's a whole other story.

A life with only small pains

It is often said that you can draw off pain or pleasure in life. I don't recall a lot of pain in my early life. We had a seemingly normal life, from my perspective. Of course, there were times when the electricity and water were turned off because of missed or late payments, but that happened to everyone, I thought. Didn't everyone have to heat up large pots of water to fill the bathtub to take baths at times? I remember doing homework by candlelight when the power was off. I also remember breakfast being served as dinner many times because all we had in the kitchen was eggs, grits and toast – cool!

It is often said that you can draw off pain or pleasure in life.

Our neighbor "Pops" was our family's short-term lender. My dad would get on the phone, make a quick call, hang up, then send me or Fran next door to pick up a "package." After doing this several times in our lives, we knew when we heard "bring yo butt right back," it meant we were going to pick up $20 in cash. Even when the reality of not being wealthy set in, we never felt like we were missing out. My parents would take us to Lincoln Park Zoo, the free one. When they had some extra money, we'd go to Brookfield Zoo, where you had to pay an entrance fee. Brookfield was way better because it was about 45 minutes from home, so it would be like a mini road trip and we knew we'd probably have to eat out that day, usually at McDonalds. My parents would also take other kids from the block with us to various places. This was my first experience with learning how to share our blessings and seeing the joy it brings to others and ourselves.

Some of our cousins lived on the north side of Chicago, spread out over the Humboldt Park area and a little east of there. My aunt Virginia and uncle Fellow lived in a public housing project for a period. At that time, it was simply an apartment to me. We'd visit every so often, and my sister and I loved to see our cousins Betsy, Junior, Ricky, Danny, Jose and Bobby. My parents valued family time, and whether it was the north or west side of Chicago, Georgia or Puerto Rico, we remained in touch and visited family as much as possible.

A first loss

I don't recall the exact circumstances, but my aunt Virginia died when I was in early elementary school. This saddened my mom and whole family, as she was the first of the siblings to pass. After her death, uncle Fellow was left to raise six children on his own. I never recall Fellow smiling.

Back in the day, the phone or doorbell ringing were major events, so much so that several people would go to the front door of the house to see who was there. Many times, a couple of us would answer the house phone at the same time and both say "hello" simultaneously. Even if you didn't answer the phone, you kind of listened to the tone of the conversation to try to figure out who was on the other end. There are a few phone calls I remember in my life, and this was one of them. My dad answered. He had a serious look on his face and a concerned tone in his voice. He quickly yelled upstairs for my mom to pick up the phone that was in their bedroom. Now both of them were on the same line during the call. A few minutes later, they got off the phone and quickly packed Fran and me into the car. There was a serious mood in the front seat and not much talking at all. They did not tell us where we were going, and after what I remember being a long drive, we ended up at a hospital. I was confused because we never went to a hospital together. I was trying to think of any reason why we would be there. After getting out of the car and arriving inside the emergency room, I saw my cousins and other family members sitting down, all with sad looks on their faces. My young cousins were crying, but I still didn't know what was happening. Mom went to talk to my aunts and uncles, who were huddled up in a corner having a conversation.

My dad told us that Uncle Fellow had committed suicide. I did not know what that word meant and kept asking dad or mom to explain. They said he took his own life. I felt confused and wanted to understand why he would do that. Still, I couldn't fully understand any of what was happening; all I knew was that my cousins were crying and wouldn't talk to anyone. Now there were six children without parents.

On the way home from the hospital that night, I could hear my parents sharing information they heard from other family members and trying to figure out why my uncle would commit suicide. It was either on or near Thanksgiving Day, which should be a happy time. There were so many unanswered questions related to uncle's death, and it was difficult for everyone to put the pieces together as to why he took that path.

Later in my high school days, my cousin Junior, who was in the house at the time of my uncle's death, provided some information. He said that he was sitting on the couch with my other cousin watching television when my uncle came in the room with a mad look on his face. Uncle pointed the gun at him and his brother, and for whatever reason, decided not to pull the trigger. Junior still had deep trauma from his dad's death, but I don't recall him ever blaming his father for anything. When he spoke about his dad to me, it was about things he used to do that were not related to his death. From being close to this experience, I can see the results of children losing not just one but both parents at such a young age and in such a tragic manner. Each of my cousins still carries the deep wounds and, in some ways, is stuck in that point in time emotionally—and is still seeking the parenting today that they missed back then.

This was the first time I encountered death in my family. I can still remember being in line to view the body at the funeral. I was holding mom's hand as the line slowly moved forward, waiting for the people who were in front of the casket to say their final goodbyes. After each person walked away from the casket, their heads were hung low and had the look of unbearable pain on their faces. When we approached the casket, I remember Mom crying and letting my hand go as she clutched the side of the casket. I stared at my uncle, still not knowing how to process everything. He looked as if he was asleep, but I knew that was not true. I glanced up and down the casket, noticing the suit, the flowers, his hands folded on top of each other. It was not real in my mind. It felt that he would "come back" at any point. I also felt the fear of being near a dead body for the first time. Nobody prepared me or Fran for this moment. We were never told what to expect, how the flowers would give us a queasy feeling in our stomachs. Nobody said we would be in a small room with an entire group of people crying. We didn't know that our cousins, who were always happy to see us, would not speak to anyone.

My aunts and uncles were trying to figure out not only how to console my cousins, but how to keep them together and raise them. Which one of them could handle this enormous responsibility that was thrown into their lap? The decision was eventually made that the cousins would be taken to Puerto Rico to live with my grandparents. The majority of my mom's family was there, and it was probably the level of support they would receive on the island that made it the best choice at that time.

The thing about suicide is that no one seems to talk about the act or person that committed it. Uncle Fellow is never mentioned although Aunt Virginia is when reminiscing about their group. I can't explain why, and maybe there are other factors outside my knowledge as to why this is. Without counseling or some way for my family to discuss the circumstances surrounding my uncle's death, the open wound is left for everyone to try to mend on their own. The family had to look forward and focus on the children, their lives and continuing their education.

At our house, we seemed to get right back into our routines after the funeral. There was never a discussion about suicide after that point. I think my therapy was lying in bed at night, trying to answer my own questions. There is also an unwritten rule that no one talks about it to others outside the house. I do remember Mom talking to family in Puerto Rico a little more after this point in time and her letting Dad know how everyone was doing. Both Junior and Ricky moved back to Chicago while I was still in elementary school.

Learning leadership in Boy Scouts

My mom signed me up to join the Boy Scouts in Troop 712 at Holy Name of Mary. My friends from school were also Scouts, so it was fun to go to meetings with them in the basement of the school. Our Associate Pastor, Fr. John, was our Scoutmaster. Scouts was my first experience with organized leadership. We learned to pronounce the alphabet the way the military does and were broken up into squads and platoons, just like the Army. We had uniform requirements with surprise inspections, strict formation times and getting "dropped" when we were out of line. Dropped means quickly falling to the ground and cranking out dozens of push ups when we were out of line. I learned to march, call cadence, hike, canoe, rappel, hunt, administer first aid and lead while in the Scouts. Fr. John would work with the parents to have fundraisers from selling popcorn, fruit and car washes to be able to buy camping gear. With the funds we raised, our troop was able to buy tents and equipment for the entire group. We had to buy our own personal gear such as sleeping bags and backpacks, however. My parents put great faith and trust in Fr. John to teach me and prepare me to be a man. He treated the youngest and oldest in our group the same and disciplined us equally. I still lean on some of the skills I learned during this time.

During elementary school, we took camping trips to North Carolina along the Appalachian Trail. After driving 14 hours from Chicago, we would arrive and find parking at the base of the mountain. We unloaded our gear from the vehicles and lined up in formation with our backpacks on our backs. Our leaders took a head count to ensure we knew how many of us were heading onto the trail and how many needed to be with us on the return. Hiking on the Appalachian Trail was tough. There are certain areas along the way that seem to go straight up, while others have a more subtle incline. My backpack seemed to get heavier every 10 minutes. As we ascended, I remember looking down only to notice that we were above the clouds. I found it harder to breathe as altitude increased, compensating with deep, gasping breaths every few steps.

We ultimately hiked many miles before reaching our designated campsite. One of the first priorities was to pitch our tents in a circular formation, positioning our doors to face toward the center of the campsite. Fr. John's tent was right in the center, so he could easily see the entire troop. Each person was assigned to a small group, tasked with various responsibilities such as wood gathering, cooking and KP (which stands for kitchen patrol, or dishwashing in layman's terms). Once our tents were set up, Fr. John would gather all patrol leaders to the center of camp. They would have a brief conversation, then disperse to their respective patrols to provide direction for the activities of the day.

I looked up to the leaders and saw how everyone respected them. I wanted to be respected just like they were. I looked at how our leaders saluted, how they led their team and knew I could one day be just like them. Each morning, our patrol leaders would inspect our tents. They made sure our tents were set up correctly, stakes were properly secured, the insides were neat and organized, and each of us was prepared for our assigned tasks. Once each patrol leader indicated to Fr. John that their patrol was ready, he'd come to do his final inspection. Seeing Fr. John walk toward my tent was a horrific feeling. My mind was racing. Did I secure my tent correctly, did I leave anything out of place, would I be dropped and made to do 100 push ups? It was terrifying up until the moment he moved on to the next person's tent.

Once all tents were inspected, Fr. John would stand in the middle of the campsite and provide his assessment. If he found faults with any of our tents, we were all held responsible. All of us would be dropped to do push ups or a dying cockroach. I'm not sure where a dying cockroach originated, but Fr. John used it as an effective way to make sure we fixed whatever problem got us in trouble. We dreaded lying on your back, knees bent at a 45-degree angle with our toes pointing up and our heads and necks lifted off the ground facing our knees. He would make us do these for 2-3 minutes, while he loudly told us we had to work as a team and how he expected excellence from the group, not individuals. I never imagined doing a dying cockroach in thick grass on the Appalachian Trail with ants and bugs crawling on me, while mosquitos were buzzing in my ears. This is the difference between being disciplined back at the school and outside at a campsite. If anyone broke form, he kept the entire group on the ground longer.

During the day, we were taught valuable skills that counted toward merit badges that we prepared for during regular meetings back at home. We had field tests on first aid, role-playing injury from an axe or knife cut, a heart attack or other emergency. We also tested for land navigation, cooking, hunting and more. We played games, too—traditional football games as well as games like "stalk," a modified game of tag spread out over a large wooded area at night. What made it more fun was the knowledge that there were all types of wild animals nearby, including black bears. Our team always consisted of the same few people. We were always the ones that went overboard like we were in Vietnam. We'd set up homemade trip wires using fishing line. We would run electrical tape between trees at head level on paths to snag people walking past.

I loved every minute of these camping trips. Being in the woods, among the beautiful trees near streams and rivers was so relaxing. Looking up at night was a different experience than back at home in the city. I never saw so many stars as I did high in the mountains of North Carolina.

I loved the feeling of being with my friends, with all our energy focused on one thing. There was nothing to do but enjoy life and take it second by second.

At the end of each trip, we would break down our camp site and prepare to pack up. This was a very stressful time and the saddest time for me. Once everyone's gear was packed and moved to the staging area, we were given a certain amount of time to "police up" the area. This meant make sure there was nothing left on the ground unless it was created by God. We were told that we had to leave our area cleaner than it was when we arrived. We had to do better than anyone else and not to make any excuses for us not taking care of our responsibilities. If the paper was there before we arrived, it didn't matter, it was our job to dispose of it. Fr. John knew that our troop was filled with young men from the city, and there was no room for error; we had to represent ourselves as respectful, responsible humans, no matter what the circumstances were.

We also went on extended camping trips to Canada, Wisconsin, Southern Illinois and many places in between. Another fun activity was canoeing. This activity was new to all the Scouts, and that's what Fr. John wanted. He wanted to expose us to things the average young person on the South Side of Chicago didn't get to see or do. Canoeing was very intimidating for many of the scouts who could not swim. The person in the front is more of the power behind your speed. Once we got in sync, it was pretty fun. I loved the outdoors, the smells, sounds and the views. I felt free and limitless, being in the midst of nature.

> *Scouting prepared me in so many ways for the road ahead, some that I recognized right away and others that I never knew were coming.*

Scouting prepared me in so many ways for the road ahead, some that I recognized right away and others that I never knew were coming. I was building a unique set of skills that are valuable in civilian life, military life and both urban and rural environments. The interesting thing about building a good toolkit is that I never knew when and where I would need any of them. Every experience had value, and I developed a desire to be more adventurous during these years and to run toward challenges as opposed to away from them. I had to use some of my newly learned skills earlier than I expected.

Real pain hits home

My dad was rock-hard, both mentally and physically. It seemed there was nothing he couldn't do. He was very wise despite never finishing elementary school. Being an old-school Mason, he seemed to know a little something about everything. He was street smart, a cool cat that everyone loved. He would ride up and down the block on his Schwinn bike with a battery-operated FM radio playing, with a white tank top, aka "wife beater" as we still call them, sporting some ankle-high black boots with no socks, looking Mike Tyson below the knees. Friends called him Charlie Brown, partially because his name was Charles but mostly because he was a natural comedian and could tell a story that would have everyone laughing in tears. I never saw him cry until my great-grandmother died, during my college days. This man from the South with very little education knew more than anyone I knew.

The thing about heroes is that sometimes their vulnerabilities show, which is what I experienced when he had a seizure early one morning. I remember being awake, lying in the bed but not moving yet. I could hear Mom's voice calling my dad, *honey, honey, honey*. I laid still, not moving an inch, so I could hear better. *Honey, honey honey*, I heard again. I imagine Fran heard the same thing but was also paralyzed by the uncertainty. I felt the desperation of Mom's voice and had to go see for myself what was happening.

Fran must have experienced the same feelings, because both of us ran into my parents' room at nearly the same time. I saw my mom on the left side of the bed, leaning over, trying to get my father to respond. His body was shaking uncontrollably, and no one knew what to do. The only thing I knew to do was what I had learned in the Boy Scout first aid class. I reached down and placed my left hand on his forehead and my right hand under his neck in order to lean his head back. I was trying to clear his airway as I thought he was having a heart attack. I then starting chest compressions, which had no impact. I continued to apply what I had learned and turned his head to his right side toward me. I then tried to use my two fingers to clear anything that may have been in his mouth that would obstruct his breathing, but his teeth were clenched so tight I could not open his mouth. I'm not sure who called the ambulance, but they eventually arrived. It seemed he lay there shaking forever. His eyes were wide open staring aimlessly toward the ceiling and there was nothing we could do to help him.

Once the paramedics arrived, Fran led them to the bedroom where Dad was. They asked us what happened and what his symptoms were. The only response I had was that I tried CPR and he didn't respond to it. The paramedics were able to stabilize Dad and place him on a stretcher. As they moved outside, a neighbor from across the street, who happened to be a retired fireman, came over to check on us. He spoke with the paramedics briefly to get a prognosis. They indicated that he had a seizure. This was the first time in my life that I could not execute anything in my physical body or brain to help a situation, and it was awful. This was my first experience with real pain within the walls of my home.

I don't recall how long it took my dad to recover, but I remember the house was more somber for a while. We continued to live, but I think all of us walked on eggshells because the neurosurgeon told us that seizures can reoccur at any time. He also explained that even moderate levels of stress could trigger one, which left us concerned. This was a tough time for me because my personal superman experienced kryptonite for the first time in my memory. Dad could have been taken away before I graduated from eighth grade, just like his mom. I spent many nights, in my bed, praying that dad would outlive me. I couldn't imagine life without him. While Dad was in the hospital, I was lonely, even though I was surrounded by people. I was the only boy in the house now and felt like all responsibilities would be passed down to me. I grew up fast once I had experienced how fragile life really is.

As much as he meant to me, he was closest with Fran. They were thick as thieves. How was she processing this? As a kid I didn't want to ask her about it, and we never did talk about our feelings around this devastating event. For me, I almost felt like talking about it would make it happen again.

All the lessons I was taught as a kid started making a little more sense, like washing dishes. When Dad was in the hospital and even home resting, Fran and I did even more chores and chipped in to help Mom to take over for what Dad used to do. We also saw the strength and faith Mom had. She held everything together and maintained all the normal routines of home and school life. There were no excuses that prevented us from moving forward and staying focused.

Learning to swim in the deep end

Life eventually got back to normal, as it always does. We started to laugh and have outings like we used to. I played baseball at Kennedy Park on 114th and Western

Avenue and was probably only one of two Black kids in the whole baseball league. My skin complexion is light due to my mixed blood and my parents never talked negatively about anyone, especially other races. I'm not sure how this played into me being able to adapt to situations around all Black people, being the only Black person in a room full of white people or being in a crowd of people of all nationalities, but I always managed to be myself and not try to sound or act like anyone else.

I remember when Black people would speak at times, and the octaves of their voices would get a little higher when talking to a white person. The same applied when a white person was speaking to a Black person: they felt the need to use certain words to make it appear they could relate. People still mimic this behavior today. My parents were not afraid to expose us to the things that would make us better, regardless of who was in the room or on the team. I developed friendships during these years at Kennedy Park because of a mutual interest in baseball. Before practice, we would meet at Coach Sheehan's house across the street from the park to get equipment. They lived just like we did: both parents worked, they had two sons and their house was about the same size as ours. Coach was as blue-collar as everyone else I knew. He would wear the same clothes he came home in from work to baseball practice.

Kennedy Park was also the place I learned to swim. I swam in the pool several times each week, and on Sundays, during "family swim", I'd stay in the water for the entire four hours they were open. My mom would join us and mostly sat on the pool deck, reading a book, while I was teaching myself to swim. I always went to extremes, and I figured that by jumping in the 11-foot end of the pool, I would have to learn to swim or drown. I didn't feel like I had limits, and we weren't taught to live within a box or go through life being afraid and hesitant to try new things. Mom saw me jumping in the deep end and never told me to stop. I carry this spirit with me, even today, and don't impose mental or physical barriers on what I want to achieve. The days spent at Kennedy Park were a vital part of my life and gave me the experience of being comfortable in any environment, even when no other person around me, looked like me.

The importance of family

My parents were able to sacrifice and take us to visit out-of-state family members each summer. One summer we would do a road trip to Georgia to visit my dad's side, and next summer, we would fly to Puerto Rico to visit my mom's side. Family was and still is extremely important to me. I remember our trips to Georgia and how much I looked forward to them. We would pick up my grandma from the west side and bring her back to our house to stay overnight the day before the trip. Grandma would cook fried chicken, hot-water cornbread and fresh personal-size fried hot-apple pies.

I tried to stay up if I could the night before road trips, knowing that I could sleep during the drive. This was easy, because the adrenaline flowing through my body didn't allow me to sleep, knowing I'd be seeing my cousins soon.

We would leave early in the morning before the sun rose. My dad would pick up Fran and me from bed, still in our footsy pajamas, and gently place us in the back seat. I can still smell his Brut cologne. I'm telling you, this dude dressed up even to go to the bathroom.

My grandma would place the fried chicken that was wrapped in aluminum foil in the back window on the ledge, so it would stay warm from the heat of the sun. The drive was long but never boring, because I got to talk to grandma and listen to her and my mom catch up on soap opera updates. When it was light outside, we seemed to drive past cornfield after cornfield and endless numbers of cows. The only other entertainment we had was picking out our favorite cars along the way.

We always seemed to arrive in Georgia during the nighttime. I remember pulling up to Aunt Lula Mae's house as the car's headlights lit up the front porch. Uncle Stovall would come walking out to greet us and help with bags and, at the same time, lights were turned on in the kitchen of the house. This was my grandma's sister's house. Aunt Lula Mae always starting cooking right away, even though we kids weren't hungry; we were just excited to be in Georgia.

We always stayed at the same Days Inn approximately 15 minutes from our Aunt Gloria's house in Athens. Our days were filled with driving to various family members' houses for a visit. We also went to a lot of historic landmarks while in Georgia, which I believe ignited my interest in visiting museums today. Each day we were in Georgia, come hell or high water, dad took us to "The Varsity." This is a long-standing drive-in style restaurant, started back in 1928—and one of his favorites. Every day, he would get a chili dog, fries and a pop and tell the waiter at the counter to "drag it through the garden," which means to load it up with all the fixings. I was so tired of seeing hot dogs that I wanted to jump out of the car and throw myself under the tires every time we pulled up in front of that place.

Other summers during my childhood, we visited Mom's side of the family in Puerto Rico. This was back in the day when people dressed up to fly on airplanes. My parents would iron our clothes and sometimes get us a new outfit to fly in; for me, it was an airline pilot shirt. We took Eastern Airlines every time we flew and usually sat near the wings. I loved to sit in a seat that had a window so I could see the flaps of the airplane wings move in, out, up and down before, during and after the plane landed. I remember having to lean forward and being barely able to see out of the window at that time. Puerto Rico was much different than Georgia, of course, with palm trees, beaches and Latin music, but the experience of seeing family was the same. It's a magical place with the perfect mix of people, culture, weather and landscape, one that we would eventually call home.

A taste for business

My uncle Benji, who lives in Puerto Rico, would visit us in Chicago while attending business conferences. Benji was the first entrepreneur I was able to sit down and learn from. I remember going with my parents to pick him up from Midway airport and stopping at "Jack in The Box" restaurant near 107th and Western Avenue on the way to our house. It was a usual routine when he came to visit. I remember sitting at the kitchen table and listening to the conversations about life, family and updates on his business. I was intrigued and wanted to learn more and more about this thing called business. I didn't know exactly what type of business he ran but knew that he'd travel to different states to attend meetings and negotiate contracts, and it seemed cool. The idea of one day having my own business originated from these casual conversations I had the opportunity to listen to between uncle and my dad. Even now, Uncle comes to my house and we spend five or six hours easily talking about business while it only seems like we were together for 30 minutes. Everyone wants us to end the conversation, but we would just go on and on and on.

In November 1979, along came Maritza, my replacement as the baby of the family and the person who would elevate me to that unenviable position of middle child. At this point in my life, my older sister received attention because she was the first child in our family and each experience was new for my parents. Maritza was getting the rest of the attention from my parents, because she was the baby of the family. What was I to do? I am the only son, so that should mean something. I must admit that when Maritza came into the family, it was cool. Fran and I got to teach her the things we learned as kids, and we also had fun times being big sister and big brother when mom and dad were away from home.

School struggles

When Holy Mary went through some issues, my parents had me transferred to Murray Language Academy for seventh and eighth grade. Murray was only 10 minutes from Mom's job, so it was convenient in a way, except I now had to ride the school bus to and from school every day. A public magnet school, Murray proved a shock to my intellectual system. The students were amazingly smart and so knowledgeable about life that it was intimidating to me. There were students of all races and nationalities, some from average homes like I was, and others who were the sons and daughters of doctors and elected officials. These students scored very high on reading and math on standardized tests and seemed to know everything about everything. This, too was painful. What do I do to catch up, keep up and stay here, I thought?

I had earned good grades at Holy Name but struggled at Murray. I had to study hard and still brought home many bad grades. I dreaded the times the teacher would call on me to read or answer a question in front of everyone. I did everything I could to avoid making eye contact with my teachers, so I could just blend in and go unnoticed. I was doing just enough to get by and had not developed the thirst for knowledge I would gain later in life. My friend Tracey from Holy Name eventually transferred to Murray, and it was a relief to have someone I'd known my whole life with me again. Maritza also started attending Murray in my eighth-grade year and made those long bus rides to and from school with me.

My experience at Murray provided another time I had to decide how to deal with pain. These were the worst two years in elementary school for me. I felt out of place, under-educated and alone because all the other students had grown up together and I was new to the school. I knew Mom moved me to this new school for my good; it was tough accepting it at that time, however.

Another shock awaited me. While all my friends were going to Quigley South High School, mom enrolled me at Mt. Carmel High School. I was devastated that I couldn't be with my boys and had to start all over again making new friends. Besides, Quigley had the better color school jackets and Mt. Carmel had this baby "boo-boo" brown colored jacket. I did not want to be seen wearing that garbage. And, what is a "caravan" and why is that the name of Mt. Carmel's mascot?

I dreaded everything about Mt. Carmel before I got there. It turns out that on my first day of school, I ran into many of the boys I played baseball with at Kennedy Park. It was an instant relief that at least I wouldn't be alone trying to figure this stuff out. Why did my mom always put me in positions that were uncomfortable for me, away from my friends? Was this punishment for a rough pregnancy or payback for her and Dad having to work long hours to pay for elementary school?

Again, I had to make the best of it. High school turned out to be pretty fun, even though I was trying to figure out what I wanted to do in life. I had developed computer skills in sixth grade after my parents bought me a personal home computer. I had no clue what it was but spent many nights in my room in the dark, teaching myself how to program using sample code from magazines I received in the mail. Of all the classes I took in Carmel, computer and Spanish classes were a breeze. I had very little interest in the rest of my classes, except to get a passing grade. My mind was always focused on something more than what I was being taught between the four walls of a school. I felt like I was simply completing the steps I needed to get past school so I could follow the path I wanted, not what school wanted to teach me.

Then I was able to register for a business class. My best days at Carmel were days I had this class. Our teacher was a former marketing/sales representative who wore the traditional businessman uniform consisting of white dress shirt, tie, dress slacks and shiny shoes. He was young, smart and stood out from all the other teachers in my eyes. I received my highest grades at Carmel in business class and felt like I was finally in my learning zone as far as subject material was concerned. I also started dabbling in entrepreneurial practices, doing Spanish and computer homework for other classmates, for cash. Looking back, it was the first time I marketed and was paid for my intellectual property.

During my time at Carmel, I was able to build some solid relationships with some of my classmates, who have become lifelong friends such as Joey, Spanky, Chris, John and a few others. We shared some fun times and also got into some crazy situations. Let's just say I don't know how any of us are still alive today.

During my high school years, my parents continued to struggle financially. The sacrifices they made for me and my sisters can never be repaid or overstated. I remember every year, right before finals, I was called to the main office, along with a few other students. This overly loud, demanding and humiliating voice would come over the schoolwide public announcement system. The first time this occurred, we didn't know what they wanted. I would get to the office and sit in a chair across from the main counter until my name was called by the clerk. After a few minutes, the clerk would give each of us an envelope with our names on it. I stepped outside into the hallway, away from the door so the clerk couldn't see me, then opened and read the letter. Even though the letter was addressed to my parents, I wanted to at least know what it was about. I read the short and succinct note, informing them that unless my tuition balance was brought up to current status, I would not be allowed to take final exams. The total dollar amount required was also listed, which in my case, was usually a couple thousand dollars. I felt horrible to have to take this note home to my parents, who were already doing everything they could to provide for me and my sisters.

I'm not sure how, but they would always come up with the check so I could take finals with the rest of my class. I could always hear Dad's doctor tell us right after his seizure that his stress level always needed to remain low. The thought of taking this letter home was difficult and, I wanted the school day to linger on as long as possible to avoid that reality. I began to develop another layer of skin during these experiences. Again, I was faced with the reality that people don't care about your personal situations and generally don't want to hear them. I wondered at times if, I too, should adopt this mentality or continue to be empathetic toward others as I was taught to do. What could I do to help, what job could I get to ease the pain? I looked for any random job I could find on the weekends. Fr. John would allow me to clean the weeds from the fences and alley behind the pastor's house. I swept the parking lot a couple of times each week for a doctor my mom eventually went to work for. I did everything I could those first two years in high school to contribute.

Through all the difficult financial times, my parents never complained that education cost too much, nor did they try to shelter us from the reality that we were not a wealthy family.

2: A FORK IN THE ROAD AT KENWOOD

My friends and I had mutual friends that went to other schools in the city and surrounding suburbs. Sometimes they would meet us at Carmel after school, and other times, we would pick them up from their schools, so we could go to a game or just to hang out. Plans always seemed to come together quickly and at the last moment, and the beginning of Christmas break in our junior year was no different.

It was the last period of the day, in Mr. Daley's religion class. Chris, John, Joey, Spanky and Keys were planning to go to Giordano's pizza after school. Right after school, we met in the parking lot to finalize the details. A couple of other people decided they wanted to go with us but had to pick up one of their friends from Kenwood High School, which was only a 10-minute drive from Carmel. We agreed to follow them so we could stay together in our group. It was common for us to have multiple cars of people whenever we went out, because everyone lived so far away from each other and the school.

We pulled up at Kenwood and waited until their final bell rang. A couple of us were outside, leaning on our cars, talking as we normally did. I knew several people at Kenwood that were former classmates from Murray Language Academy, which was only a couple of blocks up the street. I specifically remember a girl named Arianna from Murray who came outside after the bell rang. Today, I'm not sure what was wrong with her, but she seemed crazy back in elementary school, so her actions weren't too surprising to me. She walked right up to one of my classmates and started talking a bunch of trash, for no reason. We were all surprised because no one said anything to her nor did the other guys know who she was. All of us thought she was crazy and simply ignored her. She turned back toward the building and yelled toward the school front door that we were there to attack Kenwood students.

This made no sense: there were only about 8-10 of us total that day, and Kenwood had a population of a couple of thousand students. We just wanted some pizza—but that wasn't going to happen. Within a few seconds, people came running, and without any words being said, fists started flying. There were people on the ground fighting, girls screaming and extreme chaos. The group was so large that I couldn't tell our people from their people; it was like a full-blown riot. Clearly outnumbered, we were trying to get out of the area as fast as possible.

I saw what was happening. I was moving physically, but the volume of the sounds got lower and lower until there was silence. People's mouths were still moving, and I could see the fear, pain and anger on the faces but couldn't hear them saying anything. I don't remember how, but a few of us made it to our cars. The streets were filled with people walking around and yelling, and none of it made any sense. I pulled out onto Hyde Park Boulevard heading westbound.

I saw my classmate David in his Toyota Supra pull out in front of me, but he stopped quickly because something was stopping him from moving forward. David tried to pull into the other lane of traffic, but it was blocked by cars and people. By this time, there was a massive crowd, not just students but people from the neighborhood who had come out of local stores and gathered on the sidewalks.

David got through finally, and I pushed the gas hard to follow. From nowhere, two guys who were fighting fell from the right side, between parked cars, into the street in front of me. I don't remember pressing the brakes or even thinking about pressing the brakes. I just remember stopping and their heads disappearing below the hood of my car. I felt like I was witnessing a train wreck: I saw their faces looking at the front end of my car. Their eyes were as big as baseballs. My car stopped hard enough for the back passenger to slam forward into the back of the front passenger seat. The adrenaline and fear of not knowing if I had hit these two guys were terrible. For what were the longest few seconds of my life, I kept looking forward, not knowing if they were alive or not. Eventually, they got up off the ground and ran toward the right of my car. My mind and heart were overwhelmed with gratitude and fear.

I started driving slowly through the crowd until the street was clear enough for me to get away from the school.

David was already coming back in the other direction, toward the scene of the fight. He was the only other person I saw from our group, so I turned around and followed him. When we got back near the school, there were a lot of police officers on the scene. We just wanted to find out where our friends were, and to make sure everyone was alright. The police pulled David over, probably because his car was easily identifiable, as the new model sports car that initially fled the scene.

We headed to Giordano's, not to eat, but to regroup and find out what happened. Arriving at 98th and Western Avenue with adrenaline still flowing and hearts beating fast, each of us was eager to recount what had happened from our own vantage point. The only real update was that one of my best friends was being taken to the hospital with a broken nose. We didn't have cell phones, so there was no way to find out which hospital he was going to or where everyone else was.

What we did know was that situation was bad. How did going to get pizza end up like this?

At Carmel, students could be disciplined and expelled not only for incidents that occurred at school but also outside of school, even during holidays and on vacation days. I think all of us were aware of the potential consequences. Word spread fast among other classmates and that started the bad blood between Carmel students and Kenwood students that would last until we graduated.

Looking back, I see that this time could have been a fork in the road that sent me on another path. What if I couldn't stop the car and killed those two boys? What if one of my friends had seriously hurt or killed someone in the fight? What if we got arrested and now had criminal records? I think of my wife and son and thank God things didn't end up differently.

Like all times of pain, I would eventually draw on this experience again along my journey in life. I believe this incident really allowed me to learn to make thoughtful decisions over emotional ones during important times. I can quickly imagine best and worst-case scenarios and the consequences

There was grace in my life at this time.

of the actions I may or may not take. I'm able to see how a choice may play out. I've learned to ask myself, would I make this decision again?

Grace

There was grace in my life at this time, something that I did not work for but was granted. There are plenty of times that I was as thankful for the things that did not happen as I was for what did.

3: I'M IN THE ARMY NOW

During my junior year at Carmel, I decided I wanted to join the Army. Our family had an established tradition of service in the armed forces. My two cousins Jimmy and Junior were both active duty soldiers. My cousins Chris and Pam were in the Navy, and my uncle Benji had also served in the Navy. One of the amazing things about my parents was that they allowed us to spread our wings, which is so important. I don't know how they truly felt about me enlisting, but on the surface, they supported my choice.

The Army had a program called split-training where I could enlist while in high school and attend basic training during my junior year summer break. After graduation, I would attend my Military Occupational Specialty (MOS) training. Because I enlisted at the age of 17, my parents had to consent. I stopped by a recruiter's office not far from Carmel on the way home from school one afternoon. There was only one person in the office at the time: Sgt. Smith, a recruiter for the Army Reserves. We spent a long time during that initial visit, discussing options and the benefits of being a soldier. Sgt. Smith also visited our home many times, meeting with my parents and making them comfortable with the path I decided to take.

One of the first steps prior to enlisting was the take the Armed Services Vocational Aptitude Battery (ASVAB) exam. The results of this test would determine what jobs I qualified to do. I did well enough on the ASVAB that I had my choice of nearly any job. I wanted the "grunt" life, sleeping in the field, hiking for days at a time; in other words, I wanted to be in an infantry unit. Little did I know (and was not told by my recruiter) that the Reserves didn't offer infantry slots—he had his own quota to meet. Ultimately, I chose to be in an engineering unit because it was one of the closest things to a combat position.

In the early summer of 1988, I was on a plane heading to Fort Leonard Wood, Missouri, also called Ft. Misery by many people who attended basic training there. Sgt. Smith did his best to prepare me mentally for what I could expect. His message was clear: there would be lots of running, don't volunteer for anything, don't quit and most importantly, don't embarrass him.

After the flight landed, a bus picked up a group of us and drove us to the reception station. It was late, I had been traveling all day, and I wanted to get some sleep. We were told to wait quietly. A man in camouflage fatigues boarded the bus and—with a no-BS attitude—gave us very specific instructions. Some people learned right away to never call an enlisted person sir or "ma'am". When someone on the bus said, "yes sir," that sergeant lit into him and said, "never call me sir, I work for a living." Rule number one in life; learn from others mistakes.

We were instructed to exit the bus and walk inside the building where other sergeants were posted, pointing us in the direction of a large meeting room. I followed the other recruits in front of me to an empty chair and took a seat. I was nervous and excited at the same time, not knowing what was next, but already loving the organizational structure. A few minutes later, a sergeant walked into the room, his jump boots hitting the floor, click, click, click, click. He took his position at the front of the group, and I could instantly tell he had done this 1,000 times. The sergeant explained that we had five minutes of amnesty. He said if we had anything they considered contraband—like cigarettes, drugs, knives, guns and food—to get up, move to the rear of the room and place it in the box. The sergeant then gave us an introduction to the Army and dismissed us into the care of another group of sergeants.

We were taken to a large dormitory area and assigned our individual "racks," also known as bunks or beds. During the two or three days I was at the reception station, more recruits would appear and go through the same process. Our class was being formed now, with recruits arriving from other states; our training would not begin until all 240 recruits were on the base and ready. The days were spent drawing the gear and equipment needed for training such as duffel bags, clothing, rucksacks and much more. We got haircuts as well, which were over in less than a minute. The Army had every process I could imagine down to a science.

Basic training seemed a breeze compared to what I'd heard back at the recruiter's office. We took our class photos. We spent time learning to spit-shine our boots, shape and blouse our uniforms the correct way, and how to march and other basic military protocols. What I didn't know was this was simply the waiting area until all the recruits arrived, and then we would begin our formal training. In other words, the pain was yet to start.

The real work begins

Our group was awoken early one day, before daylight, by the sergeant assigned to our class. We were instructed to pack everything we owned in our duffels, make up our racks and be outside in 15 minutes. This sent the room into a frenzy. I knew inside that today was different; there was something on the horizon, and I had to get my game face on.

Once outside, we were told to stand in formation with our duffel bags placed strategically in front of us. Sergeant said our transportation was on the way and that we better stay still, be quiet and pay attention. The butterflies fluttered in my gut. I could feel the adrenaline flowing, and my mind started trying to picture what the next hour, day and week would be like. I stood there daydreaming for a while.

In the distance, I could see several trucks coming down the road, followed by a couple of cars. I specifically remember a white sporty Chevy Camaro trailing them. The trucks were kicking up dust from the road, and the image looked surreal. As the trucks got closer, I didn't think they were our ride because they were cattle trucks, like the ones I used to see on the expressway in Chicago hauling cows and pigs. I stopped paying attention to them, figuring our ride would arrive a little later. The cattle trucks came closer and closer to the reception station, then made a right turn into the parking lot where we were. The drivers pulled right up near us and stopped. That cool Camaro behind them was driven by one of the meanest people I ever met, Drill Sergeant Dewey, who I would later discover was an Airborne Ranger.

These were the drill sergeants who would transform us from recruits to soldiers. They screamed, gave conflicting commands and got right in our faces with those large round "campaign" hats that only allowed me to see their eyes and below. I could feel the spit and hot breath as they yelled instructions. My heart started beating fast because I wanted to make sure I did exactly what they told me to do.

We were told to bear-hug our duffels, run as fast as we could to the cattle trucks and get inside. Once I climbed into the truck, I looked for an open space to move to. Once other recruits boarded the bus, there was no room to move in any direction. I was pancaked against a wall, packed like a sardine, not able to take a deep breath. The other recruits' sweat was dripping on me, and mine was dripping on them. We were stepping on each other's feet, trying to keep our balance as the truck made its way through the winding back gravel roads. Even though the trucks had vented walls, the temperature felt like 200 degrees.

The drill sergeant kept giving us orders to squat, stand up, then down, up again, then down. We did this for what seemed to be 30 minutes nonstop while being driven down a bumpy, dusty road. I remember the sound of coughing, vomiting and hard breathing. The outside of my legs was rubbed raw from the friction of rubbing against the next recruit while doing these crazy punishing squats. At some point, the trucks stopped, and we were instructed to exit.

I had never experienced anything like this. The yelling got even more intense and was coming from all directions. The noise was so intense that I couldn't hear most of the commands the first time they said them. Once everyone was off the trucks, we were told to line up facing the open field, drop our duffel bags and lay them on the side. Then, we were told to take our uniform shirt and fold it with our name tag facing away, so they could read it as they faced us. For the first time in my life, I wondered why I was born with the last name Kitchens. Even though my actions didn't stand out in a bad way, my name did. They immediately gave me nicknames such as bathroom, kitchen sink, toilet, chef and all kind of other names. I didn't care I was sweating like someone poured a bucket of water on my head, and I needed to catch my breath. There were about nine drill sergeants, two per platoon, and our senior drill sergeant, who looked like he was chiseled out of granite, assigned to our company. Our XO, or Executive Officer and CO, Commanding Officer, were there. Each one introduced himself and told us this was home for the next nine weeks. They said to forget everything we knew before today because they would teach us everything we needed to know from here on out.

After this peaceful conversation, they introduced us to this thing called pain. All hell broke loose, and they treated us like we were the scum of the earth—in a professional manner, however. They ran us to the back of the barracks, where they made us experts on a punishing exercise called mountain climbers. Mountain climbers are done by placing both hands on the ground, both feet on the ground and moving your legs up to your chest on the ground like you are climbing a mountain. More punishing calisthenics followed, like the side-straddle-hop and "dropping" and "front leaning rest."

One recruit named Stevens, who was just slow and uncoordinated, stood out because they believed he was "faking the funk." In other words, he was trying to look like he was working hard but not putting out. Stevens was pulled aside, yelled at beyond belief, then directed by a drill sergeant to run and count every tree in front of the barracks. There had to be 100 trees out there. He had to run and touch each one, count it, then run back to formation. They made all of us watch this process so we could see what not to do. This was the only break we got that day. Stevens came back and gave the sergeant a count, which made the sergeant even more mad and yell even louder, saying that he had more trees than that so go back and count again. This happened three times until Stevens couldn't run any longer.

We learned our collective lesson to push ourselves to the limit.

We learned our collective lesson to push ourselves to the limit.

Once we were finally allowed to go inside the barracks, we were taken either to a smaller eight-man room or a large open bay where dozens of recruits would be housed. I was assigned to a small room, and my bed was the lower bunk on the rack. There was a wall locker next to my bunk that was where everything I owned would be stored while at Leonard Wood. Inside the wall locker, there was a paper diagram illustrating how everything was supposed to be positioned. We were shown how socks were to be rolled, hangers placed two finger widths apart, how to make hospital corner bed coverings, and how the floors should look after being stripped, waxed and buffed.

Our company consisted of four platoons for a total of 240 recruits. The barracks were like college dorm rooms with only a few stalls of toilets, showers and sinks. There were only a few washers and dryers for all of us to use. We spent the rest of the day and evening getting our barracks "squared away." Everyone was extremely quiet. No one was talking, nobody made eye contact with each other; there was just a group of fast-moving people trying to get their lockers set up correctly so they wouldn't become the next example, like Stevens.

By the end, I was exhausted, both mentally and physically. All my friends were having fun back in Chicago. I knew this was a tough road, but I wanted it and was already seeing how it would make me stronger in the future. I kept thinking that if it doesn't kill me, I'd be OK. I also saw that if I didn't operate at the top of my ability, the sergeants would quickly see it. I couldn't let them down, nor myself, so on that first night of basic training, out in the deep woods, I promised myself that I would be the best soldier in my class.

Days in basic training

Each night at the same time, it was "lights out," which meant we were supposed to be in our rack, standing for fire guard duty or pretending to be asleep. The first night, however, people in my room used "lights out" to describe how they were going to kill their recruiters when they got back home—with detail, too, not just generally speaking. After they got tired of talking about this, they fell asleep, and all I could hear was crying and snoring.

I was good with my recruiter. I don't feel he oversold me or sugar-coated how basic training was going to be. It is what it is. Wake-up call was at 0430 with a formation time of 0500. This means that 240 men had to shave and shower, get dressed, make up our bunks and be outside in physical training (PT) clothes and ready for roll call. Once everyone was accounted for, we marched to the street in formation, anticipating the sound of the lead drill sergeant to order us to "double time," or begin running. During runs, the shortest recruits were in the front and the tallest in the rear to ensure the pace was consistent.

There was no better sound during basic than hearing our senior drill sergeant call cadence. His voice was loud, clear, deep and powerful. He commanded respect by his neat dress, spit-shined boots, and deep, reverberating voice. I wanted to make him proud and wanted my voice to reach his ears to let him know I was in lock step with his guidance. We typically ran a few miles to a parade field, where we completed our first PT test. At the time, the PT test consisted of a timed two-mile run and minimum push-ups and sit-ups performed within a two-minute time limit. I always passed my PT test even though I dreaded running. I performed my best on the last test in basic, due to all the weeks of conditioning and punishment. I ran two miles in 13:15, maxed out 72 push ups in two minutes and maxed out 82 sit-ups in another two minutes.

Basic training was hard and painful but also a lot of fun. We did road marches up to 32 miles in one day with full rucksacks of about 50-60 pounds of gear, plus my M16 rifle, blank ammo and full water canteens. We had live fire shooting days, obstacle courses, live grenade training, first aid courses, classroom training days and much more. Basic was vital to who I am and taught me a great deal about what I can accomplish through hard work. It also instilled many lessons that I still draw on now. In fact, I still organize the clothes hanging in my closet from darkest colors on the left to light colors on the right, with each hanger positioned two finger widths apart.

Much like in civilian life, we had to quickly adapt to new ideas and better ways of accomplishing our goals. Security was an important lesson. While we were at PT the first few days, some drill sergeants would be back at the barracks conducting inspections. Each wall locker was secured with a padlock, and most of us kept the key on our dog tag chain around our necks. Everything had to be "secured" and placed in the exact position each time. After PT, we'd run back to barracks, riding high on endorphins. We lined up in front of the barracks in formation, standing at attention until commanded to stand "at ease." The senior drill sergeant would give us details about the time to be outside in formation, and once dismissed, we'd run inside to get showered, changed and back in formation; 240 recruits in 30 minutes was tough, but doable.

As I entered the barracks, I always peeked into the first open doorway on the right side, which was the main sleeping quarters. This time, something was different: It looked like someone had ransacked the entire room. There were wall lockers knocked down on the floor, mattresses thrown all over the place, blankets everywhere. My first thought was that someone broke in and robbed us. Only in the mind of someone from Chicago, right? I kept moving, knowing I had a short amount of time to get back to formation. As I walked down the hall to make that left turn into my room, I wondered if we were robbed also. Yep, the same thing had happened to us. How does someone sneak onto a secure military base, get pass the military police (MPs), avoid our drill sergeants, then rob us?

I soon found out that the "thieves" were our drill sergeants. We were being disciplined for not having our barracks up to the standards we were taught and properly secured. I heard yelling from sergeants from down the hall, so I quickly snapped to getting everything back in place, helping other recruits and getting back outside. If our beds were not made up correctly with 45-degree hospital corners and the blanket tight enough to bounce a coin off of, they were flipped on the floor. If our wall lockers didn't have the padlock on them and actually locked, everything was pulled out and thrown on the floor (wall lockers are tall and heavy, so it took a couple of people to lift them back in place).

I did not escape this discipline. My bunk was flipped a few times early on. I adapted quickly to this problem by thinking ahead, however. I began to always keep my bed made. I took my showers after lights out, then lay fully dressed except for my jacket and boots on top of my blanket. When it was lights-on in the morning, I'd slip under my bed onto the floor, then grab both ends of the blanket tight and tuck them into the bedframe springs, from head to foot. I'd stand back up, then make sure there were no wrinkles, that the hospital corners were at the 45-degree angle and my rack was 100% "squared away." In Army talk, this means being on top of your game. Then, I'd put on my boots and jacket, brush my teeth, and quickly get outside into formation.

Noticed for the right reasons

I would be one of the first people outside every day. Within about three weeks, the drill sergeants noticed that I was disciplined, so they promoted me to company "Guidon Bearer." This was the person who was responsible for maintaining, carrying and securing our Charlie 5/10 (C5/10) flag. Each platoon had its own flag. I would be the person at the front of the entire company on runs, road marches, convoys and everywhere the company went. My position was right behind the company commander, senior drill sergeant and platoon drill sergeants, so I couldn't get away with half-doing anything. Once we got to our destinations each day, I'd post the flag, then fall in line with my platoon to participate in the daily activities.

I still remember mess hall. The first time going in was crazy. We would run to chow each morning after PT and line up in formation. Each of us had to run as fast as possible to the door, take off our cap and stand in line, in the at-ease position. Up front, I could hear recruits yelling their name, last four of their Social Security number and branch of service. There was a civilian lady at this podium at the front of the line who was taking attendance each day and using the information we provided to do her head count.

The line moved super fast and we had to keep our eyes straight forward or risked getting pulled out of line, dropped for push ups then having to start all over again. I could hear the screaming of sergeants yelling at soldiers to put the food in their mouths and chew later. What did that even mean? As I moved past the civilian worker and now to the area where you collect your tray, there were soldiers behind the counter serving us. I quickly side-stepped to the right, moving down the line pointing at what to put on the tray. Next, I found the first open seat I could. Once I sat down, the sergeant yelled at me to eat and leave. I shoved everything in my mouth, left the table chewing, dropped my tray off by the door and went back to formation. Never ever get caught leaving the mess hall chewing. A sergeant was right at the door watching all of us exit, looking for anyone who was chewing. That got us an instant set of push ups. I don't recall ever taking longer than one minute to eat an entire meal in basic training. Even today, I'm baffled when people take 30 minutes to eat a meal—it's insane. Nothing takes 30 minutes!

Throughout basic, we had classroom and practical instruction time. Classrooms were the worst, because being inside and sitting in a chair encourages the overwhelming urge for sleep to kick in. I did everything possible to stay awake, grabbing chunks of skin on my legs and squeezing until it went numb. I'd drink water from my canteen, dig my fingernails into my hands, anything to avoid being taken outside and butchered in the hot sun. We could stand in the back of the classroom if we were falling asleep. I remember in one class the back of the room looked like a gospel choir, lots of recruits lined up on the wall, with their eyelids opening and closing very slowly as they tried to fight sleep.

Church was the only place drill sergeants didn't discipline us, so we would go there just to sleep on Sundays. It was the best sleep ever, sitting in the pews in an air-conditioned chapel without the fear of punishment.

Toughening us up

One part of training the sergeants told us about in advance was the gas chamber. Some recruits knew people who had completed basic in the recent past and told them what to expect. The gas chamber is a part of the Nuclear, Biological and Chemical (NBC) warfare program that we were trained on. We were taught the warning signs, how to put on our protective clothing and how to decontaminate when exposed to these types of weapons. The sergeants were more humane than normal the morning we went to the chamber. They treated us somewhat like humans and would remind us of what we were taught in the classroom, such as not to touch our eyes and faces, and to keep moving toward the wind and hold our arms up at shoulder height after exiting the chamber.

We arrived at the gas chamber training area in the morning hours. The entire company fell into formation and awaited orders. By now, we knew what the process was based on our classroom instruction and were ready to get it over with. Each platoon went in order into this small room that only accommodated about 15-20 people at one time. I was in the first group to enter. We were instructed to put our gas masks on. I opened my carrying case, pulled out my mask and removed my Kevlar helmet. I placed my mask onto my face and pulled the straps on the back of it to adjust the fit and seal. Next, I placed both hands over the valves on the cheek of my mask firmly, then took a deep breath to form a tight seal onto my face. This is one of the most crucial parts of putting on the mask. If not done correctly, chemical agents can seep in and hurt or kill you.

The sergeant said, "let's go," and we walked toward the nondescript building, which sat about 20 yards away. The butterflies were having a field day in my stomach, and my mind was trying to prepare my body for this experience. I wanted to be in the first group because I didn't want to see the reactions of another group ahead of me, which would lead to even crazier thoughts. As soon as we entered the room, we were told to line up on the walls and squeeze together tightly to make room for the next recruit. There was a man in a small booth in the corner of the room, looking at us from behind a thick glass window. The room resembled a small audio recording booth. I could barely hear the orders the sergeant was giving through the mask I had on and the echo in the room.

In front of the booth was a long tube, similar to a straw, that extended from inside the booth to a little bowl that was inside the room we were in. I saw the man drop a tablet into the tube, and it slid down into the bowl. When the tablet reached the already-smoldering bowl, smoke started to fill the room. We were given the order to remove our masks and put our helmets back on our heads. We were also reminded that no one could leave the chamber until everyone removed their mask, no matter how long it took. I grabbed my mask from the chin area and lifted it up toward my forehead while holding my breath. My face got hot instantly, like I had stepped into a sauna. I held my breath as long as possible, then when I couldn't any longer, I exhaled. My throat immediately locked up; I couldn't take a breath, and it felt like my mouth and lungs were plugged. I couldn't exhale or inhale. The tears, mucous, saliva and every other fluid in my head started to drain instantly. My eyes were on fire, even though they were closed. Through the coughing and gasping for air I heard from all sides, I remember the sergeant screaming at somebody to remove their mask. Until they did so, all of us had to suffer.

Finally, a sergeant told us to grab the person next to us and to move outside. I grabbed for anyone I could and followed them, taking baby steps so I would not trip and fall. I refused to open my eyes in the chamber. Once I made my way outside, the fresh air hit my body and began to provide a cool sensation on my face and skin, which was the best feeling ever. Sergeants kept yelling, reminding us to keep our arms up, don't touch our faces and eyes and to keep moving. I wandered around the woods, walking until I could finally start to see figures, which turned out to be other recruits. What seemed like an hour was in reality only five minutes between entering and leaving the gas chamber.

There were other situations in basic training that stood out as things that most people would never have the opportunity or desire to do. These included battle simulations with instructors shooting real bullets and setting off explosions. Drill sergeants are not allowed to put their hands on recruits during training. However, while we were at the shooting range, using live ammunition and the grenade pit, they could do whatever was necessary to save my life or the lives of others.

Range days were fun. They typically started with a road march for a few miles to our destination. The atmosphere was more formal than usual. Paying attention to detail was stressed over and over, and safety was the most important factor to keep in mind. We shot our M16A1 semi-automatic rifles at self-sealing targets shaped like Russian soldiers. For final qualifications, we shot targets from between 25 and 300 yards and had to hit 23 out of 40 pop-up targets in order to pass.

During our live fire obstacle course, the range cadre and our drill sergeants created a war-like environment. We had to put into practice many of the skills we learned during basic. We started out the course running, then low-crawling, then high-crawling in muddy areas, moving through tunnels and over barriers. The course seemed to be a mile long and never-ending. We had full gear, including our rifle, as if we were heading toward assaulting an enemy objective. We carried blank ammunition during this part of training, but the range cadre used live ammo. There were flash and grenade simulations going off all around us, explosions, screaming and the heart-pounding sounds of the M60 machine gun spraying rounds above our heads. This exercise took place at night, and we could see the tracer rounds going overhead. Tracers are bullets that have a red tip on them, and when fired, they glow bright red. The sergeants were shooting way above our heads, but we were warned before this part of training to keep our heads down and only stand in designated areas. I remember the thoughts I had after the live fire course. My mind wondered what a 17-year-old from the South Side of Chicago was doing in the woods in Missouri, dodging bullets and crawling in the mud? I was having a blast, that's what I thought.

Another potentially deadly part of training was the hand grenade course. We had classroom and field practice to teach us the skill of carrying and using grenades. This was one of the parts of training that I looked forward to. Recruits in my company came to learn that in June 1988, a few training cycles before ours, a recruit and a drill sergeant were killed at Fort Leonard Wood in the grenade pit. This fact made everything real for me, knowing that even though we were in a training environment, we were still using live munitions. There was a memorial outside the barracks of the company where the two were assigned, which I visited right after graduation from basic.

The day of the live-fire grenade test was typical, except for how quiet the recruits were. Handling loaded guns was no problem for us, but this was a little different. While we were at the range, I remember being lined up inside a tunnel of sorts behind a wall that had a large, super thick, explosion proof window. I could look out into the pit where my instructor and I would be positioned. As another recruit in front of me threw his grenade, I could hear and feel the blast. Soon it was my turn. I was escorted into the pit by my sergeant and positioned to receive my grenade. With the observation window positioned to my back, I was facing the opposite direction toward a wall that was approximately 20 feet from left to right and was probably 8-10 feet tall. A portion of the wall shorter in the middle provided enough room for me to see the Russian soldier silhouette, which was my target. I was given a live grenade, which I strapped onto my utility belt. Once instructed to throw it, I pulled it from the pouch, placed both hands together at chest level with the grenade in my right and my left hand on the safety pin. When holding a grenade, there is a small handle that sits on one side called the spoon. I pulled the safety pin while holding the grenade and spoon together. With the grenade in my right hand, I pointed my left hand and arm like a straight arrow, aiming at the Russian soldier target. I raised my right hand, holding that spoon tight against the grenade for dear life, into a position like I was about to throw a baseball. I threw the grenade toward the target and dropped into the safety position—on the ground, head down, my thumbs in each ear and hands covering my closed eyes. The grenade will explode approximately three to five seconds after the spoon is released. The explosion from the grenade was loud, and I could feel the concussive blast on the ground. When a grenade explodes, it blows up and outward, so the lower you are, the better your chances of not getting hurt. I was relieved that everything went well that night and felt ready to do it again.

Completing basic training

The rest of basic consisted of more classroom lessons, lots of runs and road marches. The drill sergeants didn't let up on the discipline or intensity of training, but as we developed into soldiers toward the end, they gave us a little more respect and even shared some personal stories and laughs with us.

After graduation, I flew back to Chicago, dressed in my Army Class A uniform. I felt proud of what I had accomplished and happy to be committed to a cause greater than myself. Mom, Dad and my sisters came to pick me up from O'Hare Airport. I remember sitting on my duffel bag waiting on them near the gate my plane deboarded. This was when non-passengers could enter an airport and go all the way to the gate to see people depart or arrive. There were no TSA checkpoints like today. I could see them approaching the gate, with their eyes focused on the people walking off the plane. They walked right past me without recognizing me. Apparently, I had lost weight and looked like a little frail old man, according to my mom. I walked behind them and tapped Dad on his shoulders and surprised them. I had missed the big hugs we exchanged and felt so happy to see my family again. That was the longest time I had been away from them at that point.

Coming home was different. In the Army, I was taught to move like I had a purpose. Put my food in my mouth and chew it later. Everything was about efficiency, direct action, speed and agility. The day after I got back, there was an outdoor church event where everyone was sitting around talking, eating and drinking. I specifically remember how anxious I was and how out of place I felt. I kept wondering why these people were just sitting around like the world was on pause. Didn't anybody have any place to be? Why are they taking so long to eat the food on their plates? What are these men doing with their hands in their pockets? I had to leave that event because everything seemed out of place and out of sync. I think it was a transition for my parents and family as well. I recall another time the first week back when my parents needed something from the store. They were talking among themselves, deciding who would make the trip, so I volunteered. OK, Dad said and reached into his pocket to give me his car keys. I said that's alright, I'll take a quick run. Everyone looked at me like I was crazy. Um, you do know we have a car, is what they seemed to be thinking. So, I took the list and ran the three miles from home up to the store and back. No sweat.

I learned many lessons from basic training, about how far I could push my physical limits, how to develop and follow processes, understand nuance, and adapt and overcome difficult situations. I learned about chains of command, teamwork, punctuality and much more. Most importantly, I learned that you don't ever quit. If I fail at a task, it means to try again. If I fall, get right back up, dust myself off and try again.

GAINS FROM PAIN:
Thinking positive thoughts

There were many times during training as well as during the years I was enlisted that I encountered something that was totally foreign to me. There were times that I felt I didn't have the experience, training and courage I thought, when I was told by a superior all the activities I would participate in. I was uncertain. I was afraid of the unknown.

The first time the drill sergeants announced during formation that we were about to do a short seven-mile run, I panicked inside. I had never run this distance. The feeling of doom, the fear of not finishing the run and the humiliation that came with that all began to fill my head. Once we started to jog, I glanced at the recruits to my left and my right and noticed the looks on their faces. If expressions had words, they would have said the same things I was thinking: I'm nervous.

I began to feel comforted by the fact that I was not alone. The energy in my body and thoughts in my mind moved from fear to resolve. Each step brought determination and enthusiasm for making the best of the situation. I understood that my fear was simply about not having answers to my questions. I pushed through the fear with each step and each word of the cadences we were singing. Positive thoughts now filled my mind as I looked forward to not only finishing the run but being able to share the story of how I overcame fear with others. This one run, the longest I had completed in life, gave me one more bit of proof that I could utilize fear as fuel to take on and accomplish new goals.

4: SETBACKS IN COLLEGE

Learning what you don't like

Senior year came around, and it was good to see friends again. I still felt like I was living in two separate worlds, however, now that I had military service one weekend each month in addition to my civilian responsibilities. Joey, Spanky, Chris, John and I connected every weekend, ending up at Spanky's father's house. Spanky's dad was a Chicago police officer who allowed us to hang out in his basement instead of us being out on the streets. He only asked that we keep it as clean as it was before we got there. Our typical night was going to a basketball or football game if Carmel was playing, or catching a show at Evergreen Plaza, then grabbing chicken from Harold's.

There was one time during my senior year that brought me great pride. I was now able to help my parents out instead of them always sacrificing for me. I was able to give my mom a $1,500 down payment from my Army pay and after-school job to buy her new Toyota Camry. This was a rewarding time that also emphasized that my pain in basic training brought reward. I drove my mom's car everywhere, more than she did. The Camry was a brand-new 1988 LE Model, navy blue with nice shiny factory silver wheels, a sunroof and power everything. I still remember how good I felt doing something for others, and this feeling would never leave my consciousness.

Carmel life was good, and I established excellent friendships during those years. There were several soon-to-be professional athletes at our school. Chris Calloway was my gym aide in freshman year and went on to play for the New York Giants football team. Donovan McNabb, who became an awesome quarterback with the Philadelphia Eagles, attended Carmel after I did, but I had already known him and his family from elementary school. Donovan's older brother Sean was a good athlete, and all of us expected he would go pro. He was good at basketball, baseball and football and dominated during gym and pick-up games that we played. Donovan was always smaller than us, if you can believe that, but still had the desire to play ball whenever he was around. The last time I saw Donovan was during a visit I made to Carmel as a graduate to see my old teachers. He was in Coach Nick's class, and we waved at each other. The McNabbs are a great family: Their mom and dad were active in church and our school, and we are all glad to have called them friends.

As graduation neared, everyone was excited about going to college. But I was more excited about going to my Advanced Individual Training (AIT), which started one week after graduation. I flew out to Fort Dix in New Jersey, spent eight weeks learning to drive everything the Army had and graduated at the top of my class. I landed back in Chicago on August 2, 1989. One week later, I was on my way with my parents to Southern Illinois University (SIU). My mom had taken the time to complete all the required paperwork for me during my absence, including dorm room, phone service, meal plan and whatever else was needed.

The college life isn't for me

College life was not for me, as I quickly discovered. There were a couple of people that I knew from Carmel who attended SIU, which made the transition a little easier. I started college in August and was working in the Computing Affairs department by September. My job was at the help desk, assisting students with technical problems they were having using IBM personal computers, Word Perfect and Lotus 1-2-3 spreadsheets. I spent way more time working than going to class.

Because my job was a work-study position, technically there should have been weekly limits to my job, but I quickly found a way around this. My manager would schedule me for a small number of hours, but I let other workers know that I was available to take their shift if they had exams or other scheduling conflicts. There were three computer labs on campus, and we could be assigned to any one of them during our shifts. Working with IBM computers was totally new to me as my experience since sixth grade was in using Apple products. I dove headfirst into the job and read everything I could about the computers, the software and how they were connected. When a student or faculty member came to the counter at the help desk, we would take turns supporting them by answering their questions and going to their computer and showing them how to do certain tasks. Each time someone came to the counter, I would jump up to be the first person to help them. I was hungry to learn and wanted to take on the challenge of solving their problems. My priority in college was to get work experience and practical knowledge, and I focused less on classroom instruction. I remember being in class, whether it was COBOL programming, accounting or English, and feeling the anxiety of waiting for it to be over. I wanted to learn all I could, but through hands-on practice, not by reading about it.

> *I wanted to learn all I could, but through hands-on practice, not by reading about it.*

While at SIU, I still carried the same, olive green Army rucksack I used in high school and occasionally wore some cut-off Army camouflage pants also known as "cammies." Every so often, I'd see a few soldiers jogging around campus, and we'd speak or nod our heads as we passed each other. I had the opportunity to meet Cadet Frisch during one of these encounters. We could instantly tell we were soldiers and started talking about our past and current military lives. Frisch was in a National Guard Infantry unit in Woodstock, Illinois. This immediately got my attention, and I let him know that was the type of unit I wanted when I enlisted. Frisch told me that I could transfer from the Reserves to the Guard, and he could help make that happen. His words were like a cold bottle of water after a 10-mile run. I couldn't believe the possibility that was in front of me at this moment. A few months later, I was with my dad and sister Fran at the National Guard Armory in Woodstock, being sworn in by Sgt. Woods into an infantry unit. I would now have the opportunity to do more exciting activities in the Army. My new unit was approximately seven hours from Carbondale, so I would drive to Chicago late in the week to be able to get to drill on time. The unit was great: They had good leadership, slots for Airborne and Air Assault schools and much more.

Weekend drills included some cool stuff. I felt the adrenaline and excitement of finally getting to do what I wanted to, which was being a soldier, in the field doing adventurous stuff. One of the best experiences was flying in a helicopter for the first time. The landing zones were simply flat land areas, typically tucked into wooded terrain, out of the view of civilian traffic. We were divided into chalks, groups of four to eight soldiers that would ride together on a "bird" or "helo." We'd line up on both sides of a long, wooded area that had tall trees on both sides, probably 150 yards apart. We faced the tree lines to ensure enemy personnel were not approaching. I could hear the distinctive low growl of the UH-1H Huey rotor blades from a distance. Seeing a chopper passing above while you drive down the road is one thing, but knowing I was about to ride in one was an awesome feeling.

Once in the bird, I sat in the small canvas seat, which was on the left side of the bird. The crew chief instructed us to point the muzzle (barrel) of our weapons down, then he helped to secure our seat belts. Seat belt is not the word

I'd use to describe this thing. It's more like a piece of canvas about 1-2 inches tall, and pretty thin. The Hueys are small birds, unlike the newer Black Hawks, which are more spacious and modern. As I sat there, my butt was in the seat, which feels like a steel box with canvas tarp on it, and my upper body was leaning forward, as my rucksack wouldn't allow me to sit back completely. The tips of my combat boots were hanging over the metal doorsill a few inches. The crew chief boarded the bird, and we began liftoff, with the doors wide open. Life couldn't get any better. I felt the weightlessness as we lifted off the ground, which was much different than being in a plane. We started to pick up speed, and I noticed we never gained much altitude. The sound from the engine, coupled with the winds blowing past, made the ride even more adventurous. My eyes, ears and whole body were focused on the experience. I felt every movement of the bird, up and down, and side by side. ,We were flying what I later came to learn was "map of the earth." This is when a helicopter flies a certain altitude above the terrain, not at a constant elevation. Our birds were going up and down, just above tree lines, then diving back down along flat areas, then back up to clear more trees. This is a tactical maneuver used by pilots to avoid showing up on enemy radar. I looked forward to riding in the Hueys every time we had the opportunity to do so.

Back on campus, life wasn't that exciting by contrast. There was the occasional party or small group get-togethers with friends. I rarely went to parties because of the countless hours I spent working, but one I remember was organized by my Carmel friend John for students across the country. John was involved in the Student Union, and they were hosting a national conference that included panel discussions, meet and greets and other events. This was a party associated with the conference.

I was one of the coolest dudes on campus, just leaning against the wall and bobbing my head to the music. My wardrobe was hot: freshly ironed jeans with a crisp crease, fancy puffy sweater with vibrant colors on it, casual loafers and a diamond stud earring, courtesy of the hard work I put in during my high school years. We met a group of girls from the University of Wisconsin–Oshkosh, who happened to be standing in the same part of the building we were. We spoke and introduced ourselves, then made small talk. Now remember, I'm the coolest dude on campus, so much so, that this fine young lady walked right past me and asked my roommate Fred to dance. Dang, can a man get any attention around these parts? I just kept listening to the music and nursing my bruised ego. I felt like everyone in the building saw what had just happened. *"It's ok, I'm good"*, I thought to myself.

Meeting Monique

We wound up meeting up again with the same group of girls the next day and sat around and talked for what seemed to be hours. A few of us, including John and me, had our eyes on different girls in the group, so we didn't have to negotiate between each other who would pursue whom (this is how it works in the real world, ladies). We discussed heavy political and social issues, like most college students do, thinking we were going to change the world. We were pointing out injustices, debating elections issues, what our potential careers were going to be and the option of attending graduate school. I was part of the conversation but was more focused on my next ride in a Huey and buying the Porsche that I had dreamed of since elementary school. During the conversation, Monique and I discovered that back in Chicago, we lived only about a mile from each other. I never recalled seeing her in the grocery store or gas station or even at the mall like I did other people from SIU who lived near me.

Monique and I kept in touch via the phone and letters after she went back to Oshkosh. I remember driving up to a pay phone in the parking lot at school. I dialed the number using my long-distance calling card, waited to get connected, then rolled my window up so the cord and handset were inside the car, so I wouldn't get wet from the rain. Amazing what someone will do to pursue someone who wouldn't even dance with them.

During the same period of time, I was getting further and further behind in classwork. I was working at the computer labs, then started a sales job selling clone computers with this shady character that built them at home, I think. I made ZERO sales. I did manage to set up a few sales meetings with potential customers. Our clones cost approximately $3,500, which was a big discount from the name-brand computers that were available then, but ultimately still a lot of money.

I was ambitious and busy all the time and didn't waste time on anything else except reading business magazines and books and working. During downtime in the computer labs in the evenings, there were only a few students that would come in to work, and they were typically grad students. I used this time to get more practical experience using the school's resources. One of my favorite things to do was to

I was ambitious and busy all the time and didn't waste time on anything else except reading business magazines and books and working.

create spreadsheets and list all the things I dreamed about owning. My parents would drive out to Matteson, Illinois, on Saturdays to visit model homes in new subdivisions, and I would go with them while on breaks from school. Matteson, Olympia Fields and Country Club Hills were what we called semi-affluent suburbs. There would be three or four different styles of model homes that a person could buy and have built in each subdivision. We spent hours walking through the homes, and my parents would each pick the ones they like. They would ask for brochures from the salesperson and a list of options that they could add to new construction. Home shopping was a ritual for our family. I wondered why my parents were creating the pain of seeing something they could not afford, discussing and dreaming about it as if they were going to buy it next week, without the means to do so.

When I was creating my spreadsheets, I specifically remember listing a new home in Matteson with a monthly mortgage payment of $1,300. I had $800 for a Mercedes and $800 for a sports car. I didn't know how much Porsches cost back then, and there was no Internet yet to find out. I knew the price of a Mercedes because my mom's boss had one. Later in life, I came to learn that my parents were visualizing their desires and talking them into existence. They understood the law of attraction, and looking back, it worked for them.

Between National Guard drills and work, I found time to take a road trip to visit Monique in Oshkosh. This was an eight-hour drive in my 1983 Supra that already had well over 120,000 miles and a coolant leak. I knew how I got to Chicago, but still can't explain today how I found her school. There were no GPS devices for our cars nor cell phones with Google Maps at that time. I had a real map printed on paper that I used for directions. I read and followed signs on the expressway and eventually found her school, nine hours later in the dead of night. The trip was a surprise to Monique. Whether this was smart of me or not, it shows the level of determination I have. It kindled a very important tradition that I still sustain today with Monique. The foundation of our relationship all hinged on my willingness to do what other men would never lower their standards to do. I had to think long and hard as to whether this slippery slope would put an end to my manhood and leave me emotionally defeated. I decided to go for it.

I started carrying her camera equipment.

Yep. Monique was into radio/television, and that weekend, I had the great privilege of lugging heavy bags and cameras to various locations to get some B-roll footage of woodpeckers or some other random nonsense. It didn't matter, because we enjoyed the time together. Still to this day, I carry Monique's camera equipment from time to time, more than 29 years later. Now that's a solid foundation.

Transitions and my truth

In my guard unit, I was lucky enough to get a slot for Air Assault school. This is a 14-day class that teaches you how to rappel from choppers in addition to other helo-related skills. About two weeks before I was supposed to head to Fort Campbell, Kentucky, for class, my slot was cancelled. This is not uncommon in the military. Things change so much, and priorities get pushed to the back burners for various reasons; in fact, this is the source of the popular phrase— among all branches of the military— "hurry up and wait." Over time, my work schedule became all that was important, and I missed a few guard drills, which went on my record. Eventually, I was moved to Individual Ready Reserve (IRR) status. As an individual assigned to the IRR, I would receive no pay, nor was I obligated to drill or complete annual training. It did mean, however, that I could be activated by Presidential Reserve Callup Authority, which is exactly what happened to a few soldiers from my unit. The first group of soldiers were being deployed to participate in the Gulf War for Operation Desert Shield, then Operation Desert Storm. I was in the second of three groups that would be deployed, but as history would prove, the conflict only lasted 100 hours.

As a soldier, I trained, then trained, then trained some more. It's like going to basketball practice and playing against my own teammates but never playing in an actual game against a rival team. I was not eager to go to war, nor was I against it. This is what I signed up for, and I understood it was part of the job while serving in a combat unit. I recall looking at the invasion on CNN in the student center among a lot of students hanging out, playing pool, eating and talking. My perspective was different from others' that day. I would be going soon, and my cousins Chris and Pam were being deployed by their Navy units as well as my cousin Jimmy, who was already in theater in the Persian Gulf. I had many surreal moments like this in life where I'm in the room with others and we're looking at the exact same thing but having vastly different internal feelings and perspectives.

I was thinking that if other members of my unit were there and I was sent, I wanted to be there to help and protect them. The military lifestyle is very close to my heart, and I have the highest regard for the soldiers, sailors, Marines, airmen and Coast Guard personnel while at their duty stations, on leave, retired or down-range.

The lessons and experiences I gained during my Army time are priceless. I learned leadership, how to do more than I ever thought I could mentally and physically, how to build and maintain strong bonds based on a joint purpose and so much more.

With this chapter of my life complete and upon my eventual discharge, I had little patience or desire to stay at SIU. I was ready to get into the real game and start my practical education. I went to two teachers to request an incomplete in their classes. The first teacher understood and granted it without a problem. The second teacher shared an office with the teacher I just met with from my other class. I had to schedule a meeting. I approached her closed office door and knocked gently. She opened the door and directed me to sit in the chairs just outside of the office. A few minutes later, she opened the door and directed me to enter and to have a seat across from her desk. I greeted her and thanked her for taking time to meet with me. Without

going into too much detail, I explained that I ultimately was requesting an incomplete for her class. She went ballistic and began to scream and holler. I was shocked by her lack of professionalism and inability to control her emotions. The other professor who shared the office with her was shocked as well. We made eye contact, and I'm sure he saw my utter disbelief. One thing she said stood out above everything else, and I can remember it as if it occurred yesterday: She told me that I would never amount to anything if I didn't finish her class.

While this was uncomfortable, I recognized the kernel of truth, which was if I didn't complete college, I wouldn't be able to get hired at Eli Lilly or State Farm or other large companies as a computer programmer. She was correct, and the reality was, I didn't want to be a programmer. I wanted to be an entrepreneur. I ignored everything she said after that, partially because her wig kept slipping down onto her forehead and she had to keep putting it back in place. It was an embarrassing meeting. The other teacher sat there in horror as he listened to her dress me down.

When I walked out of her office, I didn't feel bad or like a failure. I felt the opposite. I knew in that moment that she had the problem, not me. She never asked what I wanted for my life, what gave me joy and pleasure; it was all about her and her school. I had the same feeling other entrepreneurs wrote about in their autobiographies, as if no one understands them and their crazy ideas. I was in good company and had an overwhelming sense of freedom after that. My soul was unchained, and I was now going to pursue my dreams, not someone else's. I did think about sending her a letter a few years later including a photo of me, with a big smile on my face, standing next to my new Porsche, but I didn't want to put that negative energy into the universe.

Always be prepared, no matter what

I have a few recurring nightmares that continue to visit me at night, even though the frequency has decreased significantly over time. One is from Carmel while I was in Ms. Ryan's Spanish class, sitting in the third seat on the left side of the classroom. The windows are on my left side and there is an empty row between desks on my right. Ms. Ryan's desk is directly in front of the row I'm sitting in. The dream is as follows: There are less than five minutes remaining in Spanish class. Inside, my mind is focused on the clock, hanging on the wall near the door. I'm watching the second hand move slowly, tick by tick by tick. At times, it feels like the clock hands stop. Ms. Ryan gets the class's attention to let us know what our homework assignment is for tomorrow. She then announces that she is coming around to collect our completed homework from last night. The problem is, I didn't do mine and have no excuse why. Horror is all I feel. Ms. Ryan stands up and moves from behind her desk.

She walks to the right side of the first student's desk and reaches out for his homework; he hands it to her. She takes a couple of steps toward the second student and reaches out for his homework; he reaches toward her and turns in his assignment. She takes a couple more steps toward me and stands at the right side of my desk and reaches out for my homework. I slowly lift my head in shame to look at her. Our eyes meet as my heart beats through my chest as she leans toward me slightly, extending her right arm to receive my completed assignment, and the dream ends. Each time I have this dream, I wake up in terror. It's extremely vivid. I can feel the same feelings I had then, being faced with the consequences of not being prepared and not performing at a high level at all times.

I figured out later in life that therefore, I am always overprepared. I have a burning desire to always be prepared. If I am supposed to be somewhere at a certain time, I'm always there early. If I'm supposed to produce a work product, I'd better produce it, without delay or excuse. I was taught a principle in the Army that two is one and one is none. In other words, always have way more than you need because if you have the bare minimum, you essentially have nothing. I used to wake from this nightmare, sit up on the side of the bed and take a mental inventory of everything. Are the bills paid, do the cars have gas, are the doors locked, is

> *I was taught a principle in the Army that two is one and one is none. In other words, always have way more than you need because if you have the bare minimum, you essentially have nothing.*

the alarm on, did I do everything I was supposed to on my checklist yesterday, what meetings or calls do I have today and am I ready for them? The nightmares were painful, but I now use them as way of remembering to always be prepared, no matter what.

I called my mom and told her that I was dropping out of college. These must be the some of the last words my parents ever wanted to hear. The only way I could have made it worse was if I would have followed up with, "I'm also going to join the circus." I had spoken it into the universe, and I had to live with the consequences no matter what. I sat in my apartment and thought about what was next for me. What did my dad think when my mom told him? What would my sisters think, and would my younger sister see this as me giving up and ultimately never achieving anything meaningful in my life? I also wondered what Monique would feel. Did this decision destroy a future with her?

I focused on what I needed to do to make sure the dreams I had and goals I set for myself were achieved. My dreams never included being a college graduate; as a matter of fact, college was simply the next step after high school, not something I had a strong desire to do. Just as they did when I decided to enlist in the Army, my parents allowed me to succeed or fail on my own. They didn't criticize or tear me down. They trusted me to make the decisions that were right for me. I'm sure inside, however, they had doubts and questioned themselves and their parenting.

I packed up the Toyota and headed back to the "Chi." There are times in life when sobriety comes fast and without mercy. I had choices and met the forks in the road that forced me to make decisions that affected the rest of my life, in a positive or negative manner. One thing I knew then and continue to know now, without exception, is that no one will knock on my door and give me anything, without it having conditions favorable to them. I could not sit in a corner and worry, complain, blame others or talk about how the world was not fair. The world is not fair, and I will only receive from life a proportional amount of reward for the work I am willing to invest. If I spent my time reading, making calls and trying to get into the tech world, that's what would eventually happen. So I spent 100% of my time on that goal.

Starting a career

I looked for work everywhere, including the classifieds in the newspaper and asking neighbors and friends if they knew of any company that was hiring. I didn't just want any job, I wanted to get into the technology arena so I could continue learning and getting hands-on experience. I'm not thinking about the theory taught in school; I'm talking about touching and feeling technology that was being used in businesses and corporations around the world.

One of my cousins would stay with us from time to time. At this particular time, it was my older cousin Ricky, who made his home on the couch in the living room. It was cool to have a cousin around and my parents always opened our home to a family member who needed some help in life. It was about 2:30am or 3:00am one morning when I heard the car alarm blaring on my Supra. Ricky yelled up to me, "Tony, somebody is stealing your car!" I jumped out of bed and ran downstairs. Ricky had already unlocked and opened the back door and was heading outside. I grabbed the car keys for my mom's car off the hook in the kitchen and followed.

Ricky told me it was a tow truck, which we spotted heading southbound on the opposite side of the railroad tracks. I made a quick right onto 111th Street, crossed the tracks, then another right and we were on the same street as the tow truck. We hit 115th Street quickly, blew through that red light and weres catching up with the tow truck. We intercepted them just past the red light on 119th Street and crossed over into the city of Calumet Park. I approached them on the right side of our car, while Ricky was waving a bat at them. My car and the tow truck were swerving side to side, trying not hit each other.

Before we made it to 123rd, which was a hard-left turn, a swarm of Calumet Park police cars pulled in front and behind us. There were so many guns pointed at us that I couldn't even count. The police were yelling and giving commands that all seemed to contradict each other: hands up, get out of the car, don't move, show me your hands, keep still. Both of us were directed to exit the vehicle, keep our hands up and slowly back up toward the sound of their voices. We were detained but not put into the police cars. My heart was beating fast because of the adrenaline. I felt we were in the right, because these guys just stole my car and I was following them to get it back. The three guys in the tow truck were standing and speaking with a couple of officers. One of them must have called the police on us sometime during our chase.

I told the cops that these guys were stealing my car, so we chased them. The police replied that they were repo men. That's when you go from a righteous high-speed chase to Holy @#$%, this is all because of me. The police were cool, and once everyone understood what was going on, the repo guys got back in their truck and left with my car in tow. Ricky and I were left there talking to the police. We had to show our identification to them, which I had on me, but Ricky didn't. They ran our info and shortly after, a couple of them walked over to Ricky and told him to put his hands behind his back. I was thinking I was next. It turns out Ricky had a warrant due to unresolved traffic tickets, so they were taking him to jail. I was eventually allowed to leave.

When I returned home, Dad was already up and wondering what all the commotion was about when I ran out of the house earlier. I explained what happened and he had that look of "where did I go wrong" on his face. My dad and I went to bail Ricky out later that morning. I had to get on the phone with the bank in Carbondale to see what I could do to get my car back. It turns out I only owed about $200 for the payoff but with tow and storage fees, it was in the $500 range. My dad somehow made the payment to the bank and we went to get my car. Man, I really appreciated that car more than ever after getting it back. I went to the self-serve car wash on 124th and Western Avenue, in the city of Blue Island, which was only 10 minutes away, and spent all day washing the Supra inside out. If you looked past the rust, worn out seats and bad windshield wipers, it was beautiful. We actually threw good money after bad as the same week I got the car back, the timing chain broke and would cost more than the value of the car to get it fixed. My dad and I had it towed to the same junk yard that towed it and sold it for parts for a couple of hundred dollars.

Bricks in the foundation of life

Let's take stock. I dropped out of college, my car got repossessed, I'm living in my parents' basement, I have no job and no money, the student loan people are sending letters almost daily and I needed a haircut. Thank God I began cutting my own hair in seventh grade, otherwise my life would be in shambles. None of these setbacks was able to snuff out the burning flame I had within me to be an entrepreneur.

I read several books during my college days that gave me examples of others who had achieved greatness despite facing seemingly overwhelming odds. I gravitated toward books and stories of success about people who started with little to nothing, and I stayed away from those that portrayed the child of wealthy parents or those that attended Ivy League universities and started their own businesses. These stories didn't resonate with me, because I couldn't relate to their realities. Were there stories I could draw upon during this time for guidance and inspiration?

Were there stories I could draw upon during this time for guidance and inspiration?

What had I learned from my experiences up until this point in my life, and how could I apply them today so I could figure out a solution and move ahead? What life lessons did I learn from my parents, and how did they deal with tough situations?

My parents were strong people, but in different ways. My dad had so much practical wisdom from his life experiences, and Mom had so much faith in God. This was a great balance that I would be blessed to have in my DNA. No matter what was going on in their lives, they never said things like, I can't, it's not fair, why me, what did I do to deserve this or anything that took the responsibility away from them. Every day, my dad got dressed like he was going to prom. This guy wore jeans with a belt just to cut the grass. My mom always had a positive outlook and said, "If it is God's will, it will happen." My heroes were in the same house I lived in and instilled these values in me and my sisters by their actions. I didn't sit around and think about my current position in life; I focused on my dream and those things I listed in my spreadsheet back at SIU. I developed a mindset that allowed me to quickly move from shock, to options, to defiance, then to action. Then as today, I will not allow my current circumstances to dictate what my emotions and future look like. I will not sit in a corner and play the reruns of challenging past experiences in my mind and throw away my shot at greatness.

There were many painful times during my early life, but thankfully not as many as the joyful ones. I can say that I learned more during the painful times and can look at each one as a brick in the foundation of my life. By 18, I had already experienced many events that built character, determination, resiliency, faith and many more qualities that I would need in the future. If I had missed any of these experiences, I would probably be crushed under the weight of the events yet to come.

GAIN FROM PAIN:
Setbacks in college

One of the most valuable lessons I learned during my college years was to trust my gut feelings. Since childhood, I was on a path to attend college because that is what my parents understood as the road to success. They had good reason to believe this to be true. Have you ever wondered why you are doing a certain thing? Why you have the career or job you have? Why you like certain foods or hobbies?

If most of us look at where we are at any given point in our lives and are honest with ourselves, we can attribute it to someone else's influence and/or vision of who they thought we should be. I had this revelation after my first year in college: that I was there because it was what my parents thought I should do after high school. I went to college as a "next step" not because I had positive thoughts and feelings about it but because it was what was expected of me.

It wasn't what I wanted. I learned, at great financial and time expense, to go with my gut. I allowed myself to question where I was and why I was there. I released the fear of disappointing my parents by not finishing and embraced the freedom that came with having positive thoughts about what I wanted for my life. A new world opened up inside of me when I let go and accepted who I was. This was only possible after being true to myself. This lesson is invaluable and has guided me toward success more times than I can remember. I struggled at times when I chose to go against my "gut" to do favors for individuals and business partners. I found myself doing what they wanted me to do for their gain as opposed to what is best for me and my interests. I learned to wake up each day and think positive thoughts and embrace positive feelings. It is your conscience leading you to greatness.

5: BROTHERS FROM OTHER MOTHERS

My support system

The notion that no one can be successful in any endeavor without a strong support system is an understatement. Besides blood family members, I have a core group of friends. Three I have known my entire life: Jerry, Tracey and Spoon.

Let's define "friend." To me, a true friend is a family member, except they have different parents. These are people who I will do anything for and vice versa; they don't ask why, they just need to know when, and they are there.

Jerry and Spoon are a few years older than I am, and we grew up on the same block. Tracey and I are the same age and lived only a couple of miles from each other and attended elementary school together through eighth grade. Later in life, the three of them would become friends with each other and connect without me being the central figure in the relationship.

As my family's only son, I sought out close relationships with guys that I felt were like brothers. Today, my son TJ calls them uncle, and they each communicate directly with

Monique as well, which provides that feeling of a complete circle of support. Along life's path, we have shared some of the most important moments with each other, including the births of children and the deaths of parents. We have a group text among the four of us for sharing laughs, important updates and checking in on each other's mental health.

We share a love of motorcycles. Jerry and Spoon had been riding ever since I was a young boy. Jerry had a dirt bike, doing wheelies up and down the block. Spoon had a dirt bike as well, and I often rode behind him up and down the alleys in our neighborhood. Seeing them riding all those years made me want to ride.

After starting my company, I was able to buy my first motorcycle. Jerry took me to a few dealerships and explained the important parts of buying a bike. He guided me on what size I should get and the right engine for riding enjoyment and safety. We spent lots of hours in and out of shops until I landed on a Kawasaki Ninja 600. It was a mix of purple, dark blue and fuchsia colors and had a chrome exhaust pipe with some nice chrome accents. I bought a purple Shoei helmet to match.

The only problem was, I didn't know how to ride a motorcycle. Monique's father had to ride the bike home for me on the pickup date because Jerry was at work. Of course, it's already clear from my story that when I wanted to accomplish a goal, I would set it, then figure out how to achieve it later. This time was no different. Not knowing how to ride a motorcycle is no reason for not buying one, right?

I rode up and down the freshly paved alley, learning to change gears, take off from the stopped position in first gear and eventually lean into 45-degree turns at the end of the block. After a couple of days of doing this, I enrolled in a motorcycle safety class, which also taught me how to ride as well as prepared me to complete the requirements to get my Class M – motorcycle license.

In the meantime, my big brother Jerry took me out on the street for some real-world experience. This guy has the patience everyone wishes they could have. We would pull up to a red light, wait for it to turn green, then I would slowly let off the clutch on the left hand grip while with my right hand, pulling the throttle grip back to give it some gas until the bike slowly pulled away from the intersection and moved smoothly down the street. This was one of the hardest adjustments I had to get used to. If I let off the clutch too fast, the bike would cut off. If I gave it too much gas, the power would lift the front wheel off the ground and do a wheelie. I don't remember how many times my bike cut off at red lights and stop signs, but Jerry would stop his bike, tell me not to worry or rush, then tell the people behind me in the cars that were beeping to go around, sometimes in not-so-nice terms. His patience is what gave me the space to learn how to ride, without the stress of panicking in traffic.

Out of my comfort zone

He also led by example, providing the safety net I needed to grow and learn. For instance, the first time Jerry took me on the expressway, I remember him turning to me, talking loudly so I could hear his voice inside my helmet, saying to relax, take my time and it will be fine.

My hesitation about riding on the expressway was about having to lean into curves and turns; the stakes are just far higher than on the streets because you're at high speed and so is everyone else. The light changed, I slowly let off the clutch with my left hand and pulled the throttle back with my right, and off we went. I followed Jerry down the ramp. While continuing to look toward my left side for a place to merge with the oncoming traffic, I remember feeling the sense that this isn't so bad, even though we hadn't hit a turn yet. That would come, with Jerry leading the way. I leaned a little to the right, and the bike moved smoothly without any problem, as I pulled back on the throttle a little more to increase my speed through the turn. Jerry gave me a thumbs-up with his left hand and we kept riding for a long time that day.

Spoon, Jerry and I put a lot of miles on our bikes over the years and did a lot of crazy stuff. We rode with many police officers back in the day, meeting up on Montvale, then heading up to Rock N Roll McDonalds' downtown Chicago, which was one of the popular meeting spots. We also spent a lot of time on 79th and Stony Island, sitting on the side of the street, talking and laughing. The biking community was tight back then, and we would see the same riders every weekend. There is a sense of camaraderie with bikers, no matter if you were riding a sports bike, a Harley or anything in between. When we would see the old guys with long beards and leather sleeveless jackets riding on the big dresser Harley cruisers, we would stop and talk with them or wave when passing each other. I knew they enjoyed the same open road feeling I did and faced the same dangers as well. This was a bond that most of us had. There was always a mutual respect that we enjoyed.

The thrill of the open road

All three of us upgraded bikes at some point. Jerry and I bought Honda CBR900RRs and Spoon got a new Yamaha R1, which was the hottest bike out at the time. Normally, bikes weren't supposed to go through any heavy-duty riding until they hit at least 500 miles, in order to break the engine in. Well, none of us listened to that nonsense. We rode hard and fast right out the front door of the dealership. One year, Interstate 57 southbound from 147th street through the connector to Interstate 80 was freshly paved. The road was smooth, flat and dying to be broken in. I was living in a suburb about 15 minutes south of my parents' block at the time. After a long day or night of riding, we would stop back at the "block" to check on Jerry's and Spoon's mothers. I rang the bell and let my parents know I was heading home for the night. We met back up in front of Spoon's mom's house, so they could ride to my house to drop me off. That's an example of how my brothers always took care of me.

I was wearing a long-sleeve green Nike windbreaker pullover with a large Nike logo on the front, black Nike baseball batting gloves, short pants and gym shoes. Spoon had on a long-sleeve windbreaker as well, but I can't recall what Jerry was wearing. We made our way around the corner and merged onto Interstate 57 heading south. It was probably around 11:00p.m., nice night, a little breezy and very little traffic. Motorcycles perform better with cooler air as it keeps the engine at a good lower temperature.

Our bikes were lightweight: The CBR900RR weighed only approximately 408 pounds with a full tank of gas. With this light weight, when I twisted the throttle grip back with my right hand, the bike slammed forward, ready to go. We merged onto the expressway and moved over to the left-hand lane and continued toward 115th Street, then quickly to 119th Street, then toward 127th Street, passing the city of Blue Island on our right-hand side. This is the part of the interstate that was elevated, which allowed a breeze to come across the expressway, moving from our left to right side. Even with my helmet on, I could hear how well the engine was performing, it was a beautiful, consistent, whining sound. I loved this feeling. It was perfect.

As we approached the new pavement just past 147th Street, we took off. We were so experienced and confident riding together that we would often ride in the same lane, with only 24-30 inches between us, side by side doing 100 miles per hour. We knew when to lean together and were able to anticipate each other's next move just by reading body language. If Spoon was riding in front and he tilted his head to the right side slightly, that meant he was looking to change lanes. We had such a good chemistry that we trusted our safety level and knew we were always aware of each other's position and how our moves would affect each other. We rode fast and hard, but never in a reckless manner, swerving in and out of traffic.

That night, I remember all three of us leaning down on our gas tanks as flat as possible, bringing our helmets down so low that the chin would touch the tank. I could look at the road ahead beneath the tiny windshield that was only 8-10 inches above the gas tank. I glanced down at the speedometer as it was at about 115 miles per hour, then 120, then 130, then 135, then 140, then 145, only moving my eyes, not lifting my head or body because at that speed, I would instantly be ripped off the bike by the headwinds. We slowed down slightly to make the gradual left curve at the Interstate 80 overpass, but we were still going above 110 miles per hour. Once we passed it, we were on the final straightaway on Interstate 57 again, heading toward our exit at Vollmer Road, which was about four miles ahead. We picked our speed back up, and I remember glancing down at the speedometer and it was at 155 miles per hour, and I kept twisting the throttle harder with my brothers. The last speed I saw was about 160, then we had to let off the gas to prepare to make that hard-right turn onto the off-ramp. We pulled into a parking lot right on Vollmer Road to the left side, which was our usual rally point. Once we came to a complete stop, we took our helmets off, and Jerry was laughing so hard. He told Spoon and me to look at our jackets. Both of us saw that the sleeves had completely ripped off and were hanging down near our wrists. We had gone so fast that the threads had been torn to pieces. This was one of the best rides I ever experienced, and the adrenaline was flowing so hard that I couldn't go to sleep until a few hours later. To put it into perspective, the maximum speed of the Huey helicopter I use to ride in was approximately 127 miles per hour. This night, I was moving more than 30 miles per hour faster than a helicopter—but on land.

I share this story for two reasons. First, I would have never trusted anyone else on earth except Jerry and Spoon on that ride. Second, looking back, that was probably my most reckless action in life. I didn't feel that way at the time—we were good riders, we knew the roads, we knew our bikes, we knew our skills and we were pushing the limits of both the machines and the men. It was similar to taking a leap of faith to start a business or jump into 105 feet of water in the middle of the ocean with no land in sight or leaning out of a helicopter flying just above tree level. My biggest rewards have always come after I took my biggest leaps of faith. I stared fear right in the eyes, and it blinked before I did. It was eerie at the time that we were going so fast that the streetlights that lined the sides of the interstate almost blended into one continuous line of light. During the ride, I remember screaming in my helmet with excitement like I was on a roller-coaster, having the time of my life.

My biggest rewards have always come after I took my biggest leaps of faith.

Growing through life together

Tracey and I always found time to sit and contemplate life and spirituality. As we are the same age and started kindergarten together, we spent the most time together between then and high school. We were Boy Scouts, altar boys and members of other organizations over the years. For every milestone as young men, Tracey and I were always in the same place, physically and emotionally. Our first jobs were even right next door to each other, mine at a grocery store and his at a pharmacy.

The four of us have also spent a lot of time together with our families on cruises and in the Caribbean. We would sit and talk about life and what was happening in each other's lives. We knew each other's families and most of the circumstances each of us faced. To this day, there has never been any judgement between us, nor have we let the others be lonely during tough times. All three of my brothers had children before me, so I could turn to them for guidance and advice from a father's perspective. I leaned on them for relationship advice as well, what to do, what not to do. The relationship is also cool because of the age difference. Jerry and Spoon are retired, and Tracey and I are still of working age, so I am listening to them plan the next years of life and how they want to spend it. I can see the transition from young guys being proud of our clean cars to now wanting a quiet, sunny place to relax and enjoy life.

This brotherhood isn't unique—I hope that other men have a tight group of friends like us that they can trust and rely on—but it has been essential to me. These guys can hear in my voice when something is off, even a little bit. I can be totally vulnerable and open and feel secure that they will always be in my life, no matter what. They bring so much stability and security to my entire family. I feel that I lean on them way more than they do on me. I don't remember a time that one or all of them have not been present when I needed a brother to turn to.

Success has always demanded rock-solid foundations, and this includes my family and friend structure. Beyond the brotherhood are other close friends, like take for example my friend Spanky, with whom I went to Mt. Carmel High School. Spanky and I have also moved through life together. He was married one week before me, and we have stayed in touch and worked together on charitable giving efforts. He's a great husband, father and leader in his church and community. I look up to Spanky in so many ways and reach out to him for guidance, and I know he has experience that can help me.

My friend Joey out in California is raising three amazing children with his wife. His children are younger, so I can share not only my lessons but also those I've learned from others. We talk philosophy and share Army stories as well. Joey was a soldier in the Army and was Airborne qualified, which means he jumped out of a lot of planes back in the day. We ran the streets in high school, hiked the Appalachian trail in the Carolinas and shared a cool ride in a helicopter as well. My friend Curtis, down in Florida, is someone whom I met later in life who has been an inspiration to me as well. I gain strength and insight from him as well, and we pray together. Yep, two grown men on the phone, thanking God for the blessings we have received over our lives. Without fail, Curtis and I check in on each other with a text or call, even with our busy schedules.

Mike B, who I've known for a number of years, is also a good friend. I met him through his dad, who was one of my most valuable mentors. Mike and I have been in some interesting business situations, and I leaned heavily on his long experience and wisdom. When we speak now, we still laugh at some of the things his dad used to say and do. I'm talking about a man who was a pioneer in the Chicago grocery market space when there were little to no community stores available. "Nap," as his friends would call him, took me under his wings many years ago, teaching me about politics and how to navigate the relationships between it and the business world. I can call Mike right now with a challenging problem, and he literally will not go to sleep until he figures it out. He has a quick way of computing numbers and is one of the most compassionate people I know.

These are my guys. The most interesting part of the relationships with these long-term friends is that they pretty much all know each other, whether they have met in person or not. I can speak with Joey in California, and he asks about Jerry. I can speak with Spoon, and he asks about Tracey. This is a wonderful group that I cherish and hope that they have found me to be half the friend that they have been to me.

The gifts and lessons they have instilled in me have prepared me for the future challenges I would face. In each part of life, I have been blessed with new tools. Some I would need right away while others I would not need

> *In each part of life, I have been blessed with new tools.*

until much later down the road. During the most difficult times, knowing that someone cares about me unconditionally allows me to strive to be all I can be. If I fall, they will always be a strong safety net for me to land on. They will inspire me get back up and try again.

6: VOLUNTEER TO MOVE AHEAD

Rethink your strategy

Back when I was trying to jump start my career, I sat down with Mom and told her about my efforts to get a job. She recommended that I volunteer to get some practical experience. This would show my work ethic and desire to succeed, which could lead to a permanent position.

I hadn't even considered this—but it seemed like a great idea. With renewed enthusiasm, I grabbed the same Yellow Pages that I had been using and changed my strategy. Calling smaller firms to let them know I was willing to work for free in exchange for experience felt so much easier.

But it still proved hard to break through. I spent a few days calling companies, with no success. I kept calling and kept looking for non-technology related opportunities as well, just to get some cash. I gave my mom updates on my activities each day. I would contribute to the house by cutting grass, doing dishes and anything else that was needed.

My parents never babied me and, at the same time, never criticized. They had an amazing gift of never looking back, as I believe they didn't see how it would change anything. The blessings that came from supportive parents were not lost on me and gave me a deeper resolve to stretch my mind and achieve more than I set out for initially. I always felt like at any moment, things would change for the better. I kept hope and faith and pushed away any thoughts or ideas that job hunting could take months.

Finally, a break

I eventually had an extensive conversation with a small company name Nexus Unlimited located on 1300 South Michigan Avenue. I scheduled an appointment with a gentleman named Nathan, who was the head of the technical services team. I dressed in olive-green dress slacks, a white dress shirt and a green and maroon patterned tie. I remember this because it was one of the only dressy outfits I owned. The shirt was one I borrowed from my friend John while at SIU.

The interview process was new to me. My high school job at Fair Play hadn't required an interview; neither had the computer lab help desk. My mom explained what to expect and how I should present myself. I arrived at the parking lot very early and sat in the car for an hour, just to walk up to the front door at exactly 15 minutes before my interview time.

Nathan was a very upright and stuffy guy who walked like a robot, very formal and rigid. The interview was more about the job I would be doing instead of them getting to know me, which is fine by me. I was offered the job, without pay of course, so I started the next day. It felt right. I liked the fact that I would be working for a smaller firm that would provide me with a chance to be part of a team and not just another Social Security number at a big enterprise. I recall going straight home and telling my mom, who was very excited (and relieved I'm sure). When Dad got home from work, I told him, and he was proud, too.

My next stop was Monique's house. At this point, Monique was so in love with me that she couldn't see straight. Maybe it was my Latin charm or my irresistible caramel brown eyes or my confident swag. Whatever it was, she was hooked. We went to our local favorite Chinese restaurant, Chan's, to celebrate.

Starting out at Nexus was a great experience. It was a small family-owned business, focused on technology in the education space. The owner was a PhD named Dr. Iva Carruthers, who was a very smart business owner and educator. Iva's mom and nephew Marvin also worked for the company. I was assigned to work with Nate and was thrown into the hard stuff from day one.

At that time, networking computers was new, and not many people had experience designing, installing and supporting networks, including me. I had to learn fast, and I saw how different learning theory at college was compared to real-life work in the tech world. Every now and then, Iva's brother Skip would visit the shop. Skip was in sales at IBM, and everything about him intrigued me. Marvin looked just like him, and there was no denying they were father and son. I had the opportunity to speak with Skip and ask him what it was like working at IBM and how he got his start there.

Back then, I could spot an IBM worker from miles away: they wore navy blue suits, bright, highly starched white dress shirts and blue ties with shiny dress shoes to match. The marketing representatives drove nice cars like Mercedes or BMWs and always had fancy ink pens that they used to sign big contracts. Skip was no different, except for the fact that he had a Porsche 928, which was my favorite car. Man, this guy was a model of what my professional life looked like when I dreamed at night!

The other thing that made Skip cool was his openness and willingness to sit down and speak to a young, green, inquisitive man. He never came across as arrogant or privileged; on the contrary, he was very humble and soft-spoken. I now could see what my professional path could be.

While working at Nexus, I came to learn that our company was an authorized business partner with IBM. This meant that we provided technical services to their customers on their behalf. Nexus sold new computers and networking equipment to schools and also sent technicians and engineers onsite to unbox and complete the installation process. This was what I was being trained to do. Marvin and I were constantly reading documents and manuals to learn how to build networks. At that time, there were training CDs that we would put into a CD-ROM drive and run on the computer. It was like an hour-long PowerPoint presentation with some images, lots of text and boring graphics.

Learning fast

During lunch breaks, Marvin and I would sit in a back room and talk about business. He was an idea man, always thinking of ways to make money and developing new ways to think about solving the problems customers were experiencing. I loved being around someone who thought beyond their current circumstances. We continued to run ideas by each other even while we went onsite to customer locations to deliver technical services. Marvin was also very good at desktop publishing and graphic design and he helped with creating product literature and advertising material for the company. Learning did not stop at 5:00PM: I would borrow technical manuals and books so I could study at home.

Monique was working in downtown Chicago at this time, and we would ride home together when we could. If we couldn't meet after work, I'd try to rush to the Metra train stop on 115th Street to catch her. Even though the ride from the train station to her parents' house was less than two minutes, we would stop and grab dinner or sit and talk for hours. Her mom, Pam, was always so much fun and exciting to be around. She would come to the door with a big smile and greet me warmly. When I first saw her dad, Tom, I had just come into the front door and was standing in the living room. I could look up to this opening on the second floor where a small overlook was positioned, with a wrought iron style railing. Tom looked down and said, "You're not one of those Jeffrey Dahmer dudes, are you?" referring to the serial killer who was headline news during that time. I remember laughing and saying to myself, *"I'm glad they are cool."* I enjoyed spending time with Monique's parents while we sat in their kitchen and talked for hours. Tom was a fireman at that time, at a fire station only a couple of miles away from home. With their schedules of 24 hours on duty and 48 hours off duty, I didn't see him very often, but when I did, he always had some good knowledge to pass on.

Learning to make money with my mind

This was another formative time in life for me, as it was the beginning of my journey of using my mind instead of my hands to make money. This wasn't a conscious decision; it was simply the environment I was fortunate enough to be in. I do recall thinking that brain work can be just as tiring, or more, than physical work. I would be exhausted sometimes from reading work material and books for pleasure. Life quickly became wake up, go to work, learn everything I could, go home, spend time with Monique and my family, study some more, then rinse and repeat.

During this time, Clarence, a consultant that provided work for Nexus, would visit Iva at the shop. Clarence was probably in his 50s, and like Skip, always made himself available to speak with me. I remember Iva taking me to a business partner meeting with IBM and Clarence driving us there in his dark grey Volvo. This was my first experience being in a conference room at the table with executives from a Fortune 500 company. The IBM team seemed organized, intelligent and intimidating. I had never heard some of the terms they used, such as Service Level Agreement (SLA), Scope of Service, Blanket Purchase Agreement and others. I took handwritten notes while still trying to keep eye contact and pay attention to body movements and facial gestures. I studied the IBM team down to the most minute detail, such as the style of cufflink one man was wearing and how they used these corporate phrases such as "par for the course" and "stay in your swim lane."

On the way back to the office, I was sitting in the back seat, and Clarence asked me if I had questions about the meeting we just left. I confessed that I didn't understand half of what they were referring to and he promised to explain everything to me. During this time, the Internet was not what it is today. We had America Online as the way to connect. Trying to learn about business and the terms I heard at the IBM meeting was a losing battle. The information available was extremely limited to a few web pages, which was mostly text without photos.

Planting the seeds of entrepreneurship

A few days later, Clarence did come back to Nexus, and we had the chance to speak at length. He explained about the meeting we attended together and other business topics. The difference between Skip and Clarence was that Skip was an employee and Clarence was an entrepreneur. I told Clarence that I wanted to be an entrepreneur. I wanted several businesses in my lifetime but didn't know where to start. I also wanted to learn about what I didn't know, meaning I could see the upside to being a business owner, such as having the freedom of not being tied to a desk all day, being able to afford the things I desired in life and charting my own path. What I didn't know was the sacrifice an entrepreneur like Clarence had to make to be successful. Iva was very supportive of me and the other workers on her team. I believe she knew I was hungry to learn and be the best I could, so she allowed Clarence and me to spend as much time as possible together, in this mentor-protégé relationship.

You never know when the seeds you plant will grow. A couple of months after starting my unpaid position at Nexus, I received a call from a temp agency that I had applied to while looking for work. They had a position available with a large corporation downtown Chicago on the technology team. The position required me to document the entire network, with other team members in a high-rise office building. Basically, I'd be going room to room, floor to floor, taking note of the label name and number on each network outlet on the walls. The starting pay was $21 per hour. I had no income,

You never know when the seeds you plant will grow.

drove my mom's car to work each day and had student loan payments that were due.

I still turned down the offer. I looked past the financial benefit that would provide short-term relief for me because I saw the job was a dead-end position. I trusted my gut, which was telling me I would end up working as a programmer in a basement with no windows for the next 30 years, just like my professor wanted me to do back in college. I am an entrepreneur at heart, and limiting myself was not an option.

What I had at Nexus was a small, nurturing environment, with an owner that wanted me to succeed and provided me the opportunity to interact with her brother

Skip and Clarence and Marvin so I could develop into an employer, not an employee. The next day at work, I asked Iva if we could meet for a few minutes. I explained the offer I was given and told her I wanted to stay at Nexus but needed to make some money to support myself. Iva understood and began paying me $400 every two weeks. I was and am still appreciative of her giving me a solid foundation to nurture my dream. Iva also knew that I worked very hard for her and represented her company professionally while at customer locations.

Monique and I both had pagers or beepers back then. One afternoon, Monique paged me and when I had time to call her back, she said she was going to bring lunch so we could eat together at Nexus. She showed up with fried rice. Looking back, we ate Chinese food because we liked it, but also because it was inexpensive. We sat and talked for a while before she had to head back to her job. Shortly after she left, my stomach started hurting bad, and it was getting hard for me to breathe. I had Iva's assistant call my mom, who worked about 15 minutes from our shop. Someone from her workplace dropped her off at Nexus, and we got into her car to head to the hospital. I knew the feeling from a previous experience in Georgia with my parents. My father took me to a fresh fish market, and we bought some crab and other fish. I had a very bad allergic reaction, and we later found out that I had a shellfish allergy.

I was having a hard time breathing. My mom drove me to St. Francis Hospital in Blue Island, about 30 minutes from Nexus. Mom was already a fast driver, but this time, she was breaking every rule of the road. I was taking deep breaths, trying to get any little bit of air I could, but my throat was swollen enough that only a little wind would get through. I heard my mom keep calling my name, over and over again, just like she did when my dad was having a seizure. At some point I must have passed out, because the next thing I remember was opening my eyes in the emergency room. Mom and Dad were sitting in chairs on my right side. I was in that twilight state where I could see and hear, but not really move.

I could hear the conversation between my parents. Mom was telling my dad about the car ride from work to the hospital. She said she thought I died, because she kept trying to wake me, but I was unresponsive. It was a surreal moment to hear Mom say that. I also remember the female nurse talking with them and saying that it appears like I had a drug overdose. My dad had a temper and very convincingly explained to her that her clinical assessment was incorrect. It was in his Athens, Georgia tone, however. My mom explained that I had Chinese food and must have had an allergic reaction to it. I remember thinking, *why do people always assume the worst? Why does a drug overdose have to be the first possible explanation?*

Later that day, when I was more alert, the doctor came to speak with us and explained that my allergy may be more sensitive than previously known, meaning that the food could have been cooked in the same pot or with the same utensils that were used to cook another dish that contained shellfish. Now, on the rare occasions we eat at restaurants, we always let them know I have a shellfish allergy, and they will prepare my meal separately.

Life continues, and so does work. I went to the job the next day like nothing happened. I get my resiliency from my parents, especially my dad. He just didn't look in the rearview mirror a lot and give much thought to the things that didn't work out in his favor and why. He focused on the future and what he needed to do to provide for his family. I had no choice but to think this way; it's the only thing that made sense. Things happen. I was well enough to get up, put my shoes on and drive, so why stay home and reminisce about yesterday? It would not change anything.

Hard work plus opportunity can lead to success. Marvin and I had an amazing opportunity to work closely with IBM system engineers during the time I spent at Nexus. Periodically, we would attend training classes at their Chicago office. Other business partners that focused on the education market were also invited. To have the opportunity to work with IBM, the industry leaders, and not give it my all, was absolute idiocy in my mind. This was my first time meeting one of the marketing reps from IBM whose territory included the schools our company was servicing. George Gower fit right into the mold that Skip and Clarence were made of. While Skip was a very laid-back IBM marketing rep, George was like the Energizer Bunny, with lots of energy, constant motion and great stories. George was also all about business and told all of us in the room that we represented IBM, we represented him, the engineers and our respective businesses and ourselves. We must be prepared, knowledgeable and extremely professional in our manners, technical proficiency, look and overall presence in front of customers. George's comments resonated with me because he was hitting on traits that each of us needed not just to deliver services, but to be successful in anything we did in life. I saw the path and had to do whatever I could to stay on it. I could not throw away my shot at this invaluable opportunity.

There are times in life that I want something so bad, I can't contain my ambition. The adrenaline is pumping, and it seems that I have only a few minutes to take advantage of the opportunity or it will cease to exist. I won't allow anything get in the way of me achieving my goal. This was one of those times. I realized the path into the big league, corporate America was through my technical aptitude, and I had to learn everything I could to be the best. Once there, I then had to shift to learn the business side and how to navigate and maneuver the relationship-building process. I dug in even more and looked around to see what resources I had available to create a plan.

> *I realized the path into the big league, corporate America was through my technical aptitude and I had to learn everything I could to be the best.*

The next day, I again went to Iva and told her I needed to buy a computer. Because I could not afford one, I suggested that she could take money from each of my paychecks to cover the cost if she would buy it for me through Nexus. She agreed, and I made my first important business deal. Iva told me to go to our sales rep Sheila's office and ask her to place the order. I didn't know what specifications I would need to run the software required to start a business, so I consulted Marvin. We decided first on what I needed the computer for, which was Internet access, word processing and something to create flyers and marketing material on. Sheila looked for a computer in a thick catalog on her desk and ran it by Marvin and me. Once we decided on the best one for the amount I could afford, she ordered it. I was on fire with excitement. This would be the second computer I owned in life and the one that would help move me from technician to entrepreneur.

Marvin and I continued to work hard on Nexus'" behalf, servicing our customers and learning everything needed to be good technicians. Every other free minute including breaks and lunch time, we sat in front of a computer and designed logos using PageMaker. We also designed trifold brochures listing the services I offered, along with the associated fees.

Doing my best, always

My next opportunity came at a conference on networking that IBM was hosting at Northwestern University in Chicago. IBM tapped local business partners to send a few workers to help unpack and assemble Local Area Networks (LANs) that were being shipped in from the corporate offices in Atlanta. Iva approved our attendance, and we were told be to at the campus at 8a.m., in business casual clothes. Marvin and I arrived an hour early, even beating the IBM team to the location.

This was a big event for IBM, and there was a lot of work to do. We got to work unpacking huge crates that contained computers, networking gear, cables, file servers, monitors, printers and other equipment that I had never seen before. We completed both technical tasks and labor tasks such as helping them put computers on tables and connecting cables. Our supervisors Bob and Dave shared the fact that out of all the business partners IBM asked to send workers, we were the only people that showed up. He said that the project would have gone a lot faster if we had extra hands, but it didn't work out that way. He also thanked us several times during the day for simply doing what they asked and not complaining. He said this was the part of the life of an engineer that did not involve sitting in front of a computer doing brain work. The job also required manual labor from time to time, and he was glad we showed our dedication to the craft.

Marvin and I continued to work tirelessly that day until we completed everything Bob and Dave required of us. At the end of the day, Dave asked us if we would ever consider working at IBM. Marvin said it was not for him as he had other plans than a technical career. I said 100% yes and that I would start tomorrow if given the opportunity. Even though Marvin was Iva's nephew, he knew I had bigger plans and would not want me to limit my destiny, even if it meant leaving his aunt's business. Dave asked for my contact number and said he would be in touch. He also gave me his business card and told me to call him if I needed anything.

Even though Marvin and I were tired, I could not stop talking about the opportunity that was now in front of me. I imagined myself in that navy-blue suit and crisp white dress shirt. I already saw my photo on the IBM employee badge. I didn't know what the next steps were, but I knew my future would be bright because of the dedication and determination that drove me to show up and do my best when others wouldn't.

A few months went past, and life continued while I wondered when Dave would call. The longer I waited, the less optimistic I felt that I would get a position at IBM. I didn't understand human resources and everything it takes for large companies to hire people, so I had no perspective on a typical hiring event. Eventually, Dave did call me and asked to meet him. Dave and Bob greeted me in the lobby of the IBM plaza to escort me upstairs past security. We then went to their work area, with cubicles in an open bullpen setting. The office was on the 26th floor, and from this side of the building, we could see as far west and north as our eyes would allow.

Dave explained that the reason it took a while to bring me on was because his team was in transition between managers. I was hired as a supplemental worker on the service delivery team with the systems engineers, which was a part-time position working each weekday from 8:30a.m. to noon. I was fortunate that Iva allowed me to change my work hours to 12:30 to 5p.m. My job was to help Dave and Bob conduct pre-sales planning, implementation and post-sales support of the networks and systems our sales team was selling. As an example, we would review quotes to ensure all the technical components were included, so that the desired outcomes of the customer could be met. We would also provide a level of local technical support for our business partners installing our systems.

Our team was focused on both K-12 and higher education customers and consisted of a sales team and a technical team. We had systems engineers that worked on local area network (LANs) and others who worked on mainframe systems. Our sales teams were divided by territory and each team had a marketing representative, system engineer and trainer to support them. Bob and Dave were assigned primarily to the large public schools, and I would work most of my time with them. These guys couldn't be more different, but they worked very well together and provided a level of balance that was needed for the job.

Bob was tall, spoke very fast and was super smart. He could calculate numbers without much thought and had a photographic memory. Dave was a former educator who could communicate without technical language so anyone could understand. I could tell both read tons of books and manuals because they always had a solution to any technical challenge that arose.

Their level of excellence set the bar even higher for my desire to learn. In the tech world, you either know it or you don't. Setting up networks at that time required me to manually type in commands as opposed to simply clicking on icons and buttons like today's world. To be good, I had to memorize hundreds of commands, programming codes, the correct syntax of operating systems and much more. There was no Google or tech support line for us to call; there were only manuals and the firsthand experience of my teammates to help resolve issues. Because networking was pretty new at that time, there were many things that would go wrong, including customers accidently knocking cables loose, people losing CDs and floppy disks and the never-ending need for them to be trained to manage their networks and overall IT environment.

Becoming a sponge

This was the beginning of my experience with multiple revenue streams: I was working at IBM, Nexus and had my own business at the same time. I wanted more than anything to learn everything I could about technology, delivering services to customers and how to get new customers. Looking back, I'm not sure when I slept, because Monique and I spent a lot of time together after work, then I would study all night and start all over the next day.

Working at IBM was a crash course in developing both technical and professional skills. Our team eventually met the new manager, Kai, who was relocated to Chicago from the Atlanta office and came with a lot of experience, leadership expertise and professionalism. I was the youngest person on our team and the least experienced, but I thrived in the environment of learning and nurture created by all the team members. I was like a sponge, talking with everyone I could, every time I could. There are benefits to be the newest and youngest person in the room, as long as you are eager to learn.

I was curious about everything: my job as well as others'. I took the opportunity to ask others about their roles, and what their days were like. At first, lunch time was the only opportunity we would have to focus on a conversation outside of our workspace. During many conversations with our marketing representative George, I learned that being a good, even great, technical resource would not get me to the level he thought I could get to. I asked George if I could participate in a few customer visits with him in the future, and he happily agreed.

This was one of my first tastes of how corporations require that everyone fit into a category or silo. The marketing reps had to sell a certain number of products, and if they didn't, they could lose their jobs. The technical team had to design, implement and support the products the marketing reps were selling, or they could lose their jobs. The higher a person moves up the organization chart in a major company, the farther they are from the customer, both literally and figuratively.

I also learned about the tension that can arise when team members crossed over into the other's "space." For example, a marketing rep would put together a quotation to present to a customer that included several components that, once tied together, would create a total overall solution. Well, marketing reps would often submit these proposals, and the customer would buy them. Then, either the internal technical team or an outside business partner was tasked to go to the customer location to put the pieces together and make everything work. The problem is, there would often be parts and pieces missing that would prevent the customer's order from being installed correctly, and in several cases, installed at all. This could have been prevented if the marketing reps first sat down with a technical resource and said, "The customer is looking for the following result: Tell me what components and services I need to quote to make it work."

With and through George, I started to learn about building relationships with customers. George seemed to never be selling; instead, all his customers were friends. We would sit in a decision-maker's office and talk about their children, retirement, current events and everything else except how many computers they wanted to buy. As the conversation would be winding down and we would get up to leave, the customer would always say something to the effect of, by the way, send me a quote for 100 computers and George would always reply with a very big thank you and promise to do so.

As important as I knew technology was in general, I learned it is simply the vehicle to achieve the desired outcome. Nobody purchased computers in the early '90s just because they liked the way they looked. Customers bought computers to run software applications to educate students, to process complex calculations and to create databases to enter, sort and generate reports. A salesperson's job is to introduce customers and prospective customers to solutions to these types of problems. Focusing on the desired outcome and how the customer benefits is the way to show you are concerned with what is most important in the relationship-building process. I also learned that the role of a salesperson is ultimately to guide a customer in making a good decision.

Shadowing George gave me the ability to learn these important skills in a protected environment, before having to learn them in front of my customers. George also deferred to me during conversations with customers when technical questions arose. This showed his confidence in me and provided a level of depth to our team dynamic. This lesson also stuck with me over time and was evident during my company team meetings when I would speak on certain topics and let others lead in areas they were subject matter experts in.

This approach made me a better team member at IBM because I developed the ability to sit in front of customers, get an understanding of their needs and be able to deliver on the technical design, implementation and support required to make the solution work. I learned that using technical terms in front of customers had no benefit. I also changed my dress style to one that was more customer focused than functional. I began wearing suits to customer visits, even if I had to crawl on the floor to locate cables. I would take off my suit jacket and work for hours doing both manual and technical tasks. I believe that customers took me more seriously when I was dressed for business.

Before our tech team began working on any project, the customer would have to sign an agreement that included the scope of services, which is simply a description of the services that we would be providing to them, the pricing, the estimated time all the tasks would take to complete and the desired outcomes. If a customer did not have a signed agreement on file with us, we would not schedule the visit to begin the project. This became an important lesson for me early on and ensured we would get paid for services provided. When we sell a product or even a monthly subscription to a software application, if the customer does not pay, we have the right to repossess the product and even suspend the software until they make a payment. When we deliver services that are vital but intangible, you cannot go back and repossess "brain power."

I also learned the disadvantages of charging by hourly rates as opposed to a project fee. If I trade my time for a dollar, I will never grow beyond the amount of money I can generate based on several hours in a day. To further illustrate this point, I can quote a customer a per-box fee of $10 to move 50 boxes to a specific location. I could also quote them $25 per hour to move the same 50 boxes. If it takes me 3 hours to move the boxes, I would generate $75 total. If I use the per-box pricing model, in that same 3 hours, I would generate $500.

This same principle applies to almost all business models. The important thing to remember is that intellectual property, also known as the sum of the things you have learned through study and experience, is far more valuable than trading time for money.

A well-known secret that I came to learn early is that most large corporations, even today, outsource many of their primary service offerings to other smaller companies. The large company has the huge marketing dollars to convince customers to do business with them, but the actual work is performed by others. I was also introduced to this business model early on. Our tech team at IBM consisted of very high-level systems engineers who are subject matter experts in the solutions the company was offering to customers. They could design, deploy and support any of these systems with their eyes closed. As a result, they were extremely valuable to the company and they were able to command large salaries and benefits in order to stay part of the team.

When the engineers were required to provide services to customers, however, it was rare and expensive and took time away from being in the office working on the next product and system releases that would be even more profitable to the company. How did they provide the onsite deployment of the systems that were still too complicated for the average customer to do on their own, in a cost-effective manner? They outsourced this service to a company that could do the work for much less. This sounds good, but why would a large company simply give a good portion of it's service revenue to another company? The answer is simple: because they now have a way to make money without providing any service or product. Yes, that is correct. Here is how it works.

Company A sells washers and dryers to consumers. They explain that the customer will need to pick up the equipment from their store, take it home, connect the gas line to the dryer and correctly run the exhaust pipe outside so they don't die of carbon monoxide poisoning while washing clothes. They also stress to be careful because if someone is smoking when the gas is turned on to the new dryer, their house, and the next few houses on the street, can go up in flames. Then, they say, we can help eliminate all that risk for a small fee and have our team perform these services. What choice would a customer make? They agree to the $65 fee and work with them to schedule the delivery date.

Company A already has a few small businesses they partner with to provide onsite delivery and installation services for products they sell. The prices are agreed upon, scope of services outlined, and terms and conditions set for the overall relationship. Now, when Company A sells a fridge, large TV, washer and dryer or other appliance that a customer needs delivery and installation of, they will simply use them to provide the service. Back at the store, the salesperson checks the system for an available delivery date, which is really a calendar that includes the schedules for all their partners.

On the day of the delivery, someone shows up, confirms the delivery information, installs the items and requests a signature that everything was completed successfully. The business partner then sends the completion records and an invoice to Company A and awaits their payment, depending on the terms they established in their agreement. Here is the beauty of the deal for Company A. They sold a product and made money from that sale, then, they made money from the delivery and installation and performed ZERO work. The customer paid $65 to Company A, but Company A only paid $25 to the small delivery company. The other $40 is pure profit. If they only sold 25,000 delivery/installation orders each year, that's $1 million in profit, with ZERO overhead, no expenses and the liability falling completely on the smaller deliver company.

IBM had a similar business partner program that I participated in while at Nexus. We were the small company that did the work and were paid based on our contract terms. Now, I was on the side of the large company that owned the program. While scrubbing new orders to ensure the parts and pieces were correctly quoted to successfully complete a project, I had the opportunity to see the pricing we were paying to our business partners for the services they rendered. It was not hard to do the math and determine that the grass was much greener on that side of the fence.

While in meetings with our partners, I listened very closely to the issues and concerns they raised as well as the successes they experienced. I took notes while paying careful attention to facial expressions and body language to see if others were agreeing with the tone of the meeting. I also noticed the differences in sizes and scale of the different partners. Some partners were small and only provided installation services while others were larger and had sales teams that sold and installed IBM solutions. The smaller partners needed very little in the way of business tools; they essentially were using their brain power and physical labor and not much else to generate a lot of money. My path forward away from IBM was clear based on this knowledge.

The beauty of starting from zero

In college and after, I read many biographies and autobiographies. I was attracted to people who started with very little and gained some level of success. I stayed away from stories about people who achieved high levels of formal education and started a business and even people who were born into wealth and simply kept the legacy going. These stories did not resonate with me. The people I was drawn to were—and in some cases still are—business legends. They transformed life, overcame unbelievable odds, persevered when others gave up and taught me how to do the same. Their wisdom and knowledge were available to those of us who picked up the books and listened to their words and life stories. Even now, whenever I face a tough challenge or want to get perspective on a situation or want to know how others

succeeded at any cost, I find a book on
that topic and read it. Sometimes I read
several books at a time while listening to
an audiobook as well, if my current life
situation requires me to tackle several
challenges at once.

*In college and
after, I read many
biographies and
autobiographies.
I was attracted to
people who started
with very little and
gained some level
of success.*

The next time George and I got
together, I asked him to explain how
I could become one of the business
partners. Of course, George knew what my ultimate plan was:
to grow my part-time side hustle into a profitable business.
He also knew that this meant I would have to leave the safety
net that was IBM and survive on my own. George agreed to
help me with the process of becoming a partner.

The first step was to let our manager know that I would
be leaving soon. I remember meeting with our manager in
her corner office and telling her my plans. She was mostly
supportive but there was one comment she made that I
remember even today. She said her name had value because
it had the IBM logo under it. If she didn't have the affiliation
with IBM, it would not have the same value. I understood
what she meant and conceded that her rationale made sense
to some people, but not me. The beauty of starting from zero
is that there is nowhere else to go except up.

There is a relationship between corporations that
employ salespeople and corporations that sell to these
people. A large company will pay a seemingly large salary,
then encourage their employees to look the part. They
want them to have the nicest suits and the $250 ink pen

so clients take them seriously when they are signing new contracts. Be sure to drive up to the customer location in a BMW or Mercedes and throw a few dinner parties at their downtown condo, they would suggest. Part of this uniform is for the company to show its customers that they are doing well financially and to trust that we will be in business for the next 50 or 100 years.

The dark underbelly of these companies encourages employees to spend on these important business "uniforms" to the point where their large salary can barely cover the costs of their newfound lifestyle. At any given time, the salespeople would have $1,500 suits on, Mont Blanc ink pens, Rolex watches, gold cufflinks, the latest cell phones and the largest Mercedes. They lived in affluent neighborhoods and put their kids in the best private schools. There were companies that catered specifically to selling parts of those uniforms to the high-earners, and they knew they would have repeat customers.

Recognize the trap? Corporations pay employees more, then they go out and spend up to that new limit, then they must work twice as hard to maintain the corporate lifestyle. Now the corporations have them on the hamster wheel, never able to leave. They will do anything and everything to perform, not because they love the work but because they have so much debt and so many recurring expenses related to their corporate persona. Now, they are trapped on a path that leads to a 30-year career, simply navigating the corporate maze of the organization chart, hoping to be able to outperform the new hires who are hungry to take their place on that treadmill.

GAIN FROM PAIN:

I cannot overstate how powerful your feelings are and how much you have to protect them. How many times have you had a feeling to take a different route to work or to not reply to that email claiming to send you "free" money? Have there been times when you went against your feelings and had bad outcomes?

I didn't have experience starting a career, nor did I know all the different paths I could choose in my field. I was guided partially by how I felt when I considered my options. I asked questions of those who were experienced and sought the information I needed to help me make the best decisions in life, but ultimately, I went with my gut.

The lesson is: Trust yourself. Everyone around you will have an opinion about what you should do. People generally mean well but can never know your inner desires and dreams. They can see a path that they would take and try to convince you it is good for you as well. When you lay your head down at night, peace will only be present if you follow your heart and live the life you want for yourself.

7: MASTERS OF BUSINESS

In practice, not theory

In 1991, I looked into the abyss and took a step in the unknown. I didn't have a large amount of money saved nor a long career to fall back on. I didn't have a list of prospective customers ready to sign up, nor did I have many of the other resources one would desire when going all in.

What I did have was hunger, a life of always being the youngest in the room and the experience of having a different path from others I grew up with. I developed and embraced the mental toughness instilled in me by my parents along with their unwavering support. I also had an unbelievable partner in Monique and mentors who gave me the foundation I needed to succeed.

Now I also had a company on record with the State of Illinois as a sole proprietorship.

George had already put me in the position to work with IBM's business partner team, and I was able to join the program rather quickly. For IBM to direct orders to my company, a marketing rep had to list us as the business partner of record. I had good relationships with all the reps on our team, including those that covered other cities in Illinois, not just Chicago, and they immediately started to give us work. George took me to visit every one of his best customers and asked them to give me a chance to earn their business and asked nothing in return.

This is the essence of a mentor-protégé relationship. Someone with experience, wisdom and a whole host of other essential qualities decides to give someone else a chance by sharing their time and knowledge in hopes that they will grow and learn from it. I am eternally grateful for not only George but all the people who helped me in my life. It's a humbling feeling to know that someone else, with all their responsibilities, challenges and priorities, would care enough to put faith in me to protect their investment in the relationship.

The company started out with me as the sole employee working with customers to design, install and support LANs. My schedule was filled months in advance just by the work the IBM reps were giving me. I put a lot of miles on my car driving between customer locations in Illinois, Michigan and Indiana. Although I now had a company, it was more like a very high-paying job without a boss at the beginning. There were no marketing, sales reps, reports and human resources issues to deal with; it was just me, my car and the knowledge I had gained over the years. The work was exhausting mentally but not physically. I already had so many lines of code and computer language commands in my mind; then I would study the information being released by IBM for new products as they came along all while still reading every book I could on business and successful people. This is the pace I set for a few years. I still needed to make time for new customers that the IBM team would bring me as well.

I've learned many lessons while operating a business, some the hard way and others from the stories that mentors shared with me. Our company had both direct and indirect customers, meaning that we would provide services in some cases directly to organizations on their own behalf. Indirect customers were those relationships where a company would hire us to provide services for their customers. I stress to anyone who is willing to listen to always pursue direct customer relationships when starting or growing a company. This way, the contract will clearly spell out what services you are expected to deliver, the terms surrounding the engagements and what the final compensation will be. Everything is clear in hindsight, but when I was building my business, I took on every new customer I could.

I've learned many lessons while operating a business, some the hard way and others from the stories that mentors shared with me.

We built a very strong reputation over the years and were sought out by large companies looking to enter or bolster their presence in the market we operated within. This included some of the largest technology product manufacturers in the world. When new opportunities arose, these companies would request a meeting with us to strategize on how to get on new contracts or how to position themselves to submit winning proposals in response to bid and Request for Proposal solicitations from prospective customers.

I was now far better at business than performing technical services and had built a good team of young, hungry technicians and engineers who were anxious to do the work. My job was to convince the large companies to partner with us and ensure the contracts we would be awarded were serviced to the best standards. I learned quickly to distrust these companies and to document every email, note and correspondence between us and them. I always had a senior person in our company on calls and at in-person meetings, not only to have a historical record of events but also to hear things that I may have missed during the negotiations and to read the room for body language and facial expressions.

Navigating uncertainty is a skill

After meetings and calls, we would perform a "post-mortem" or debriefing to ensure all action items requested of us were completed as well as to review the entire relationship to determine our future positions when certain contract negotiations would occur. I would also study the news and announcements that all these public companies would issue. What products and offerings would they be releasing in the next six months, what new team members were they hiring, how were their international sales doing? Were there regulatory issues, trade disputes, lawsuits, patent infringements, tariffs and other external factors that would create workflow issues for us in the future? Also, what was happening with our partners' customers, the ones we delivered product and services to? Were there government strikes, elections that would cause contracts to be put on hold, budget constraints? When were their fiscal budget years starting and ending? All these factors had to be considered for each of our customers.

To do this research, I read local newspapers, national trade periodicals and articles and followed political races for each territory our company was delivering products and services to, which was ultimately the entire United States. If our customers performed an upgrade to a new operating system before completing thorough testing, this action could bring an organization to its knees. We would be affected because our production line would have to stop, sometimes for weeks and months until our partners and their customers conducted proper testing and certification of the new equipment and software, which is effectively a work stoppage nationally for us. If we were not staying abreast of these potential changes in our industry, we could not prepare our finances and human resources to weather these times. Also, when we have large corporations as partners, issues like this affect not just our local office but all the customer locations across the country. During our 29 years in business, we experienced many of these potentially devastating events. It was essential to be prepared.

Defending revenue & growing a business

When not dealing with industry changes, we had to deal with excessive greed by so-called partners. I always viewed our company partnerships as relationships of convenience more than true partnerships. When they needed us, they loved us; when they felt like we were tied in long-term under fixed pricing, they would take advantage at every turn. We never took this personally and never felt sorry for ourselves, as this was the norm when I would speak with other business owners that I had developed personal relationships with over the years. This is part of the game, so accept it and figure out how to work within the rules and boundaries of the game. There were times over the years when the partners would have leverage and they used it— and we did the same when it was our time.

Large corporations typically add language to contracts that put them in the position of dominance and control, all while we were making them millions of dollars. Some of the clauses we have seen are:

- **Most Favored Nation:** This means that we guarantee the customer that we will provide the lowest pricing to them, lower than any of our current and future customers for the same type of product and services we are providing for them.
- **Unlimited Liability:** If we provide a service, be it installing a computer system or a network, if somehow a device catches fire and the entire $20 million building burns down, we accept responsibility for it.
- **Intellectual Property:** If we create a software application to help us update software or a process to make another task move along faster while we are working under contract with them, they will own the intellectual property. This also means that if we funded

the project on our own, did not have any input from them and they were never aware of it, and simply developed it during our two-, five- or seven-year contract, it was theirs. In essence, at the same time U.S. companies complain that China is stealing their intellectual property, they are doing it themselves to other US companies.

- **Non-Compete Clause:** Most indicate that once our contract with this partner expires or is not renewed, we cannot compete with them to win business for a customer that we mutually serviced. Some agreements have taken it even further by indicating we cannot compete with them in a certain geographic area or market, such as finance, housing or medical. These non-compete clauses can last for two-three years after our partnership agreement has expired.

Besides these contract terms and conditions, partners will drive our fees and prices down to bare minimum while promising volume over a period of time that never seems to materialize. A few times over the years, our partners would tell us that their customer was seeking price discounts, so they were coming to us to help save the contract. Our management team would huddle up to see if we could provide a discount while maintaining operational costs and modest profits. We would extend a price discount, in fears that if we didn't the entire contract may be terminated, based on the guidance our partner provided. Later down the road, we would discover that customer never asked for a price discount and the contract was never in jeopardy. As a matter of fact, our partner would raise the price to the customer without us knowing. So, ultimately, they lowered their cost from us, raised their price to the customer and were now making even more profit while we had to do the same amount of work for less overall revenue, resulting in lower profit margins.

I would see news reports and stories in financial publications about how these companies were the darlings of Wall Street and doing so well for the U.S. economy, while I had friends whose companies had partnered with them and were going out of business left and right due to shrinking profits. I personally stopped buying products from these companies after that. This painful lesson about working hard to gain additional customers, especially those of scale, in order to grow our company, was one I had to learn repeatedly. It is not easy to find new customers, and the big guys know this, so they constantly hold it over our heads.

Never take this personally; it's business, right? I never expected a handout or to be treated any differently than other companies, so we took all the changes in stride. Most of our contracts were long-term and required renewals every two to three years. Once I learned what I didn't want to agree to, we would have to wait until the next contract term, then work to renegotiate. We always honored our agreements, no matter if we didn't realize the full potential of the estimated revenue we were anticipating.

Renegotiation and constantly protecting my business's bottom line were challenges that I was willing to take on— and I loved the idea of building our value to these partners so that we would have leverage next time. We were able to have certain clauses removed from our upcoming agreements, such as favored nations and others.

The lesson is: Never run from this type of challenge, and again, don't take it personally. Large, publicly held corporations have boards of directors, shareholders and stakeholders to answer to. They are under constant pressure to increase revenues and profits—each month and each quarter—to make their company more attractive to outside investors. This is a constant cycle: Investors buy more shares, the company makes more money, and valuation increases.

> *Renegotiation and constantly protecting my business's bottom line were challenges that I was willing to take on—and I loved the idea of building our value to these partners so that we would have leverage next time.*

Despite these headwinds, my company was thriving financially, increasing our revenue and profit margin annually for 28 years in business. Who would feel sorry for us when some of our competitors were going out of business? As the herd of small businesses thinned over the years, new ones would emerge and try to enter our space and take over our position on contracts. One year, a company filed a complaint against us for installing fire alarms without a license. An armed inspector showed up at our office to take photos of the building, vehicles and personnel, openly telling our receptionist that we were illegally operating a business, which of course created a panic in the office. Our management team started immediately investigating this so-called inspector, assuming that it was a case of mistaken identity. After a few days of calls with our accounting firm asking about licensure, our attorneys and state investigators, it was revealed that a competitor had made these false allegations in order to blemish our record and poach our customer.

I learned that as a business leader, you must develop thick skin quickly or get out of the game. Nothing can shake your focus on running the company. I never pursued getting even or treating others in this way. We were not competing with others; we were focused on the job our customers were paying us to do. I stressed laser-like focus with my management team and employees as much as possible. It's not easy to put aside the negative feelings and introspective thoughts I had when others were trying to do us harm, but I had to drive on.

An invitation to join the Masters of Business

In 2001, I was invited to join a business organization named ABLE which, at the time, comprised more than 50 of the smartest and most successful business owners in the U.S. These were the Masters of Business, in my opinion. By this time, my company had enjoyed modest success and was growing as I wanted it to, in order to maintain quality and successful relationships.

I was invited to a prospective member reception at an art gallery in downtown Chicago. There, I was greeted by the executive director of ABLE and given my name badge. I was early of course, probably 20-30 minutes before the start time, so I was able to have a couple of conversations with other prospective members. ABLE was such a secretive organization that I didn't know what to expect, and neither did any of the other invitees. The room slowly filled with a who's who of people that I had read about in some of the most prestigious magazines and seen interviewed on national news shows about world and financial events. What was I doing in this room, and what could I possibly offer to the group? I had to look like a groupie, as everywhere I looked, there was another person I recognized but never thought I would meet.

This was a turning point in my business leadership, and I had to do whatever I could to join the group. One of the founders (and then-president) of ABLE was Ralph G. Moore, who gave the opening remarks. Ralph spoke about the mission, values and direction of the organization. He also invited a couple of the new members to share their experiences. One of them happened to be in the IT space, and I knew his company well. He was also a former well-known IBM manager who had many successful public projects under his belt.

The formal structure of the group, the low profile they kept, and the caliber of the members were intriguing to me. Some notable members at that time were John W. Rogers Jr., chairman of Ariel Capital Management; Quintin E. Primo III of Capri Capital Partners, LLC.; and Melody Spann-Cooper of WVON Radio, who was responsible for inviting me to the reception. I vividly remember thinking that night that I would be the president of ABLE one day. I had a new goal.

This is how quickly I came to love the organization and what it stood for in that two-hour reception.

I wasted no time in requesting and submitting my membership application, along with the $3,000 annual dues, even before my application was approved. I called the executive director a few times for updates during the two-month interview and vetting process they conducted. I was eager and would not accept no for an answer. After being accepted into the organization, my first general membership meeting took place right after the September 2001 terrorist attacks. There was a long discussion about our members, their families and employees and if anyone was physically hurt. Some members had offices in New York, and most members traveled to Washington, D.C. with some regularity. There was also discussion of how our organization could support victims and their families at this time. This was such a powerful time, as I was able to see these business giants for their human side as well. It was one of the first times I experienced compassion in the business world, a refreshing change from the constant focus on profits and growth projections.

Listen first

I learned early in life that you don't learn from speaking, you learn from listening. A constant flow of Fortune 500 CEOs, elected officials, and government leaders attended our meetings discussing ways for us to grow our businesses and become better corporate citizens. In the early days, I rarely spoke, choosing instead to listen to the tone of the voices, delivery styles, posture and finesse of other members as they interacted with these powerful people. There were protocols to be followed when addressing prospective customers and discretion required when working with elected officials, nuances that I could only learn at this table. I knew that the skills I was building would be needed in the future, so I made sure to pay attention to every detail possible.

Whether these 73 members knew it or not, I considered each of them to be a mentor. For example, Quintin Primo shared with me with the importance of establishing trusts to protect business and personal interests. He was vulnerable enough to discuss the ups and downs of business and how everything could be going very well today and then the bottom falls out tomorrow without warning (especially apt advice as I write this during the COVID-19 pandemic). When I visited John Rogers at his office, I recall his young daughter running around without a care in the world—and no one seemed to mind. These bits of information and experiences can't be bought, but the people in my life at that time selflessly shared them with me.

I had two questions I asked every successful person I came across, whether it was my first time meeting them or if we already had a relationship:

1. If you could turn back the hands of time, what would you do differently in life?

2. Give me some advice on being a good father and husband.

Here is some million-dollar advice. Having asked these same questions for years, and even today, the overwhelming responses are:

1. I would do what I love, not what I was educated to do. Whatever made me happy, I would do it, regardless of whether I was paid for it or not.

2. The men say that they wished they would have focused on family more than their businesses.

Nearly 20 years later, I still get similar answers from people I ask. At first, I was surprised that many of these top performers, who had very successful companies or long political careers, were saying that their careers were not necessarily in line with what their hearts desires were. It didn't make sense on many levels, but the more we talked, the clearer the message became.

This is when I learned about the "hamster wheel." Famous people walk away from their career for no apparent reason. Successful people who had "everything" commit suicide. Why? What was so bad in their lives that caused them to give up? Here I was getting the answer from high achievers, who fit these exact profiles. ABLE members had some of the largest homes I had ever seen, some of the most expensive cars; they flew private air, they vacationed in the most exotic destinations. The lesson is: Achieving financial success does not necessarily satisfy your heart's desires. I would hear people saying that they would rather be running a charter boat business in Florida, which one member decided to do. Others wanted to paint beautiful works of art, while still others wanted to help students learn to fly airplanes. One elected official wanted to move to Africa and help local villagers by creating a micro-loan program to help people start businesses.

I always asked the question: Why don't you pursue your dreams? Again, the answers were enlightening and somewhat frightening. Some people were concerned about what their peers would think of them giving up their businesses to do something that didn't make much money. Others openly admitted that they were on the hamster wheel: Their businesses could not function without them, so they could not be away from the office. Some said that the contracts they were on were so labor-intensive with such low profits that they had no choice but to service them, hoping for better days in the future. They were in a vicious cycle of waking up, going to the office, having phone calls and meetings, going to fundraisers and networking events, back home to sleep, then back on the hamster wheel in the morning.

While not the case for all ABLE members, this was the case for most high performers I have come to know over the past 30 years. Eventually, I could look at a person's eyes and see the pain of being in a position they wanted out of. This was a gut punch for me. It shattered my preconceived ideas of how successful people viewed life from the inside. This was their perspective, not the public's glamorous ideas of what a CEO's life was like. It's tough, and I would one day find myself on the same hamster wheel, spinning at a different pace.

The answer to my question about parenting and marriage also took me by surprise. I recall speaking with a civil rights leader's son about life in general. I remember asking what it was like to live with this person that we saw as bigger than life and who was always on the front lines when it came to voicing concern about important social and political issues. The answer was that he felt lonely. While his father was out fighting for everyone else, he longed for his father to be with him at home, having dinner and playing a role in what mattered to him and his siblings. While this person understood the important work his father was doing for the nation, he still felt that he had to share his father with everyone outside his home, and that created pain and a lonely feeling for him.

The message was similar from others I met. Many high performers were divorced two and three times. They had strained relationships with their now-adult sons and daughters because they were never home to help and watch them grow. In many cases, their families were pushed to the back of the priority list. Some of the conversations were clearly painful for the men I spoke with, but they seemed to welcome discussing anything except business at the end of a long day.

Many of them told themselves a common story to justify the time they spent away from home and the disconnect from their families. They had somehow convinced themselves that they were working hard for their families. Many legitimately felt that their role was to make money so everyone could have what they wanted, and they were very successful at being providers. This was evident by the size of the million-dollar homes and Mercedes, Bentleys and Porsches parked outside of our meeting venues. I would follow up with another question: Would you do it all over again, knowing you would lose your spouse and intimacy with your sons and daughters? No one said they would make that choice again. They would prefer to have a successful family life if that meant their businesses were less successful. They also echoed the same feelings that having a business in a major city such as Chicago comes with: living a certain lifestyle that is attractive to others but draining on the soul.

I could see the pattern of the hamster wheel of success: the office in the central business district, where rent and lease prices were terribly expensive. The status-symbol car, designer or custom-tailored clothes. The challenge became, how do I achieve a level of success and maintain a healthy work-life balance? At the time, it was easy for me because my wife was on her grind as well, reaching to achieve her career goals, so we understood long work hours and how to enjoy each other in between.

The challenge became, how do I achieve a level of success and maintain a healthy work-life balance?

This is the part of business that many people don't see. It's the sausage being made on the floor of the factory, so to speak. I can say that each of the people I met through ABLE, whether inside the organization or guests of ours, taught me something, and I am eternally grateful to them.

One of the people I had the opportunity to meet was a tall, thin, light-skinned Illinois state senator. As big as Chicago is, the business community is a relatively small group of men and women. The business leaders, community organizers and elected officials often work together to achieve certain goals and solve important issues. Of course, I'm talking about Barack Obama. I first met our former president at a meeting where he was simply listening in on the discussion between business owners about their challenges and successes. He was quiet and always eager to listen and learn. We had met previously with many other officials, including state and national leaders, so all of us were pretty laid back and not overly anxious about being in the presence of elected officials. They had the same challenges we had, and we considered them to be just another human being, no better or worse than any of us.

The thing that really stood out about Barack—more so than any other elected official—was his gift of self-confidence. He did not have to dominate a conversation or a room. Some other elected officials were always trying to prove they were valid and legit. I don't believe any of us imagined at that time that Barack would be interested in running for president, but eventually he did, and of course we know the rest of the story. Our members always carried a great amount of pride knowing what the rest of the United States and the world would later discover about Barack: that he is a very smart, dedicated and thoughtful person and always provided a sense of calm and stability when he was in our presence.

Barack and I share a special place in our own personal histories. He realized his dream of being elected president of the United States in November 2008, and I realized my dream of being elected president of ABLE in November 2008 as well.

Finding purpose as business grows

The early years of business are exciting because everything is new. I was moving fast, building something from nothing and putting teams and processes in place. At a certain point, once the systems are working together, the next phase is to grow it, or at least that's what society would have me believe.

Business was going well, and we were growing our staff and revenue. Having access to ABLE members provided me the relationships and resources needed to get guidance and advice on business situations that would arise. I also now had perspective from people who were in their 50s and 60s and could clearly see that life in the next 20 or 30 years would be more of the same if my only focus was to continue to grow the business.

My goal was never to grow a billion-dollar business, and I had nothing to prove to anyone. I was more concerned with being the best that I could, in any situation. I never identified myself as anything other than my name. I didn't say, "Hello, my name is Tony, the president or chairman of ABC company." The company was a vehicle that I created to fulfill my real life's purpose. I knew people who were so tied to their business, job and title, that when any of those things went away, so would their self-worth and identity in other people's eyes.

I always had a plan to retire at the age of 45, so I knew that the life of my company would be limited to the years I had left before that period of time had arrived. If I limited the way I thought of myself or projected a transient position to the outside world, what would happen once I turned 45 and moved on to the second part of my life? Instead, I focused on the traits that I had developed over the years and leaned on the morals and values taught to me by my parents and mentors. Traits and philosophies like being true to myself, treating people with respect, giving instead of taking, and bringing others along for the ride.

These principles would remain with me forever, without an expiration date. I had seen the eyes of people who owned prominent businesses before and had lost them. There's an emptiness and glaze that reflects the pain of losing their identity as well as the business. Their power and influence were gone in their minds because they were now an ordinary person. I also saw how full of life others had been that made their exit from the business world and never let their position determine how they were viewed by others. Lou Holland was an example of this. Lou had a very successful investment firm and was a former University of Wisconsin Hall of Fame football player. He was the type of person who had many titles that he could use during introductions, but the one he chose to identify with was simple and heartfelt. He would always say "My name is Lou Holland, and I'm just a good ole country boy from Wisconsin." Lou was the kindest person anyone would ever want to meet and treated all of us with the same amount of respect. Lou passed in 2016, and I will remember him not as a businessperson, but because of the person he was: humble, smart and generous with his time when I needed guidance.

One thing that I found troubling in the business world was the lack of humility and willingness to acknowledge any power higher than us as being a big part in successes. I understand that it may not be appropriate to stand on a table and thank God for your achievements, but even in casual and confidential conversations, spirituality and God never came up in those circles. I did hear a lot of people patting themselves on the back for the company doing well and showing everyone photos of the celebrities and other "important" people they met. I concluded over the years that it was insecurity that prevented some high achievers from acknowledging that it was not pure talent nor superhuman intellect that got them to where they were, but a higher presence. If that secret was revealed, maybe they would not be profiled in news and magazine articles anymore as the brilliant people that everyone thought they were. The truth is all the businesspeople I personally encountered worked extremely hard and many had brilliant minds. They did put in the work required to achieve lofty goals, but at some point, the universe did conspire to help them.

8: LOSING MY COMPASS

Dad was raised down South, a place where a traditional meal included fried chicken, red meat and soul food. Even in Chicago while we were growing up, he always talked about "down South" and how he was a country boy at heart. My father carried a lot of stress, being the head of a household of five people. Even while enduring stress, he found the lighter side of life—and made time to laugh. Any time there was a group of family members together, somehow he would have everyone laughing so hard, they would be in tears. He had this gift of telling funny stories and framing things in a way that made light of it.

I remember being on the cruise ship that Monique and I got married on. Monique's mom, Pam, arranged for her, Tom, our friend Lola, her husband Oliver, Monique and me to be seated at the same table for dinner each night. Oliver was a little older than my dad, but they shared the experience of understanding the South, where they had roots. Oliver and my father wound up sitting next to each other. They started talking about old-school phrases and sayings they heard growing up. None of us but Tom knew what they were talking about. Dinner could last anywhere from an hour to two hours on these ships, and they would talk the entire time with these inside jokes. They would say something to each other, and both would laugh and laugh and laugh. The other one would reply with a counter comment that would make them laugh even harder. I'm talking about the type of laughing that makes everyone in the area laugh, even though they don't know what the origin of the laughter was. This kept on until they both were literally crying at the table. Two older, grown men, wiping tears from their eyes, mouths wide open, bent over with stomach pains, laughing.

We had a big group on that cruise, probably three or four tables of travelers. I remember Monique's aunt coming over to the table to see what the problem was. Apparently, they were laughing so loud that everyone else around us heard them. Here we are trying to be dignified, and these jokers are in their own world, just the two of them, speaking a language none of us understood. I remember Oliver laughing so hard he got up from the table to leave the dining room. When he returned, all it took was a few words from my dad and it started all over again. Lola was so mad that she refused to let them sit next to each other for the rest of the cruise, but that only meant they would talk louder so they could hear each other across the table. Both referred to each other as "partners in crime" after that, for years to follow. This same scenario played itself over and over, everywhere we went. The interesting thing is when Monique, our son TJ and I were in Georgia recently, a cousin that I had never met in person told me that I reminded him of my father because of the funny stories I was telling during our visit. I never recognized this quality until he pointed it out.

By 2006, my dad had to go on dialysis as a result of the damage stress, bad food habits and high blood pressure had done to his kidneys. The diagnosis took all the family by surprise. Of course, we had to figure out how to support him with stress management, diet and getting to and from dialysis three days each week. Typically, older men from the South are very determined people and hard to move away from their traditions. My dad was the king of hot links from the local barbecue joint, and it was tough to get him to give up these old habits. Physically, he was the same as before, just getting a little winded from time to time. We continued as always, traveling like a pack of wolves. We still hit the zoo, museums and all the activities we enjoyed as a family. Every weekend since TJ was born, my parents came to our house on Friday night to visit. They were hands-on and loving grandparents. I remember the first time they played the drums together and gave us a good concert. The problem was, we didn't have a drum set. Dad pulled out some pots and serving spoons, sat on the floor with TJ and made all kind of loud noises that was supposed to be music, I guess. First Dad would make the sounds, then TJ would try to repeat it. This went on forever. They got very creative by playing a beat, then falling backward on the floor as the finale of the performance. Of course, TJ loved this.

Every Sunday afternoon, my sisters and nephews would visit my parents at home, and we would get together and enjoy family time. This was a tradition that was not formally scheduled but always expected. Sometimes, we would host the get-together at our house, but if we had the time together, it didn't matter where we were. The same applied to birthdays: We would all meet at Pam and Tom's house in the city. Monique's aunts and uncles would show up, then friends would as well until there were 15-20 people in the house. As much as Monique says my family was crazy, hers was the same. We all got together, whether it was a special occasion or not. The only difference was, my parents were ready for bed at 10p.m. and at Monique's parents' house, the party didn't start until 11p.m. I think everyone in my family fell asleep on one of Pam and Tom's couches at some point, waiting for the party to end.

I enjoyed the days when four generations of men sat together in a room and enjoyed each other. My dad, me, my nephews Luis and Gabe and my son TJ were always close. Luis is the oldest grandson, so he spent the most time with my father, doing some of the same things I did as a child, helping in the garage holding tools during car maintenance and learning to do household chores. Both Luis and Gabe spent a lot of time with my parents and often came over on Friday nights with them.

On the Sundays that I visited my parents at home, TJ and I would stay until it was time for dad to go to dialysis. We drove him to the center in Indiana, just across the Illinois border, where he would stay until the morning. Mom would pick him up and take him home before going to work. Often Luis and Gabe would ride with us because they lived in

Indiana as well. When we pulled up to the center, TJ would already be asleep in his car seat, so Dad would whisper goodnight to him. I would watch Dad grab his portable oxygen tank and walk toward the building and think to myself that he was going through this process for us, not him.

Because he got winded fast and due to the potential side effects of the medicine he was taking, his doctors advised him to stop driving. This was hard and was not something Dad wanted to hear or comply with. I'm sure he knew it was best, but he wanted to stop on his terms, not the doctors'. I inherited his determination for sure.

My dad always gave me fatherly advice on being a good husband and father. We sat in his living room while he leaned back in his reclining chair and chatted. He could doze off, wake up 10 seconds later and jump right back in the conversation like nothing happened. He also had a unique way of interacting with my sisters and me differently and treated us as individuals. Fran was the first child, so she had the closest relationship with my father for many years. I came along and inherited the

> *My dad always gave me fatherly advice on being a good husband and father.*

only son position. The middle child is always the forgotten one. Then Maritza came along and, as the baby, took over top spot. Maritza got away with everything: She didn't have to do chores, she didn't have to clean up and no rules applied to "short girl," as he called her. Whatever position we felt like we were in as children, we were provided the same love and attention equally.

My dad called me late on Sunday, July 16, 2006, after 9p.m. He was trying to find something he misplaced for his computer. I think it was a web camera, and he was calling to ask if I knew where it was. I told him I didn't, but I would come to his house the next day after work and help him look for it. My mom's birthday is on July 18 so, on Monday the 17th, we were trying to figure out what we were going to do. Monique had an office in the same building as we did, right down the hall.

While I was in my office, two things happened simultaneously that started a chain of events that would forever change my life. I heard Monique say "What" very loudly, and at the same time, my cell phone rang. I looked at the phone and noticed it was my mom's name on the caller ID, so I answered it. With the phone on my left ear, I could hear Monique's voice in my right ear. She was still down the hall so I couldn't understand what she was saying. I could now hear her feet pounding the floor, getting louder as she approached my office, telling me, "Let's go."

I wasn't sure what she was talking about but remember saying to wait a minute because I was on the phone with my mom. I turned my attention back to my mom. She asked me to go to their house to check on dad. I got my stuff together and left the office while still on the phone with Mom. I hopped in the passenger seat of Monique's truck, and we left the parking lot. I still didn't know who Monique had spoken with, but I asked my mom what was happening with Dad. She said something about him being unresponsive and that the ambulance was on the way.

We stopped to pick up TJ from daycare, which was only a five-minute drive from the office. The drive from Olympia Fields to South Holland takes about 20 minutes without traffic. I don't remember much else about the ride. A million thoughts were going through my head. I tried to call my dad on the house phone and on his cell phone, but there was no answer. During the ride, I learned that my dad had died. I still don't remember exactly how. Shock was setting in.

At my parents' house, Maritza was there. I don't recall if Mom was there before me or if she arrived right after us. I remember sitting in the truck in the driveway confused, because I thought I heard someone tell me an ambulance was at the house with my dad, but it wasn't. Nothing was making sense, and my mind was not processing anything. I eventually got up the courage to go inside the house. I took a deep breath and tried to brace myself for what I was about to see. I didn't know where Dad was in the house: Was he in his bedroom, the living room, where? I walked slowly in the back door, climbing the three steps to the main level. I walked forward toward the hallway and glanced to my left side toward the kitchen. Nothing. I then turned in the opposite direction toward the living room, and there Dad was, lying on the floor. He was fully clothed, and nothing looked out of place, he just looked asleep to me. I walked closer to him and gazed over him from head to toe, trying to understand what had happened. I was looking at the face of the person who gave me life, lying there absent of his. I was in shock and disbelief.

My world was suddenly different. Just two hours before, we were planning a birthday party; now we had to plan a funeral. Life changed so fast and in such a dramatic fashion.

My world was suddenly different. Just two hours before, we were planning a birthday party; now we had to plan a funeral.

People seemed to appear from nowhere. I don't recall when, but I saw Fran, Luis and Gabe. I saw Maritza and my mom eventually, then Tom and Pam, then Jerry and Spoon. I don't remember crying or anyone else doing so for that matter; I believe we were all in shock. I don't recall talking with anyone, but I'm sure I must have, based on the number of people there. The only thing I do recall vividly from the time we picked up TJ until much later in the day was when the funeral home came to pick Dad up. I was sitting in a bedroom next to the kitchen on the edge of the bed. The funeral director asked everyone to clear the kitchen and area near Dad, so they could do their job.

It was my dad, and I wanted to make sure they took care of him, so I stood up and started walking toward the kitchen. Both Jerry and Spoon stopped me in my tracks. They held me so I would not see what the funeral director was doing. I'm physically strong, and I remember pushing against them with my body to move them out of the way. Both hugged me and would not let go until the funeral director took Dad away. I didn't understand at the time but trusted them completely and knew whatever they were doing was best for me. Monique's dad was a fireman, and both Jerry and Spoon were police officers, so they had experienced scenes like this before.

Everything else was and still is a blur. I don't recall going to work the next day, but somehow my car was back at home despite my having left it at the office the day before. I do remember going back to my parents' house the next day, which was my mom's birthday. We pulled into the driveway as we normally did, and that's when the realization hit me that my dad was gone. Every time I came to the house, whether he knew I was coming or not, he would always be standing either at the front door looking out or at the side door, depending where I parked. This time, I sat in the passenger seat of Monique's truck, looking at the front and side doors back and forth, hoping he would open one of them, but it never happened.

As a child, my worst nightmare was losing one of my parents. I remember praying that I would die before they did because I didn't want to have to face the pain of not having them in my life. That day had come. Once I had a child of my own, the prayer changed to praying that my child would bury me, not the opposite. I felt like my compass was off. Not my moral compass, but the one that pointed me in the direction to complete the tasks and responsibilities I had as a son and father. I had to lean on Monique more than ever to make sure our family was still moving ahead—and for support. I had an office full of workers, customers and business partners to manage, and suddenly I was the oldest male of the family and probably by no choice of my own, the one to provide some sort of guidance and leadership.

I didn't want this challenge; I didn't ask for it and didn't want to process what had occurred. It was all so sudden, so unexpected, so final. It felt like a really bad dream because I just spoke with Dad not even 24 hours ago, and we had plans for that day. None of us had planned a funeral; where do we start?

Monique stepped up and took the lead and provided stability for all of us. I can't imagine what Fran and Maritza and Luis and Gabe were feeling. I remember staying close to my mom, though, not letting her get too far out of my sight. As much as he was our dad, he belonged to her first, and they knew each other long before we came along. At some point, our good friends Neva and Allyson came over to my parents' house, which ultimately became the meeting place every day. Monique had become friends with Neva and Allyson, and they communicated more than I did with them, even though I had known them for many years before we got married. I can't recall how many days had passed between Dad's passing and the funeral, but it seemed like forever. I remember Tracey being at the house, reading Bible verses with my mom. Monique contacted her friends at Leak & Sons funeral home. Spencer Jr. and his family really helped, walking us through the process for the service and burial. The next thing I remember vividly was my dad's side of the family arriving from Georgia. I hadn't seen Cousin Chris in many years, so we sat in the living room and talked for hours. We finally laid Dad to rest soon after, in a plot under the shade from the leaves of a big tree. Dad loved being outdoors and sitting under a "shade tree" as he called them, so we wanted this type of environment as his resting place.

One of the worst times after my dad passed was when the service was over, the visitors had gone home, and I was alone at home, left there to sit and finally process the significance of the loss. This was the worst time ever. I wanted to lay in bed and not move. I wasn't sleepy, I just wanted to sit still and think about Dad. I wanted to hear his voice again, I wanted to see the smile and hear him playing with the boys. I wanted to drive him to dialysis, as bad as that was, but at least we would have time together. I called his cell phone so I could hear his voicemail greeting. It was excruciatingly painful, but I had to hear him one more time.

Monique got me up and moving right away. I don't recall taking any time away from the office or, at the very least, working the phones to keep things moving. I think Fran, Maritza and I gave everything we could to Mom. None of us wanted her to be alone. We didn't know how to help her to deal with the grief, but we just wanted her to be OK.

This was the most pain I had ever felt in life. I had to draw on everything I had experienced in the past to show myself that I could endure. It goes without saying that I prayed all the time and surrounded myself with family and friends.

I didn't feel that anything positive could come from this experience. I typically try to find the silver lining in each situation and focus my attention on it, instead of the problem. I didn't know it at the time, but one of the gifts I received from this pain was to reconnect with my cousin Chris. Chris is a few years older than me and has a wonderful wife named Pam. They have a son named Miles who is an amazing young man. Chris and Pam are Navy veterans, and both served in the Persian Gulf War, so he was a little busy over the years with military and family responsibilities. If it would not had been for my dad passing, I don't know what other scenario would have arisen that would have given us the opportunity to become as close as we are now. Less than one year later, Chris, Pam and Miles would be traveling with us and still do so, to this day. Every Sunday, we call each other and spend at least an hour on the phone checking in and sharing our life experiences. It feels like Dad's spirit brought Chris and me together, and that is his way of keeping his memory alive. Each time Chris and I speak, I can feel my dad's spirit gently saying, "I'm here and I'm OK." What a gift!

I would not know to what extent at the time, but my dad's passing made me stronger, emotionally and mentally. I chose to face the pain at a certain point and dig deeper.

> *I chose to face the pain at a certain point and dig deeper.*

When I thought about Dad, I used the feelings I experienced to create a resolve within myself to push even harder with everything I did. I knew my mom would need strength from me. She would need to know that I would provide whatever support possible for her to be at peace. This feeling was not only mine; I'm sure my sisters felt the same.

The strength to bear pain

There will be pain, sometimes more excruciating at times than others, but I know that I can get through it. I also feel strongly about the phrase, "This too shall pass." Pain and grief are hard, no doubt; going through it is a process, but if I decided to go sit in a corner and drink myself to sleep, what happens to my wife, my son, my mom, my family and friends? By doing nothing, I am ultimately creating more pain for myself and others. I have a company to run, and it's no one else's job or responsibility for it to succeed but me.

My dad's death also made me appreciate my life. I became determined that I would not waste time. Not that I did before, but seeing my dad pass in such an unexpected manner drove home the thought that tomorrow is not promised to anyone, not a single person.

One hard lesson I also learned is that others don't care as much as you do about the difficulties you are facing, so don't bother telling people outside your circle about them. Of all the business relationships I had established over the years, I would eventually speak to many of them a few weeks after Dad's death. However, I can count on one hand how many people even acknowledged his passing. They knew about it because of how closely our company worked with them every day on projects. I mention this to say that even when life is on pause, turned upside-down and torn to pieces, no one outside your inner circle really cares. This added another layer of calluses to my mind. Not my heart, but my mind. I became better at isolating my personal life and relationships from my business life. This takes practice, but I was given the gift to start the process. I would find it easier later to negotiate contracts without my personal feelings getting in the way.

My loss also made me in many ways the leader of the family. Leadership is not about giving orders and demanding things of others. In fact, it's just the opposite:

When I find myself in a leadership position, I am humble knowing that people are looking to me for guidance and support. Leadership is a privilege, not something to be taken advantage of. I already had experience leading my company, leading ABLE and working in a strict hierarchical structure in the Army. All those roles were professional, while this new one was personal; that's what made it different. I often think about Dad and what advice he would give me today when I'm facing tough situations. I also wonder how he would handle others he would be facing.

There is some pain that is a once-in-a-lifetime occurrence. This type of pain is the gift that keeps on giving. For example, I've spoken with other friends who have lost one or both of their parents, and we share the same feeling about holidays. I'm a father, and my son celebrates me each year. I also treat this day with importance because no matter what, I must be available for my son as it is our special day. Since my dad passed, the meaning of Father's Day has changed somewhat. I find myself staying in bed a little later or waking up a little earlier so I can take time alone to think about my dad and how special he was to me. It's a somber day still, all these years later. I hear about other people my age whose fathers are still living, and I think about what we would be doing on that day if Dad was still alive. In a way, I become that little child all over again, just replaying the times in my head when I felt loved the most by Dad. I have a thousand memories, but some stick out more than others, like when he would pick me up and carry me to the car after I had fallen asleep at my grandma's house.

I think about the goals I have achieved that he would be super proud of. My dad used to take me to look at boats as a young boy. I bought my first boat in 2008. Without consciously knowing it, I was fulfilling a dream he had many years ago. Of course, I wanted the boat, but it was because of the seed he planted. Remember, all of us are living out some portion of our parents dreams, perhaps those we were fortunate enough to know about.

My birthday is another day that has a different meaning now. Once, my birthday was about my parents, not me. I had nothing to do with the planning, nor did I choose the day. This day was special because it was the day their hopes, dreams and prayers came true: They gave birth to me. I view my birthday as a special day for my parents, not me. The same is true when I think of my son's birthday: It was the happiest day for Monique and me, while he just lay around under a warm heat lamp while drinking milk and pooping all over the place. We were the ones celebrating, so it's our special day. No matter how many years pass, for every success or failure in my life, I think about Dad and long to hear his joy or sage wisdom telling me it will be OK.

I am still waiting on a time in the future when I can really sit in the reality that my dad died all by himself. I need a safe place, a physical location and secure emotional state of mind to think deeply about this. I have many questions that will never be answered, but I still need to ask myself and take time to contemplate what Dad must have been thinking and feeling. I was Dad's only son, and he was my role model. I know that there was nothing I could have done to prevent his death, so I don't feel guilt. Due to the circumstances surrounding his death, I believe my dad had a heart attack. I don't feel in my heart it was an instant death, and that makes me wonder, when he initially felt something wasn't right, did he call for my mom? Did he yell out for my sisters, or did he yell out for me? How much pain did he have? Could he catch his breath? When he fell to the floor, was he conscious? If he was conscious on the floor, did he hurt himself during the fall? How long did he lay there, hoping someone would come help him? Did he think about me in those last seconds of his life?

THE GIFT OF PAIN:
You are strong enough

You can get past your worst nightmare. I learned this lesson after experiencing the most significant pain I had felt up until that point in my life. Knowing that one day something can happen can never prepare you for when it occurs, good or bad. I knew when Dad began dialysis treatment that his time with us was shortened. From the moment I received the call through seeing him with my own eyes and experiencing something I'd dreaded come true—all this was like pressing pause on the song of my life.

Some pain will be so acute that it seems as if everything around you is standing still. In your shock, your senses can't respond. Your mind tries to make sense of the unimaginable, and your heart longs for comfort. Have you been in this place in your life? Are you there now? It hurts, it's lonely and the world around you continues to function as if you and your pain are irrelevant.

A month or two may pass, or even years, but I promise you that mentally, spiritually and physically, you will reach a better place than where you are today.

The lesson is this: We have the free will to decide how to respond and react during difficult times. You will have a moment when you have to decide if lying in your pain will provide more comfort than using it to reach somewhere new. Remember, you are still alive. You will feel better. You can help others that are experiencing what you have already mastered, which is enduring, healing and living with a greater purpose.

9: THE MOST IMPORTANT GIFT IN THE WORLD

Our son

April 10, 2003, was one of the best days of my life and one that marked a consequential turning point: It is the day that our son TJ was born.

Having been married for five years at this point, Monique and I had achieved such levels of success in our businesses and personal lives that we could focus on starting a family. We still wanted to work long hours because we were doing what we loved. How would we prioritize our days after having a little person to take care of? We discussed it as a couple and thought about it from our individual standpoints. We had parents to provide the guidance we needed, who had taught and encouraged us, so we could prepare this young person to be a productive member of society. We had an excellent support system of sisters, cousins, aunts, uncles and friends, who all provided us a safety net in case we needed it. I already had experience being a presence in a young boy's life with each of my nephews, Luis and Gabriel. These were my buddies and I learned a great deal about the growing pains that boys face, which prepared me in many ways for TJ's arrival.

A perilous passage

As much as Monique and I were looking forward to meeting TJ, about five months earlier, I was in a situation that could have prevented me from doing so. Prior to knowing Monique was pregnant, we were booked on a cruise with our usual travel group coordinated by Monique's mom. At the time of the cruise, we would be about five months into the pregnancy. We scheduled an appointment with our doctor, who said the trip posed no danger to Monique or the baby, so we decided to go ahead with our last vacation before becoming parents.

We flew from Chicago, heading to Puerto Rico to board the ship for a seven-day cruise. We both sorely needed some quiet time away from work and the daily chores of life. Pam prepared her travel groups well and suggested getting to the embarkation port a couple of days ahead of time. This provided an opportunity for everyone to start the unwinding process before getting on the ship.

Anytime I traveled to an area where there was an ocean, I could not resist the urge to scuba dive. I decided to get a couple of dives in with a local scuba shop while we were in Puerto Rico those two days. I booked the excursion with the Caribe Hilton's front desk and the next morning went downstairs to the lobby to await the shuttle van to pick me up at 6a.m. We headed south, down the east coast of the island. The view was amazing, with the ocean on my left side and the tall, lush green mountains on my right.

Now, I wasn't a newbie to diving. Monique and I had previously obtained our Professional Association of Dive Instructors (PADI) Open Water Certification and had completed several dive trips in various parts of the world. I continued my training, having obtained my Advanced Open Water Certification in Jamaica and had logged about 28 dives at this point. I had conducted night dives, navigation dives and a deep dive, going down as deep as 105 feet below the surface of the water. Diving in the ocean is a lot different than in the States, where many people dive in quarries and lakes. The currents are strong, and the depths are greater, although visibility is usually much better.

The shuttle van arrived at Puerto del Rey Marina in the city of Fajardo approximately 45 minutes after leaving San Juan. The total trip should take five-six hours since we would be doing a two-tank excursion. After checking in at the dive shop, we walked toward the pier where the dive boat was docked. The captain greeted us and introduced himself and his crew. Captain Jim gave us a safety briefing about the boat, the waters and what to expect to see during the dive. During every safety briefing I've ever heard, some inexperienced newbie always asks if there are sharks in the water. Each time, the captain says, "Yes, it's the ocean. This is where they live." He then reminds them they are visiting the ocean, but it is the sharks' permanent home.

We boarded the dive boat. Each time I sit on a dive boat, the experience is different. The view, the smell, and the currents combine to create an exciting experience that can only be enjoyed on the open water. I sat quietly and listened to the two dive masters provide details of our dives. The first dive is always at a deeper or equal depth than the second to ensure your body can handle the nitrogen levels that build up. Our group was 10-12 people, all beginners without any dive experience who wanted a taste of the sport while on vacation. The only experienced people on the boat were Captain Jim, the two dive masters and me.

We headed east toward the island of Icacos, a short trip of 20 minutes. Once there, we sat and waited for the captain and crew to drop anchor and ensure the boat was securely tethered to the ocean bottom. Once we got the go-ahead, everyone was told to get their gear and equipment on. This is when my adrenaline kicks in. I'm excited to get in the water, to feel the warmth, to see the fish and observe the bright coral rising from the ocean floor. I assisted the dive masters to ensure breathing regulators were working, oxygen tank valves were open and vests, also known as buoyancy compensators (BCs), were functioning properly. The first dive master jumped in, turned toward the boat and gave the all-clear signal. He instructed his group to enter the water. Once his people were in the water, he quickly moved them to a safe area away from the boat so the next set of people could jump in. Next, the second dive master followed the same process. Because I had a lot of experience, he asked me to enter last to make sure the entire group stayed together. The captain and dive masters are always doing head counts on dive trips, before, during and after each dive to ensure they don't leave anyone behind. Also, while in the water, the dive masters continue to perform head counts, as ocean currents can easily carry a person far from the group without much effort.

Our first dive was in approximately 60-65 feet of water, with nearly 80 feet of visibility. We could see everyone in our group with no problem. Typically, divers stay close together as they want to point out fish to each other and feel safer in groups. I would say we spent no more than 25 minutes on the first dive, then began a short decompression stop on the way to the surface to allow any built-up nitrogen to escape from our bodies.

Once all divers were accounted for, the crew pulled anchor and headed off to the second dive location. Between dives, I drank a bottle of water and snacked on some fruit that was provided by the crew. The adrenaline subsided, although I was still excited about the second dive. The next dive site was located not far from the mainland, visible about two miles away. It was a little later in the morning now, and the current had started to pick up a bit. Even if water is choppy on the surface, though, I could descend a few feet and the water would be very calm. I didn't want to do the second dive as I wasn't feeling good because of the rough seas. I whispered to the divemaster I assisted earlier and told him I was going to sit this one out. He insisted that I come along to help him with the group because they were all inexperienced. I understood his concern, assessed the group's lack of knowledge with the sport and agreed to dive.

I knew managing a large group was not easy, especially with the stronger currents we were experiencing. While I was putting my equipment on, the first and second group of divers had already entered the water and were going down to avoid the rough water on the surface. I gave the divemaster I assisted an OK to let him know I was right behind. I completed my equipment check, pressed the purge button on my regulator to ensure air was flowing, then duck-walked to the back of the boat. I grabbed my dive computer and held it tight to my chest with my left hand while using my right hand to cover my mask and regulator to prevent them from falling off as I hit the water and took a giant one-step leap. Once in the water, I checked my gear again, turned toward the boat to make eye contact with Captain Jim, and used my right hand to tap the top of my head, which is a dive signal for "all good." The captain was the only person remaining on the boat.

Since the current had picked up, the visibility was a little less than the first dive, probably 60 feet in any direction. The boat was anchored in approximately 40-45 feet of water, which is a good depth to allow natural light to come into the water. As I made my way toward the ocean floor, I could not see any divers. I looked up and saw the silhouette of the bottom of the boat. I positioned myself near the ocean floor and hovered a few feet from the bottom to see which way the current would take me. This way, I could possibly determine which way the divers had drifted.

One of the important rules in scuba diving is to always have a dive partner, never dive alone. This rule is in place for many reasons, especially if there is an equipment malfunction or emergency; a dive partner would be able to assist. I was breaking this rule, technically. I was alone, simply separated from my group. My goal was to get in the water and quickly connect with the group, but it didn't happen that way. I was only a few minutes behind them, so they couldn't be far, I thought. My training taught me to surface if I was lost, to locate the boat or other landmark, then reorient myself.

Once on the surface, I looked toward the boat, which wasn't too far away. I yelled toward the captain, asking where the group was. Captain Jim looked around, moving from one side of the boat to the other. Eventually, he spotted them. Even when divers are well below the surface, the bubbles that are released from their regulators rise to the surface and can be seen from some distance. This is how Captain Jim knew where they were. I was probably 40 yards behind the boat at this point, and he pointed toward the front of the boat, off to the right side but clearly out at a distance. When a boat is anchored or connected to a mooring, the "stern" or rear of the boat will swing from left to right with the movement of the water. This means that the way the captain was pointing was a very rough approximation of the direction they were in.

I released air from my vest so I could descend, then swam in that general direction all by my lonesome. I swam just a few feet from the ocean floor in a grid pattern, like I was taught in my advanced class. I was swimming fast, which means I was burning through a lot of air. I also had an elevated heart rate for sure. I resurfaced again after swimming about 150 yards. I could now see the boat way behind me, off to my right side, but I did not see Captain Jim. He may have been inside the boat's cabin.

Here I am, in the middle of the ocean, by myself, low on air in 50 feet of water. I decided to go down again to avoid the choppy surface and do one last semi-circle or arch from my position toward the boat to meet it as its stern swung toward my direction. After probably another hundred yards of fast-paced swimming, I felt exhaustion kick in rather quickly. I was sucking air like I had done wind sprints, then decided I needed to regroup and rest a little. I kneeled on the ocean floor, lowered my head and rested. I consciously took more shallow breaths as I checked the oxygen level on my gauge. I also looked at my dive computer to see which direction I was facing, which was east, toward the mainland.

I formulated my emergency plan. If all else failed and the boat left without me, I would surface, partially inflate my vest, then swim the two miles to the shore. I wouldn't need air in my tank at that point; I would just have to avoid getting run over by a passing boat with its propeller blades swirling and slicing through the water. My air level was just above the red zone and I was spent, tired, exhausted.

Even while in this really bad situation, I felt a sense of peace and imagined that this was it, the end. Wherever the other divers or the boat were, I wasn't close to them and probably didn't have enough air to keep looking. My only options were to sit there and let my air run out in a couple of minutes or slowly surface, do a five-minute decompression stop at 15 feet to let the nitrogen escape my body to avoid the "bends," then surface and wait for the boat crew to notice I was missing and start looking for me.

As crazy as it sounds, sometimes the safest place to be is under the surface of the water when in a dive area. If I'm the only person in the water, far away from a dive boat that is displaying a flag that reads "Divers Down," notifying other boaters that divers are in the water, I could get hit by a boat, and that would ruin my day. All of this was going through my mind, but I was very relaxed. I thought about my Monique and my unborn son as I kneeled, taking slow breaths. Time seemed to stand still. I was resigned that my options were limited, and I remember looking around, just being aware of my surroundings. Little did I know I would have this same feeling on September 20, 2017. It's like I just wanted to take one last look as if to say goodbye. My oxygen level was now in the red.

From the corner of my eye to the left, I could barely see the outline of what looked like a big fish. I had come face-to-face with huge grouper while diving in Cozumel, Mexico, and thought it must be one of them. As the shadow moved a little closer, the shape was longer than it was tall, so I thought maybe it was a dolphin. As it came even closer, I now recognized that it was a diver. I had the biggest adrenaline rush ever and rose up from the ocean floor and swam as fast as I could without losing eye contact with the person.

As I got closer, the diver looked over his right shoulder toward me, and I could see it was Captain Jim. I trailed behind slightly and followed his lead and soon saw another diver, then another diver, then more, all in an area spread out over about 30 yards. I looked up and saw the boat, oriented myself toward the front and swam in that direction. I grabbed ahold of the anchor line a few feet from the bottom and lifted myself, hand over hand, slowly ascending toward the surface. Even with all the drama, I still remember having the presence of mind to make my final decompression stop at 15 feet. I checked my air gauge and dive computer to time my five-minute stop and noticed I was almost completely out of air.

After floating in 15 feet of water, holding on to the anchor line, I became overcome with the thought that I could have died right there in the Atlantic Ocean, without ever having met my son. I felt my stomach turning with despair and vomited into my regulator. I couldn't ascend yet, so I removed the regulator from my mouth, pressed the purge button on the front to clear the debris, then shook it in the water to rinse it, and put it back in my mouth, only to vomit again. I eventually surfaced, and the sky never looked more beautiful. The sun was beating upon my face, which gave me further evidence that I was alive. I removed my fins and placed them on the boat, then climbed the ladder and got on the boat. I said a thank you prayer and sat quietly by myself until we arrived back at the marina.

This was one of those times in my life where I didn't quit, but also didn't have many options. Call it luck or faith, but I know it was a higher power giving me the chance to see my wife and future son. How many times have I been in a dark place, without anyone or any solution in sight? What I had learned from difficult times in the past is to not give up. The answer or help could be right around the corner if I have faith and continue living. Like the day of the fight during high school or the high-speed motorcycle race on the highway, this was yet another time when my life could have gone in a different direction.

What I had learned from difficult times in the past is to not give up. The answer or help could be right around the corner if I have faith and continue living.

Life is full of obstacles, turns and even dead ends. I would not have stopped swimming, even after my oxygen ran out. I would have swum on the surface for days if need be, to ensure I stayed alive. It would have been painful, but giving up would have created much more unimaginable pain for others than my sore muscles. I took away several lessons from this experience, one of which is that I am 100% confident that I can remain calm during difficult times. I can control my mind enough to not allow it to wander toward uncertainty, but instead keep it focused on solving the problem.

Becoming a father

Life with a child demands a new level of focus, sacrifice and discipline. We knew our son was the top priority on our personal and professional schedules. He is God's gift to us and became our most important purpose in life. Did this mean I would not give 100% to my company? That's correct. Did this mean that our daily routines had to change? For sure. Did we mind? Not at all.

I had a shining example to look up to. I recall my childhood and how much time we spent together as a family.

My parents never traveled out of town without us, nor did they make us sit at the "kids" table when grown-ups were talking. If the conversation was not appropriate for children, they wouldn't have it in our presence. As a matter of fact, part of the reason why I always gravitated to older men for guidance is because I remember the wisdom I had gained from sitting at the table with my father and his peers when I was a child.

I had also heard the regrets of several high achievers, how they missed their children's important years. I was not about to go down that road with my son. I was away from my son overnight during his childhood twice. From the time TJ started daycare until he was 13 years old, either Monique or I dropped him off at school in the morning and picked him up after school. No matter what we had to do, we made this a priority. We always sat down at the dinner table together, even if one of us was not eating. We said prayers every night before bed, we attended every Tae Kwon Do practice and tournament and included our son in every conversation we had at home. For the rare times Monique and I would have to be away from home at the same time during the evening, my parents would come to our house to babysit. We made sure family time was sacred and ensured that both sets of grandparents had equal time with him.

Having a child focused my life deeply, as I truly embraced the gravity of the responsibility I was given. I had been entrusted to teach another person about love, loss, relationships, education, spirituality, finance and much more. If I didn't have a grasp of all these areas, I would lean on family and friends to teach me. It was also a point in my life to change behavioral patterns that were passed on by my parents and put the next generation on a better path.

People often speak about having a work-life balance. Our choice was to dedicate the next 18 years to raising our child, and everything else came in a distant second. We understood that we would have to put certain goals aside, but not abandon them. Taking my foot off the throttle—so to speak—in my business was no problem. I look back at the little things that I could have missed if I were traveling on business or spending longer nights at the office and am so thankful that I didn't: His first steps, the first-time hearing "Daddy," and even the times when TJ would have uncontrollable laughing attacks. I was present for all these moments that only come once. If I was truly working hard for my family, like so many other business leaders would say they are doing, how could I justify being away from my family when they needed me the most? I was confident that I knew how to make money and that in the world, there is always more of it to be had. The one thing in life we do not get more of is time.

> *The one thing in life we do not get more of is time.*

Travel strengthens family bonds

As my parents did with my sisters and me, we took TJ everywhere with us. He was not someone else's responsibility, nor did I ever recall a time where I felt I needed a break from my parenting duties. We also knew that beyond the lessons we taught at home and what he learned at school, it was important for our son to see the world and meet people of various races, beliefs and backgrounds. In his younger years, we went on a few family trips within the continental United States and a few outside the U.S., but we knew he would not realize the full benefits at that age.

Later, when he was 13, we set out to achieve a big goal: to visit the lower 48 states as a family. We would save Hawaii and Alaska until the college years. The planning began in late 2015, and our trip started in June 2016—the first year of a four-year project. We visited 12 states the first summer, which took about 35 days in total. We headed east, and Philadelphia was our first stop before heading down the East Coast toward Florida, then west to New Orleans, then back up to Chicago. Our goal was to stay in each state for at least one day, longer where we had family.

What an experience! We met good people in each place we visited and really immersed ourselves into the history of each location. From Boston to Florida is a coast rich in American history. We visited places that Monique and I learned about in school and learned the backstories to some historic events. TJ was learning history that was not taught in school as well as different aspects to what he was previously introduced to.

Our pre-planning informed what places to visit, where to eat, which sites we had to see and their historical connection to the rest of the states. I recall sitting in a small family-owned restaurant in Traverse City, Michigan, having breakfast. We chose this place because TJ loves French toast, and they reportedly had the best in town. There were only about 8-10 tables in the place, all seating four guests or fewer. I could smell the freshly brewed coffee as I opened the door and the fresh pastries they made in the back. When it was our turn to be seated, we were escorted to a table, and there was an older white couple sitting to our right side, probably in their 70s, already finished with their breakfast. The tables were close enough that we could hear their conversation, and they could hear ours as well. The couple overheard us talking about a couple of places we wanted to visit in the city. The wife leaned over and asked where we were from and what types of things we were interested in doing. Monique is the social one in our family and quickly engaged in a dialogue. After formal introductions, I thanked the man for his service after noticing the Vietnam veteran baseball cap on his head. We spoke briefly about our common bond as soldiers, and this established an instant rapport between us. Here we are, three Black people from Chicago now living in Puerto Rico and an older white couple living 2,200 miles away in Michigan, most likely with different political views, different upbringings and different perspectives based on our life experiences, sharing a common bond. The couple was so welcoming and helpful, and we were gracious and appreciative for the information they shared. They were also impressed that we were on a journey to expose our son and ourselves to the different people, places and cultures of the world.

I listened to every word the older man said to me, feeding my insatiable appetite for knowledge. This experience in Michigan would be repeated in nearly every state we visited with people from all walks of life and races. They have enriched our lives in many ways. One of the most important things we wanted our son to learn was inclusion, to open his mind and heart widely to people, geographic locations and socioeconomic situations. We went from sitting on park benches in Harlem, New York, eating fried catfish with our cousins Chris and Pam, to having private dinners in the desert in Dubai.

No matter where we went, there was a common thread we noticed in the conversations with others: They all wanted to provide a good life for their children, and all wanted to lay their heads down in a safe place each night. They wanted to be treated equally and to be seen and heard. This is key. Many people said as they walked through life, they felt that no one saw or heard them.

We also learned how much people like to talk and share their stories. When we'd stop for gas, someone would notice our out-of-state license plates and strike up a conversation at the pump and we'd spend a few minutes discussing how beautiful the landscape of America is. One of the jewels we found while driving across the states are the brown Historic Landmark signs that were posted along the interstates. The agreement we had before starting our travels was that we would not rush, and any time one of us wanted to stop to see something, even if it would take us off course, we would stop. Each time we saw a brown sign in the distance, we'd slow down a little to be able to read it and determine if it was something we wanted to explore. Even if we didn't stop, Monique would look up the name or location on her tablet so we could learn more.

After four years and more than 23,000 miles of driving, we had visited all the lower 48 states, many of them several times. I learned that road trips can be one of the most rewarding experiences anyone could ever have. They are one of the best ways to learn about history, gain understanding of other cultures and clarify what is important in life.

Africa

When TJ was still a baby, we decided to visit Africa once we he was old enough to endure the long flight. Monique's parents, Pam and Tom, had been to Africa several times and told us how wonderful their experiences were. They had handcrafted canes and jewelry made by the locals from different countries on the continent. Pam showed us photos of Maasai warriors dressed in their elegant red garb and described how amazing they were in person. With Pam, we began planning in late 2015 to make our first trip to the motherland.

Our local travel advisor in Nairobi, Kenya, was Rose Muya, a longtime friend of Pam's. When it comes to spending money, we prefer to invest as much as we can in the experience of travel. The reason this is important is because Rose wanted to know what our budget was for the trip. We had no way of knowing what was reasonable and asked her to put together some ideas. We wanted to have exclusivity wherever we went, so that we could take our time and set our own pace rather than being influenced by a larger group.

When we received the final proposed itinerary and booked the trip, I was very excited and had butterflies at the same time. After 18 months of planning, 12 shots and more than 22 hours of flying from Puerto Rico to Chicago, then Chicago to London, then London to Africa, we landed in Kenya in June 2017.

A cross-country road trip was an adventure, but this trip was full of many more unknowns. Taking our first steps on African ground was truly a spiritual experience: This was a land full of history, ancestral roots and natural beauty unlike any other. As we drove from the airport to the hotel at about 10:30p.m. local time, I noticed tall fences, approximately 15 feet high, with barbed wire on the top—to prevent wild animals from crossing.

That first night we could not sleep, probably from both the excitement of what was to come and the fact that we had slept a lot on the way to Africa. The next morning, we got to meet Pam's contact—and our trip planner—Rose for the first time. She is a true ambassador for her beloved country.

After a short conversation and a review of our itinerary, we boarded a small van. We were now headed to our first stop, a place named Giraffe Manor. It's a place where tourists and travelers stay before and after safaris, as a rest stop of sorts, to get travelers acclimated to the continent, including the elevation and time zone. Visitors can see wild giraffes and warthogs visiting the manor, expecting to be greeted by visiting guests.

Just before sundown, we sat outside on the patio, in the comfortable, cushioned wicker furniture. The staff made fresh tea, coffee and biscuits, which we Americans would describe as scones. Soon after, the giraffes began approaching from the wooded areas, slowly and gracefully walking toward the manor. I've been to the zoo many times in my life as a child and an adult. We knew beforehand that seeing these animals in their natural habitats would be so much different, but it is hard to describe the feeling of being up close and personal with truly wild exotic animals. The staff prepared bowls of pellets for us to give the giraffes and reminded us of the safety precautions we needed to adhere to in their presence. Giraffes can kill a lion with one kick. They can also head-butt and kill humans or another large animal if they get too close. TJ and I were brave enough to hand feed the giraffes. Their tongues are black and up to 18 inches long with a texture like sandpaper. We also stood back and threw pellets toward the giraffes and they would catch them in their mouths. We got really adventurous, putting a pellet in our mouths between our lips, and the giraffes reached down, pushed their tongues out and swiped the pellets out of our mouths. TJ and I kissed a lot of giraffes that year (sadly though, Monique hasn't kissed me since).

Rose picked us up the next day and took us to the Rift Valley for a water safari. Rose checked us in with a local mariner, who escorted us over to a wooden boat that was approximately 15 feet long with a single outboard motor on the back. All five of us put on our life vests, then slowly headed out into the body of water. The driver told us to look to the left, near the shore, just in front of the mangroves, and we would be able to see a hippo. I didn't know what to look for the first time, but later noticed other hippos with their ears and foreheads just breaking the surface of the water. These animals have huge heads! I knew from my reading that hippos kill more humans in Africa than any other animal. This is because people assume that since they are so large that they cannot move quickly, which is not true at all. They move slowly in the water, but on land they run faster than humans.

The next day was the big day: We'd be heading to our first lodge on the continent. Rose picked us up in the morning to take us to Wilson, the regional airport where smaller planes and choppers transport small groups of travelers to the bush. When traveling on safari, we were restricted to carrying no more than 30 pounds of gear to keep the weight of the airplanes and cargo under a certain limit.

Our transport was a small propeller-powered airplane that held only about 10 people. The pilot was a young Black lady who couldn't have been more than 30 years old, and the co-pilot was a young white man, probably close to the same age. We had never flown with pilots this young; they looked like teenagers. Once the bags were loaded, we taxied to the runway and made our way down it until we were airborne.

I remember having an overwhelming sense of pride that this dream Monique and I had many years ago was coming to pass. We had managed to take our 13-year-old son to Africa to experience the people, the land and the culture. As I looked out the left side of the plane, I saw huge mansions that looked like those we had seen in Atlanta and Florida and, nearby, more modest houses. I could see the tale of two vastly different worlds. There was real economic wealth in Kenya, not just from the natural resources that lie in the ground and mountain regions.

The flight from Wilson airport to the lodge was about 45

minutes. As we approached, all I could see was a mildly worn area on the ground ahead. I sat back in my seat and looked out the left-side window again, noticing we were getting close to the ground, then suddenly, the pilot pulled the nose of the plane up and gained altitude. The copilot began speaking on the radio as we made a right-hand turn. A few minutes later, we seemed to be back on the approach path to land and the same thing happened again—the pilot pulled the nose up and banked right. There was clearly something wrong, but we were not informed about it. I began to wonder if we were having mechanical difficulties or there was something wrong on the ground. Pilots don't abort landings without reason. Again, we circled, made the final approach, and as the ground got closer than the previous times, we eventually touched down on the grassy air strip. Once the plane pulled down the strip, the pilot turned around and headed back toward a group of trees in the distance. She turned around and told us passengers that she believed there were animals on the strip and had to radio down to the safari guides and ask them to drive their truck down to scare them off.

Once the rear door opened, the three of us grabbed our backpacks and cameras and made our way down the steps and walked in the "bush" for the first time. A truck that was parked under one of the nearby acacia trees slowly approached. Two tall, thin young men, dressed in bright red traditional Maasai attire, with blue, orange, yellow and white beaded bracelets and anklets, exited the truck. They introduced themselves as Konee and Moses. Konee was clearly the leader and was very professional and studied us with his eyes. I could see him looking us up and down with an inquisitive expression on his face. They grabbed our bags and walked us over to the safari truck, which was a modified Toyota Land Cruiser, with a flip-down front windshield big off-road tires painted dark green with khaki-colored canvas seats. The driver's seat is on the right side of the vehicle, with a manual "stick" gear shifter between it and the passenger side. The eight-passenger seat area, where we would spend many hours, was accessed by stepping up onto the side of the truck. There were no side windows, and the roof was made of a heavy canvas tarp like material, meaning that there was no protection against the elements nor any animal that wanted to have lunch with us. Moses offered us Kenyan tea, coffee and water.

I was in heaven. There was beauty everywhere I looked. I felt a sense of accomplishment and pride as I looked toward Monique and TJ, who were looking out of the opposite side of the truck. This is why we work so hard. This is why we don't spend money on frivolous, senseless material things that lose value the day we buy them. This experience of visiting Africa with my wife and son justified any and every tough business challenge I had faced. Life is about experiences, and we were aware that we were in one that would provide countless wonderful memories. We were truly living in the moment.

Along our 45-minute ride to the lodge, anytime we saw an animal, Konee would stop the truck so we could

> *Life is about experiences, and we were aware that we were in one that would provide countless wonderful memories.*

observe and take photos. At some point, we could see the lodge in the distance, recognizing it from the photos on the website. Konee leaned over to his left side, reached to pick up the VHF radio handset and spoke Swahili into it. Moments later, we entered the gates of the safari lodge, where we would call home for a few days. The staff members were standing at the entrance as we approached, bearing the biggest smiles we had seen. They greeted us by name, began collecting our bags and offered us warm moist face towels and soft drinks. The manager introduced herself and escorted us to the reception area, which overlooked a beautiful green landscape with Mt. Kilimanjaro in the far distance. I stood there, staring off at the trees, mountains, blue skies and brilliantly colored flowers. I was at peace. The lodge that Rose had chosen for us is very quaint, with only seven villas. As we stared out, all three of us mentioned how much like Puerto Rico it looked. The mountains, the green foliage and their acacia trees look almost exactly like our flamboyan trees. Hard work, plus determination plus saving our money for this moment, instead of fleeting material things, and God's grace got us here.

There were two watering holes positioned in front of the lodge, maybe 150 yards away. We were told that animals would sometimes gather there to drink, and sure enough, we began seeing giraffes, then gazelles and other animals approaching it. There was nothing to do but observe the raw and pure beauty. I didn't want to take a picture, I just wanted to be in the now.

We had the option of doing a game drive that night or waiting until the next morning. Animals behave differently during various times of the day, so being able to observe them in the morning, afternoon and night brings unique experiences. The cats, including lions, leopards and cheetahs, typically become more active at night because they are nocturnal and prefer to hunt at that time to approach their prey without warning. This means they are sleepy and lazy during the day, typically staying under the shade of trees to keep cool for the most part. I was anxious to do a night drive and did so each evening we were there.

We typically left the lodge at about 8p.m., just after dinner, dressed for evening temperatures that dropped into the 40s and 50s. Night after night, I felt the adrenaline high that I loved. Mix the elements of danger, darkness, an unknown environment and natural born killing machines on the prowl for prey, and the result is a night drive in the bush in Kenya. Konee and Moses are excellent trackers and stalkers. They are from the Maasai community, comprised of some 400,000 members in Kenya, belonging to various clans and villages. They are people with a nomadic lifestyle, who stay firmly planted in traditions that seem at first glance to be frozen in time. In many ways, however, they may be more liberated than most people I know.

Not too many years ago, in order to become a Maasai warrior, a young man would go out with his age-set to hunt and kill a lion with nothing more than a spear. As the young men came back after spending days in the bush with nothing but their friends, living off of the land and killing and eating their food, the first person leading the line, wearing his trophy kill, was the one responsible for killing the lion. The villagers waited anxiously for days, hoping their son was the first boy in line, which meant they would bring great pride to the family. The tradition has changed from killing lions to public circumcisions as their test to pass to become a Maasai warrior. Konee is a junior elder, and Moses is a warrior. They are now conservationists by trade as guides and encourage other members of the Maasai community to refrain from killing lions. During the dry season, lions will kill any animal it can to eat, including cows owned by the Maasai people. Warriors often seek revenge for the lions taking down their family cows and goats during the night and form up to hunt and kill the lion responsible. The elders have tried hard to discourage this practice and try to convince the younger warriors that conservation is a better choice.

On our evening rides, it was dark, and Konee would drive down a trail while Moses held his large "torch" light out of the left side of the truck, sometimes flashing it from side to side looking for animals. As we were driving, Moses and Konee shifted between Ma, Swahili and English in the same conversation. Whenever they thought they saw something, Konee would quickly stop the truck and they would flash their lights in the direction Moses mentioned and focus in on one area. I finally asked, how do you first spot an animal, then identify what type it is, in the dark? They told me that they know the color of the eyes of the animals when they are exposed to light, the distance between the eyes, the height of the eyes off the ground and if the animal was alone or in a group. Amazing!

The next day as we were leaving the lodge, the largest elephant I had ever seen came walking directly in front of the truck. Konee quickly stopped the truck and turned off the engine. Moses turned and looked back at us and said, meet One Ton. We had just met one of the most famous elephants in the region. He's a large bull with one of his tusks extending so far down that it almost drags along the ground. Monique and TJ's faces had looks of astonishment. We were in One Ton's world, and he took his time and even stopped as if to say, "welcome to Kenya." We learned later that One Ton had a brother named Tim who was even larger than he is. Tim lived near Amboseli National Park and died in 2020 from natural causes.

The jackpot of a safari is to see all members of the "Big Five," which includes the elephant, lion, leopard, buffalo and rhino. During our three weeks in various parts of Africa, we were fortunate enough to see all of them. About an hour from the lodge, Konee stopped the truck, backed up slowly and sure enough, there were three large male lions sitting under a tree off to our left side. Konee slowly pulled the truck off the trail and pointed the front end toward the lions, which were probably only 20 yards from the road. As we approached them, Moses explained that they are brothers, and the guides knew them well. The older brother wore an elegant dark black mane, long and thick. This was his reward for surviving many years in the harshest conditions in the region. He wore his robe with pride and honor. Although the younger brothers didn't have manes yet, they were nonetheless fierce warriors. There was a look of determination in their eyes and a comfort and security they displayed. Lions are the kings of the jungles and one of the only animals that can lie down without the fear of being attacked and killed.

We stayed with lions for about 30-40 minutes, just watching and admiring them. Our day was complete: We didn't need to see anything else after we experienced our first lion in the wild. I cannot imagine any material purchase of greater value than the experience that Monique, TJ and I shared that day in June 2017 in Kenya. The memory of the experience truly is priceless.

A spiritual visit

Our trip also included spiritual riches. After rising early and chatting with the staff at the lodge—who treated us as if we were family—we headed to visit an African village, Siana. Midway through the hourlong journey, we stopped to have tea at the top of a mountain. The view was breathtaking. I could turn in a 360-degree circle and see as far as my eyes allowed in every direction. Kenya is a magical place to me.

After our journey, we arrived at a place that was a few hundred yards from a two-lane road, with little to no vegetation in sight. It was dry, and lots of dust was being kicked up by the tires of our truck. Konee exited the vehicle and asked us to stay inside until he got permission for us to visit. We sat and spoke with Moses as he explained how and why each village is situated. This village, also called a Boma in the Ma language, contains 28 homes, made of mud, cow dung, sticks and branches for support and molded with water. On the outer perimeter of the village, there is a five-foot-high wall of thorny bushes from various trees and branches. The entrance to the village is left open during the day so the residents who live there can enter and leave as they please. At night, the "door of bushes" is moved into place to prevent predators such as lions and hyenas from entering.

After a few minutes, Konee returned to the truck to inform us that we were welcome to visit and to give them a few minutes to prepare to greet us. Konee explained the protocol of entering a Maasai village, which is as follows: The leaders will meet us in front of the entrance to the village. They will do a ceremonial dance and sing songs to bless the village and those entering it. Once that is complete, they will introduce themselves and personally greet each of us and escort us inside.

After a few minutes, twelve ladies lined up about 15 feet in front of us from left to right. They were dressed in bright red cultural dresses, with handmade earrings, necklaces, bracelets and anklets in blue, yellow, gold, white, orange and other brilliant colors. They sang with the melody of a professional choir and had smiles that I believed could light up the darkest nights. There were young ladies and older ones in the group, displaying generations of mothers from the Maasai tribe. After the songs, Konee walked us over to meet the ladies. We greeted them in their native language of Ma, saying "supa", or "hello" in English. This act brought even more smiles. We walked down the line, hugging each one as if they were our aunts, and we sensed a familiarity with each of them in their eyes, hair, skin texture, fingernails and facial expressions. They made us feel at home and welcomed us into the village.

The children were running around, playing as others their age do, hiding and peeking at us strangers from behind the homes. In the center of the village was a bunch of goats, loosely tied to prevent them from moving freely. The leader of the village is a precious lady named Moitanik. Moitanik invited us into her home to learn more about her community. Konee, Monique, TJ and I visited with her for about 30 minutes.

To be invited to enter a home in a Maasai village is a privilege and honor. There is one passageway, without a door, leading into each home. As I faced the home, I had to turn to my left side, so that I was now in front of a doorway no taller than 5 feet, 5 inches. I took one step forward, and now I was facing a wall, then I turned to my right, took another step, then turned to my right again, and finally I was able to walk into the home. Konee explained to us that the entrance is designed this way to prevent lions from entering the homes and attacking people while they sleep. Both Moses and Konee have had lions and hyenas enter their village at night and kill cows and goats.

To be invited to enter a home in a Maasai village is a privilege and honor.

The home was dark inside, except for the very faint glow of hot embers on the floor, set within an 18-inch circular shallow pit. This small area is used to provide dim lighting as well as a stove to cook on. There are typically one or two square holes in the walls that serve as windows, without screens or glass. The beds are little more than the same material used for the outside structure, simply elevated off the floor. We didn't know it at the time, but there were two small babies inside the home as well, sleeping behind us. Through Konee's translation, we learned that the ladies' responsibilities were to build the houses and to walk long distances, several miles in fact, to gather water for the village. The men typically went out to hunt and gather food. The children did not attend school, although education was extremely important, because they could not afford it.

We graciously thanked Moitanik for welcoming us into her home. Once outside, we were taken to the back of the boma, where the ladies had blankets neatly placed on the ground, with their handmade craft items lying on top. The ladies sat toward the front of the blankets, ready to answer questions and offer their goods for sale. Monique, TJ and I quietly discussed the fact that it would impossible for us to choose who to buy from; everything was beautifully made with such care, precision and love. Therefore, we bought something from each lady and gave them as gifts to our friends and family back in the States. Shopping is based on negotiation, and while many visitors asked for discounts, we did not.

Once the shopping experience ended, we began to walk back into the village. A few of the ladies intercepted us and pulled Monique toward them. They sat Monique down on the ground and started placing necklaces and jewelry on her. We understood from Moses that the ladies were so happy and surprised by our generosity that they were overwhelmed with gratitude. This brought Monique to tears and I believe Konee as well. I may have had a piece of dirt in my eye, but I can't remember for sure.

Once back in the middle of the village, all the ladies gathered around, and we stood in front of them to have a few words before we left. The kids were keeping their distance from us. I asked Moses why, and he said that other tourists are often dismissive of them and the ladies wanted to keep them at a distance. I asked Moses to ask the ladies if the kids could come over to join us and they agreed. Soon, there were 15-20 kids running our way with big, brilliant smiles. We hugged them, told them "supa" and put our arms around them and included them in the conversation.

Before entering the village, we asked Konee if it was OK to take photos of the villagers, and he said yes, they would not mind. Taking photos of locals can be a sensitive topic for certain segments of the Maasai people, so we wanted to respect their culture by asking first. Moitanik began the conversation by telling us that the ladies were very happy to meet us. They had never seen Black people from the United States in person. She said that she saw facial features and other similarities between Monique and her daughter. She saw the same in me and that TJ looked like he could fit in as a young Maasai warrior. TJ had twisted hair at the time, and the young Maasai warriors wore their hair in a similar fashion. Everywhere we went in Africa, TJ's hair was a conversation piece as people said how he could be one of their clan members.

Moitanik told us that they always wondered how other Black people outside of Africa lived and what they thought of their ancestors and the people of Africa in general. Konee said Moitanik felt like our visit to the village was like a homecoming for relatives they sent off many years ago. They mourned the loss of their ancestors who had been carted off to the U.S. as slaves. What had happened to them? How were they treated? Would the descendants of those slaves, who later obtained their freedom, return to Africa? Would their sons and daughters come back home to visit? Did the Black people in the U.S. forget about them, especially during droughts and famines? Moitanik said their prayers had been answered with our visit. One of the ladies who was in her late 80s never imagined seeing a Black person from the U.S., sitting in her village, playing with her grandchildren.

At this point, Monique was in full boo-hoo mode. She tried to express her feelings but couldn't get the words out. I spoke on behalf of our family and told them how they reminded me of my mom, especially in their haircuts. I also told them they looked like my great-grandmother on my father's side. I said that they were some of the most beautiful and kind people we ever met. We let them know that we would never forget this experience and that it had already changed our lives, even before leaving the village.

The children missed some of the bittersweet emotional undertones, but they were focused on shared delight.

We took lots of photos on our digital camera and hit the playback button to show the children their images. We take simple things like photos for granted, but we soon realized that these children had never seen themselves in a mirror, let alone on a photo. The same was true for the ladies that had never seen a photo of themselves. The kids looked at the photos, laughed really hard, ran away screaming and came right back to look again.

This was a magical and spiritual experience for everyone in the village as well as our family. When we left, the ladies would not leave the truck. They were on the right side, where Monique was seated and kept holding on to her, crying and saying words we couldn't understand. Even as Konee pulled away slowly, they kept holding on while walking along the side of the moving truck until they had no choice but to let go. We were emotionally spent, spiritually drained and overwhelmed at the reality that we connected to our ancestor's families, who dreamed of meeting us without even knowing us.

I had never seen a happier group of people in my life. By American standards, these people were the poorest I had ever seen, living in mud huts, no cars, no money, no televisions, no running water, no electricity, no internet, no phones, no social media, no 401Ks. How is it possible that they can dance and sing the way they do? What are they happy about? One of the ladies at the village was approximately 90 years old. Most Maasai don't know their exact ages. How is it possible that this lady could bend down to sit on the ground and get back up without help from others? What about health insurance and stocks and bonds? How could they survive without retirement accounts? How is it that people back at home with untold wealth could be so unhappy? People with all the worldly possessions anyone could ask for still jump out of windows to their death because they lost some money in the stock market. The ladies we just met had none of these things but sang songs of praise and thanksgiving so freely and joyfully. They are happy and grateful for life.

I feel that this moment will stay with TJ forever and is one of the most important experiences of his young life. What greater gift can we give our children than exposure to history, culture, ancestry, nature, giving and God all on the same trip?

What greater gift can we give our children than exposure to history, culture, ancestry, nature, giving and God all on the same trip?

The next few days were filled with more game drives and exploration. Konee and Moses showed me how to track lions as well as taught me other animals' specific patterns and behaviors. One time, Moses spotted a large baboon nearby in a tree. We tried to follow, but he moved quickly away from us. The baboon made a sound to not only let other baboons know danger was near, but to inform other animal species. They protected each other. The same happened when we were in Lewa on a walking safari observing elephants. The elephants did not see us, but several zebras came along and spotted us almost immediately even though we believed we were out of sight, behind a large dead tree that had fallen on its side. The zebras made a noise to alert the elephants of our presence, then turned and ran about 10 feet away from us, stopped, turned around and stared at us again. The elephants never did get the hint. Our guide, Kitonga, told us that the animals have a symbiotic relationship, meaning that they have relationships since they share the same land and want to protect each other from intruders.

Our stay at this lodge was coming to an end. While we sat in the truck waiting on the plane, we had time to laugh and share our favorite stories of the trip with each other. We laughed about the times we had to stop in the middle of nowhere, in the dead of night so I could "mark my territory," aka urinate. Yep, I got out of the truck, walked to the rear about 10 feet, couldn't see more than a few feet in any direction on a moonless night and peed. Another night, TJ had to do the same thing while on a game drive. I got out with him for support, we went to the back of the truck and stayed there for about 10-15 seconds and he said "OK, let's go." It wasn't until two years later that TJ told me he was too nervous to pee; nothing would come out. As a man, I totally understood.

The five of us had laughed so much during this trip and built a stronger family bond. Like for the ladies at Siana, our meeting was a life-changing event as well for Konee and Moses—they had never met Black American tourists. We exchanged phone numbers and told them we would never forget them, and we promised to stay in touch and visit again with other family and friends. We kept our promise and visited again in 2019 with five more family members. I talk to both of them every week and sometimes with the ladies of Siana when Konee visits them. This is the legacy of our trip.

Reflecting on the power of family time

A lot of our family time is spent enjoying memories of the places we visited and people we met around the world. We also look forward to visiting some of our "all stars," the places we really enjoy like Africa, Washington, D.C., New York, London, Atlanta, Philadelphia and more. When watching a show on TV or a movie, we always recognize a place we visited, even without the name being broadcast on the screen. When we meet people and ask where they are from, if it's anywhere in the states, we can quickly provide some real feedback and stories about the time we spent there.

I often tell people that it is not a parent's place to decide if they are a good parent. It's up to the child to decide what they feel about how we are or were as parents. One thing I know is that there is no greater gift in life than to make the decision to be involved in a child's life and share every waking moment, creating experiences and memories that will make them a better person, a productive citizen and someone who has compassion for other humans, no matter their race, religious belief, sexual preference, political views or socioeconomic status. We decided that sacrificing growing million-dollar businesses and buying a bunch of stuff that ultimately has no value is not worth anything if it detracts from our family time. Exposure and immersion are the best ways we can teach valuable lessons to our son.

We understood while TJ was still a toddler that formal education would only be a part of his educational plan. Between kindergarten and the end of 8th grade, neither television nor video games was included in his daily routine. At night, TJ and I would lay in bed and read books together. I would change my voice to match what I thought the characters in the book should sound like. TJ would not want the reading to stop, often asking that we read shorter books a second time, back to back. He would also read books on his own as a child, not just small ones but also some that were several hundred pages long.

We made important decisions as a family, so we could show him how to make them, not just to go along with others plans. This included small things and larger ones that had more importance and relevance. We also kept up the drumbeat of being kind to others and never looking down on anyone, regardless of their circumstances. TJ showed in later years that he learned this lesson well as we traveled. He would often, without being asked to, give to homeless people who were living on the street. He would smile and offer a tip to restaurant workers and others that assisted him in certain ways.

Our travels, in my opinion, have provided some of the best education and opportunities for him to gain wisdom. Through our travels, we have informally adopted many people and causes and consider them part of our everyday life. In Africa for instance, when we saw these amazing people and learned about their needs, I believe each of us felt in our hearts that we had to find a way to be of assistance to them. Looking into the eyes of young children who do not have access to formal education and who may not eat each day, I searched my mind to think of ways to provide immediate relief. As a family, we sat and talked about how we had so many things, many of which we really didn't need. Although we have always lived modestly, we saw that many others worldwide lacked comfort yet only desired the basics such as education, shoes, blankets and a steady source of food. We figured out a way to provide all of these for them. Giving to others and seeing the good in people were lessons TJ learned early in life so that he can continue the pattern for many decades.

10: THREE WEEKS WITH AN ANGEL

In March of 2012, Monique, TJ and I decided we would move to Puerto Rico in June 2013 to live a slower-paced life in a safe environment where TJ could do all the things a young man should be able to. We wanted to be in an environment where kids could safely ride bikes, a place that freed us of rush-hour traffic and long drives between home, the office and downtown meetings. We also wanted a change of weather—we were tired of dealing with snow each year. Part of our plan was for my mom to move to Puerto Rico in December 2013 to live with us. This would give us a few months after we arrived to get TJ in school, adapt to everyday life on the island and settle comfortably in a routine before she arrived.

In the fall of 2012, my mom flew to Atlanta to visit my dad's side of the family and stayed with my cousins Chris and Pam. Whenever mom went to the ATL, Chris would take time off work so they could run the streets. Mom had a lot of energy and couldn't sit still for very long, always wanting to be out among the people. They would go to visit family, stop by their favorite hangouts and sit at home and catch up and talk about life. My mom had a few favorite restaurants that she had to visit during each trip, but this time was a bit different. Chris called me every couple of days because he and Pam were concerned that Mom did not have an appetite. They went out to eat or cooked at home, and she would barely have any food because her stomach was bothering her. This was unusual, so they wanted to keep me informed.

Later in the year, in early December 2012, Mom flew down from Chicago with us to spend Christmas time in Puerto Rico. Although the temperature is in the low 80s in December, Christmas is really fun. Everyone has decorations on their homes, people decorate their golf carts in holiday colors and wrappings, and others are caroling. Even at the local stores, the workers and customers sing Christmas songs out loud for everyone to hear. Mom was her usual self this trip, waking up early, sitting on the back patio, drinking coffee and reading the Bible in her pajamas. I did, however, notice that she was not eating much, and when asked, she said her stomach was hurting a little, but it wasn't anything to worry about. We are a lot alike in the sense that even if there is something on our minds or happening with our bodies, we didn't want to give it unnecessary energy to allow it to grow into something more significant. This usually works to my benefit, but not always.

In January 2013, Mom made an appointment with her primary care doctor to seek answers to the lack of appetite and periodic abdominal pain. Mom also asked for a referral to see a gynecologist so she could establish a new relationship for her annual checkups.

During the visit with the gynecologist, they detected a mass in her abdominal/pelvic area and ordered a blood test. When the results of the blood tests came back, the doctor scheduled a follow-up visit for Mom to discuss them. The doctor explained that because of the size of the mass, she was concerned about it. Also, the results of the ovarian test were higher than the normal range, so another referral was made to see a gynecological oncologist, who was an in-resident specialist at the University of Chicago hospital.

Time passed between doctor's appointments. I didn't worry too much; overall, Mom was in good health. She was energetic, in great spirits and still running the streets as she always did. Blood tests and a biopsy were completed, and the results came back. My sisters Fran and Maritza went with Mom to the follow-up visit with the specialist.

We learned that Mom had been diagnosed with ovarian cancer. The doctor said the cancer was Stage IV, because it was also present on the liver, which is difficult to treat. They then discussed treatment options such as chemotherapy and surgery to remove as much of the cancer as possible. The doctor said that because the cancer was so far along that they considered it to be terminal, and she would have just two to three months to live. The team at the hospital promised to do everything they could to make Mom comfortable during the last part of her life.

Mom approved of the treatment options the doctors suggested. They left the room to allow Fran and Maritza to digest what they had just heard. Mom said that she had heard the doctor's opinion, but the final word comes from God and not them. When my sisters called and told me what the update was, I felt like someone punched me in the chest. Everything in me stopped immediately as I searched my mind thinking about what this meant. My eyes looked around at everything in front of me, but could not focus on anything. I had the feeling like I was going to vomit. I felt helpless for the first time in many years. The strategy I had relied on, of spending every waking moment working toward goals, could not give me the outcome I desperately wanted this time. I laid down in the bed, got under the covers and thought about the best- and worst-case scenarios until I fell asleep, right there in the middle of the day.

As a family, we worked out a plan to support Mom during her treatments, which began quickly after the appointment. My nephew Luis, who lived with Mom, would be the primary person responsible for her daily needs. Fran, Maritza and I would alternate going to chemo sessions. After chemo, Mom would stay at our house overnight. Mom never experienced the negative physical side effects that we braced ourselves to deal with. The only noticeable difference was that she would stay awake most of the night, reading, watching TV or playing a game on her tablet. Mom slept in TJ's room, which they both loved, because they would get into all kinds of craziness. For TJ, this was a fun time, having his friend with him for a couple of days, which meant the usual house rules were out the window.

The changes we were looking for were indicated by the tumor marker number. The oncologist indicated that the lower the number, the better her body was responding to the chemo treatment. A tumor marker is a substance that is made by the body when a cancer is present; it can also be made by cancer itself. After each chemo treatment, Mom had to go to her doctor's office for a progress report. I was anxious to get the call from Fran, Maritza or Luis to hear what the number was. Each time she was treated, the number went down slightly, which was always good news. I felt relieved and encouraged immediately and this feeling would last for a few days each time. I felt a sense of gratitude that on that day, I had a lot to be thankful for.

Mom continued to go to her chemo sessions, then run the street like she didn't have a worry in the world. We were headed back to Puerto Rico (PR) in June as we usually did for summer vacation. Several of us hiked the mountains in El Yunque rain forest, and Mom was right there. We rode ATVs along the base of the rainforest. We went on boat rides, walked for hours in Old San Juan and really enjoyed life without thinking about doctor's visits or treatments. By this time, Mom's hair was falling out, so she decided to have it cut off, which was fine, because now she, TJ and I really looked alike. A lack of hair didn't stop Mom from walking around proudly. The doctor recommended a wig, which Mom quickly refused. She didn't do anything that made her feel or appear to be anything but healthy. The word "sick" never came from her lips, and she did not complain about anything, not even for a second.

At the end of a couple of weeks, it was time for the family to leave PR. This time, the end of our family vacation had a different meaning. It was a sad time, because Monique,

TJ and I were not going back with the group. This was the beginning of our time living on the island as our primary residence, and it would be the first time I would not see my family and friends daily. It was also difficult for me because Mom was scheduled to have a total hysterectomy on July 1, 2013, which was only a couple of weeks away. The goal of this surgery was to remove the mass that was in her pelvic area. The chemo had made the mass smaller, which gave us hope that it would be easier to remove. The surgeon also removed as much cancer as possible from the surface of the liver.

Maritza, Fran and Monique's mom, Pam, were in the waiting room to support and pray for a successful surgery. My sister Maritza later said that it was very painful to watch Mom lying on a gurney, with her hospital cap on her head, covered slightly by the hospital blanket, being rolled down the hall to go to surgery. The procedure lasted a little more than five hours, and the doctors felt it was helpful in the overall fight. Recovery took a couple of days at the hospital, then once released to go home, Mom rested for a few more days.

Mom's doctors asked if she would like to be included in a clinical trial of an experimental drug, so we coordinated a family conference call to go over the positive and negative outcomes that could arise from being included in this study. Mom deeply appreciated the input we provided and ultimately decided to join the trial, which started after August 2013. Looking back, each phase of the cancer treatment brought new hope. The chemo sessions went well, the surgery helped remove some of the cancer and now the trials also lowered Mom's cancer marker number. Chemo treatments had ended at this point and she was ready to resume her travels again.

While at home in Chicago, Mom was also spending lots of time with her new great-granddaughter Kaelyn. Gabe's daughter came to refer to mom as "GG," which stood for great-grandma. Kaelyn was the first girl in the family since my younger sister Maritza was born, so everyone was super excited. Kaelyn's early years reminded me of how my sisters and I were raised; lots of trips to the zoos, museums, parks and any other activity we could do away from home. When I called Mom, I always tried her cell phone first, because she was never home. I'd call her, and in the background, I would hear the noises of the air rushing into the car windows or the sound of blinking turn-signals. "Mom, where are you?" I asked, and each day the response was different: "We're on our way to the store to get Kaelyn some clothes" or "We're going to drop supplies off at the food pantry." The only time I could catch Mom on her house phone was during the late evening hours, when she would be reading the Bible or playing brain-teaser games on her tablet.

To say my Mom and I had a special bond is an understatement. I was clearly a momma's boy in every way, and everyone knew it. Thank God Monique understood and accepted this fact. They also shared a special relationship with each other. It was common for

I was clearly a momma's boy in every way, and everyone knew it.

Mom and me to talk four or five times each day, and we never ran out of things to talk about. Our conversations were all about family and what each of us was doing each day and what our plans were for the future. I was blessed enough to provide anything Mom wanted at this point in life, but she never asked for anything. This didn't prevent me, however from still being supportive in whatever she wanted to do.

Mom spent time and money on experiences and helping others. There is no question where I get this from. Many times, I sent Mom money for groceries or to pay her utility bills ahead of their due dates—and later, I'd find out that she would not spend any of it on herself. She donated food and supplies to her favorite local charities, such as the men's shelter, women's home or food bank. Other times, she bought some coats and donated them to her church to be distributed to the homeless.

We collaborated on her travel plans. We liked to plan her trips together, sitting on the phone going over the details. I felt like her personal travel agent and enjoyed every minute of it. Mom and Maritza enjoyed going to Las Vegas together. Not having gone myself yet, I couldn't relate to the fun times they spoke of after each trip. Early in the morning, I called the hotel they were staying at and placed an order with room service for breakfast as a surprise for them. I purchased tickets to shows during their trips and emailed them to Maritza as a surprise. This is the type of fun relationship we shared. Even while she was out of town, we still spoke several times each day.

One dream that Mom had was to visit Lakewood Church in Texas, the home of Pastor Joel Osteen. During a visit that Mom and my oldest nephew Luis took to Katy, Texas, I arranged for a limo to pick them up, take them to church service at Lakewood, then back to their hotel room in Katy. This was another surprise for Mom that she didn't ask for or expect. Joel Osteen would later become one of my favorite pastors.

Mom continued to travel to Florida and Atlanta in late 2013, then back to Puerto Rico with us for Christmas 2013. It's funny how most of the traditions from childhood carry over to my adult life. Each Christmas, Monique assembles and decorates the tree, while I act as the DJ, playing our favorite holiday songs. In later years, TJ would join us in the living room as we talked, laughed and reminisced about things we had done in life and visions of what was to come. During these moments when I should have been the happiest, there was always a feeling of sobriety and hesitation when thinking about the future because my mom's health was a constant presence in my mind. I often found myself staring at her quietly from a distance, soaking up every second I could of her life, voice and presence. Having the experience of missing those things about my dad after his passing instantly took me back to those days while I fought to stay in the present moment to appreciate what was in front of me. I did not want a single moment to pass by at any greater pace than it normally did. If I could hit the pause button and just look at Mom, I would.

My mom was the only person for years who knew what to give me as a gift. I'm not a fan of gifts in general, which created problems for those who wanted to acknowledge me on certain special days. The gifts she would give me would be custom-made items, with special messages carved, embroidered or inked on them. For example, she once gave me a small decorative pillow, with a special message from her to me. I still have this pillow and TJ and I for years have referred to it as the "special pillow." This Christmas, Mom did the same for TJ, giving him a small plaque to hang in his room reminding him of the way he should treat others, with kindness, compassion and respect. It hangs on his bathroom wall today. The other gift she gave TJ this Christmas was a handwritten letter that would provide comfort at a time when all of us needed it, nearly a year and a half into the future. TJ would not let any of us read it, because that's the type of relationship he and Mom had. They would sit and talk for what seemed liked hours about important life issues and trivial things as well. They'd sit together sometimes on the couch, TJ on his laptop and Mom on her tablet, enjoying each other's presence.

A new venture

In early 2014, I decided to start a new business based in Puerto Rico that would serve two purposes. First, I wanted to give TJ the opportunity to own and operate a business. Second, I wanted an income stream to provide funds for his college years, one that he controlled.

The idea was to start a charter boat business. Although I had experience with power boats, I knew nothing about sailboats, which most charter boats are. Because I had no experience in this area, I turned to the person in my network who was best equipped to help, Captain William "Bill" Pinkney. Bill and I had met a couple of times. In 1992 while I was interning at Nexus Unlimited, our company took Bill's amazing life story and converted it to a computer-based system. Later, at the Puerto Rico airport, Monique and I recognized him and shared a brief word, and he graciously posed for a picture with her. As the saying goes, never burn a bridge. Here we are, more than 20 years later, sitting in a coffee shop in Fajardo, Puerto Rico, talking about doing business together.

Bill was the first Black man to sail solo, circumnavigating the globe the long way. His is an amazing story, the journey and accomplishments of a legend. As we sat in the bakery, I asked Bill to tell me what vision he had for himself for the next several years. In it, he and his wife, Migdalia would buy a catamaran sailing vessel and offer charters to guests for five-, seven- and 10-day trips in and around the U.S., Spanish and British Virgin Islands. During the downtimes, he and Migdalia would take the boat out for several days and live aboard it while anchored or moored near one of our Caribbean islands.

Bill's vision lined up perfectly with my idea. Bill knew my knowledge of sailboats was limited, so he agreed to start the search for one that would meet our needs. Through a friend, Bill soon found a boat in Florida's Intracoastal Waterway that was for sale. They met with the broker and viewed the boat, learning that the current owner had health issues and could no longer manage to keep and maintain the boat. Bill called me with excitement in his voice saying, "I think we found it." He cautioned me that it was an older model and needed some work, but the foundation was strong, and it had certain key features that would benefit us in the long term.

I bought the boat sight unseen. After the closing, I hired a captain to sail the boat from Florida to PR, which took about six days. Monique was in Chicago when the boat arrived, so TJ and I headed to the marina to see it in person. We walked down the long row of docks, to head over to 5T, anxiously wanting to see the boat. As we made the right-hand turn from the main dock onto the number 5 dock, I looked down toward the end, catching a small glimpse.

As we approached the boat, my heart sank, and I let out a loud gasp of air. I kept quiet as TJ also had a look of dismay in his eyes. We slowly walked from left to right, scanning every detail of the boat, up and down, looking for something that would bring relief to the overwhelming feeling I had. A thousand thoughts crossed my mind such as, "Am I in over my head?" and "What was I thinking?" and even, "I don't want Monique to see this." TJ and I climbed aboard into the cockpit, not wanting to touch anything as it seemed everything was 1,000 years old. We slid the cabin door open and got a whiff of a smell that could only come from a decomposing cat. The only reason I didn't climb to the top of the mast and just off to my death to end my pain was because TJ was not old enough to drive home by himself. This would be a long night without much sleep I predicted.

The next day, we went back to the marina, hoping the boat we saw yesterday was the wrong one. My wish had not come true: it was the correct one. I called several contractors to meet me later that day to discuss refitting the boat and making it "charter" ready. Antonio Vecino, who refits hulls and does paint work, came. Danny and his engine team came. Caesar, who does cushions and upholstery, came by as well as Martin, who does mechanical work, and Quino, who would do the sails and trampoline work. We talked about my vision for the boat and what the timeline was (everyone laughed when I said three to four months).

Each contractor said they would provide an estimate in a day or two, and they all went on their ways except for Antonio Vecino. Antonio had been in business for more than 50 years at that point and was a master artist. We had used his company to have the bottom painted on previous boats we owned, and we already had a cordial relationship. Though he is very soft spoken and of short stature, Antonio was respected by everyone at the marina. He is extremely good at what he does, an expert with a vision.

As we stood there on the dock, looking at the boat, Antonio leaned toward me and told me that if I wanted him to work on the boat, he would do it, but he said his best advice was to hope it sank. He had been the most honest of the contractors that day. The others would do anything I wanted along as I was willing to pay. I scheduled the boat to be moved to Antonio's shop to start the refit.

Bill and I met at the boat a few days later, which was the first time I had seen him after the boat was delivered to PR. As always, he had a smile on his face and was oozing with optimism. I shared my initial impressions of the boat as well as TJ's feelings. I explained that it wasn't Bill's choice of boats that concerned me, it was the length of time and amount of money it would take to refit it. I told Bill I trusted his judgement completely (and still do today).

Antonio joined us to get more detail about what I wanted his team to do. The only direction I provided was that this boat would carry my mom's name on it, so it should be made ready to carry that honor. He asked if he could use his discretion regarding paint, styling and other details, and I told him that he was an artist and I understood that artists need to be left alone to create the body of work that they had visions of and for him to follow his heart. I later found out how much that sense of freedom buoyed Antonio.

I went to visit the marina nearly every day to see the progress and updates firsthand. Bill and I also spoke often to track down contractors and parts that were ordered from stateside suppliers. Bill was amazing during the entire refit, going to the boat every day, doing inventory on any spare parts and pieces left on the boat by the previous owner, all the way down to screws and gas filters. No one knew this boat better than Bill and dedicated more time than him.

I stayed out of Bill's way as well because I knew this project represented purpose beyond his daily rituals of life. Bill is at home on the seas and on boats. We would sit on the boat while it was up on stilts at Antonio's shop and talk for hours about life and its lessons. He patiently answered all my questions about becoming a better husband and father. If Dad were alive, he would have been right there with us.

Setting sail on another journey

Monique, TJ and I already had a boat trip planned for the British Virgin Islands for the summer of 2014. Cousins Chris, Pam and their son Miles were joining us. The boat ride from Puerto Rico to Tortola is approximately three hours, depending on the ocean conditions and winds.

Mom loved being on the boat, sitting on the back, soaking up the sun and feeling the occasional sprinkles of salty ocean water. TJ sat in the cockpit with Monique, across from the captain, and slept most of the way over. Once we arrived in Tortola and cleared customs, we docked at Nanny Cay Marina on the south side of the island. I told everyone we would be staying at a small hotel located right there at the marina. After we secured the boat to the dock and hosed it down with fresh water to keep the salty sea-water from corroding it, we grabbed our bags and headed toward the hotel lobby.

Our friend and captain Javier and I stepped out of the lobby to stop by the car rental booth to retrieve the SUV I had previously reserved. Javier and I drove around to the front entrance to the hotel and told the crew to come with us. We loaded the bags and told them we were going to dinner and that our reservation time was getting near. Everyone was starving at this point: Being on the ocean for hours at a time, under the sun, leaves everyone very thirsty, hungry and sleepy.

Javier and his wife, Colette, had been on the island many times before, so he drove us to our destination. The drive was about 20 minutes, but it took us through windy and steep roads in a seemingly deserted part of the island. I remember looking back at the family and seeing this look of dismay on their faces, like they wanted to jump out and end the pain of the car ride. It was hot, the AC was not working and we were nowhere near any place that looked like a restaurant would be located. Monique asked a few times how long it would be before we got there in her "south side Chicago" voice. The road was so bumpy that at one point, Javier could not drive more than 10-15 miles per hour, constantly turning the steering wheel, trying to avoid the large potholes. Finally, we hit a small stretch of paved road that wasn't in the best shape, but much better than what we had just driven on.

Javier and I later learned from a local that the residents didn't want the roads repaired to discourage people from driving in this area, to protect their sheltered lifestyles. In Tortola, there are no street signs. We locate businesses by their names and the same applies to homes. Just ask someone where "The Butterfly Home" is, for example, and they can tell us exactly how to get there. Javier slowed down a bit, looking to his left side at names on the large stone markers, trying to locate the name of our dinner spot. There it was, a few hundred feet from the dirt road. We made a left turn onto a winding driveway and followed it up the hill for about 100 yards until it curved left and ended at a large picturesque house. Javier and I exited the truck and stretched our legs, telling everyone to come on out so we can get to dinner.

The look on everyone's face was priceless—it seemed to say, "this food had better be good!" There was only one other car in the driveway. I walked to the front door and rang the doorbell. A few seconds later, a lady opened the door and said, "Hello, love" and asked us to enter. Now the look on people's face was of confusion and probably a little frustration. Javier and I smiled at each other as everyone walked past, knowing the real reason we were there.

Once we were all standing in the living room area, I announced that this was our rental house for the week. I remember the look on Cousin Pam's face as she beamed with joy. I then introduced everyone to Ella, who I had been working with for a few months to make the vacation memorable. We had rented the home from a local family, and Ella was the person responsible for taking care of it. During our stay, she was our cook and main contact for anything we needed. Ella is a kind soul, with an accent that reminds me of being in Jamaica. Dinner had already been prepared by Ella and her cousin Paulette, who was in the kitchen. They already knew our family's favorite foods from a list I'd sent. We fixed our plates and sat outside at a large rectangular table overlooking the ocean, with Peter and Norman islands off in the distance. We asked Ella and Paulette to join us in prayer and dinner, which they did. Our family always treats others as equals. While we were in Tortola, at this house, Ella and Paulette were part of our family.

As laid back as Puerto Rico is, Tortola is much more relaxed. Life slows down, and I truly enjoy each moment. I wanted this to be an enjoyable trip for all of us, especially Mom. We did not have to cook, clean, do laundry or any of the typical at-home responsibilities. The fact that mom had cancer living inside her was a constant weight sitting on my heart. During the vacation, Mom had to visit a clinic to have tests completed and fax the results to her doctors in Chicago. Ella was kind enough to drive Mom to her visits, and they had time to bond a little during those drives in the early morning hours.

During our stay, we had many options to fill our days. One day we visited a dolphin training facility just a short drive from the house. The instructor fitted us for life vests, then escorted us to a small gate that opened onto a narrow walkway adjacent to a large square-shaped body of water that was approximately 100 feet wide and 100 long. The instructor briefed us on the upcoming activities and gave us background information on dolphins, including the fact that they shed their skin every two hours. Shortly after, the instructor blew a small whistle that he kept on a lanyard around his neck, and a huge dolphin appeared behind him and rose out of the water. The dolphin was seemingly standing on his tail in the water, eye to eye with the instructor. I was absolutely amazed, and all of us were laughing and smiling. The instructor had the dolphin perform certain tasks for each of us individually, such as swimming to the surface, standing up, and extending both front fins so we could hold them as if we were dancing with them. The dolphin went down the line and did the same for each person. Then the dolphin came back to the first person, then rose again and reached out to kiss us.

The instructor invited a second dolphin to join in at this point. He swam all the way toward the back of the pen to illustrate what we were going to do next. He laid flat on the surface of the water, toes pointed down and both arms extending outward with his body resembling the letter T. I saw the dorsal fin of the dolphins now heading toward the instructor, then diving below the surface and out of view. Out of nowhere, the instructor's body began moving on the surface of the water toward us. Each second, he moved faster and faster, but he was not swimming, he had the same body position as when he first started the exercise. All of a sudden, the surface of the water bubbled up like it was boiling and the instructor's body began to rise upward toward the sky, arms fully extended, knees locked, being propelled by the dolphins pushing him from the sole of his feet. The instructor was coming toward us so fast that I didn't know if he would be able to stop. *He had done this thousands of times I'm sure*, I remember thinking, *so he knows what he's doing*. Just as quickly as he started, he slowed down, sank gently into the water and drifted over to us. The dolphins were nowhere to be seen. Now it was each of our turns. This activity can be intimidating, especially for those who cannot swim and for anyone who fears large animals.

What an amazing gift to be able to share this special time with family. All of us, from age 10 to 66, enjoyed this priceless experience.

What an amazing gift to be able to share this special time with family. All of us, from age 10 to 66, enjoyed this priceless experience.

During the week, we went island hopping to Cane Garden Bay, Jost Van Dyke, Norman Island and Virgin Gorda. Each island is separated by a short 30-minute boat ride. I'd find myself glancing at mom, with TJ leaning on her, sleeping, and feeling the thankfulness that they had a close relationship. Whenever mom was around, TJ gravitated toward her, and this trip was no different. As much as I am a positive person and an eternal optimist, from time to time my mind would drift as I observed them together, wanting them to have many more years with each other. None of us sat around and talked about cancer, nor did we spend any time gaming out worst-case scenarios. Mom would never allow or want this. Instead, we took her lead and made the best of each moment we had together.

One day, we went to visit "The Baths." This is an amazing place where there are huge rock formations. In some areas, they lean against each and formed cavern-like formations with small pools of water, hence the name "baths." To preserve the integrity of the structures, boats are not allowed to approach the area near the main entrance, so we had to swim or dinghy our way to the shore. Javier took us by dinghy to the far end of the island and waited back on the boat for us to call by VHF radio when we were ready to be picked up. One of the precautions Mom had to take while receiving treatment was to stay out of the sun as much as possible. To help with this, she wore a huge floppy-brimmed hat, like something I would see in the movies back in the day. To top it off, she had a sassy one-piece, leopard-print bikini that exposed way too much cleavage. What else do we expect from a cougar?

We began our journey through the rock formations, some of which are as tall as 50-100 feet, winding through narrow passageways and stopping periodically to step into one of the nearby pools of water. The temperature of the water is always in the 80-degree range, warmed by the constant sun rays shining down on it. Some areas of the baths required us to climb steep staircases, while in others we had to use the ropes provided to pull our way up slippery inclines. From end to end, we probably spent 45 minutes moving along the pathway. One of the most memorable moments was near the end of the trail, when, our group was standing in a large pool of water. There were huge boulders arching overhead, forming almost an A-shaped covering and providing a cool, shaded area to enjoy. I stood back and asked everyone to turn toward me so I could take a picture. Mom was in the front and struck this epic pose with one hand on her hip and the other pointing up toward the sky, while displaying a sassy smile on her face. Cousin Pam was standing next to her, with the biggest smile ever, adoring her love of life. This picture is probably one of the best representations of my mom's spirit that I have. No matter what she was dealing with, rich or poor, hair or no hair, at home or far way, she made the best of life, never complained and always had a smile on her face. We had many more memorable moments during this trip, but this one was one of my favorites.

During Mom's visit to PR in early November 2014, she was as energetic and fun as ever. She and TJ spent time at the beach club playing ping pong and sipping on piña coladas with extra cherries. They sat on the back of the golf cart together while we rode around the neighborhood enjoying the view. Mom did not know anything about the charter business nor was she aware of a very special surprise we planned for her. She wondered where I disappeared to each day for a few hours. Monique did a good job of distracting Mom from my absence by sitting out back, gazing at the ocean having girl talk with her. The truth is, they both probably wanted me gone anyway, so they could talk in peace. One weekend when my family came to visit, my cousin mentioned that my mom's eyes were more yellow than white. Monique, TJ and I didn't notice since we saw her every day and didn't notice the subtle change. When Mom went back to Chicago a few days later, she went to her regularly scheduled doctor's visit and brought the eye discoloration issue up to him.

Monique, TJ and I had left for a short trip to St. Thomas a couple of days after Mom departed, to round out the Thanksgiving holiday. Fran called and gave the usual update on the doctor's visit. The doctor recommended inserting a tube to drain fluid from Mom's body, which should help remove the toxins that were causing the discoloration. During this short getaway, I spent many hours on the phone with my sisters discussing the doctor's prognosis, which seemed to take me back to the initial diagnosis of cancer. I had that sinking feeling all over again, and I lost focus on everything around me. I managed to drown out the voices in my head and push down the feelings, as I had done in the past, so I could remain the positive and strong leader of my family. Fran told me that Mom mentioned to the doctor that she was scheduled to travel back to Puerto Rico in a few weeks to spend Christmas with us, which he firmly recommended against. This also added to the weight I was feeling. I thought, why can't she travel, is there more to the story? She was fine a few days ago being on an airplane, what had changed?

After we arrived back in Puerto Rico from St. Thomas, I went to the marina again to check in with Bill and the progress on the boat. We were close. The boat now looked like a boat, and Antonio told me to give him a little more time to finish his work. I told Bill what Mom's doctors said about her coming back to PR and what Monique, TJ and I had as a backup plan. He understood and remained as committed and accommodating as ever. The plan was set, and we shifted timeframes a bit and proceeded. It was the first week in December, and I had to change airline tickets for my cousins in Atlanta, nephews and sisters and buy new tickets for Monique, TJ and me.

I was notified by Antonio that the boat was ready to be moved from his shop to the water and then to our permanent slip. Moving a boat takes planning, coordination and confidence in the boatyard crew. These people are responsible for hauling a 20,000-pound machine, suspended on huge rubber bands, nearly 150 yards down a gravel road to a loading dock, then lowering it evenly into the water. This "splash" as the marina calls it, was very special for Bill and my family, but probably more so for Antonio Vecino. The same man who had hoped the boat would sink overnight now beamed with pride at the artistic masterpiece that he created. Antonio walked alongside the crane as it made its way down the driveway, glancing at every corner and strap keeping it secure, like a father carrying his newborn baby. Other marina workers stopped to see the boat being moved, having remembered when it was originally delivered to the marina nearly eight months ago, looking very different than today.

The next Saturday, our long-awaited special event occurred, though my family from the states was absent. Javier and Colette, JD and Nita, Andre and Carole from Chicago, who were already in PR for a non-related trip, attended the christening of Lady Dee, the name given formally to her on this day by Captain William "Bill" Pinkney in his official dress-white uniform. Bill read the language from the document that would take the boat from being "it" to "her" and from its former name to Lady Dee. The name was displayed as large as possible on both the port and starboard sides as well on the stern so all could see. Everyone at the marina knows the boat because of the transformation it underwent and because Antonio Vecino treated her like the beautiful, graceful and kind woman she was named after. We recorded the entire ceremony, and each person had the opportunity to say a few words to the camera for Mom. TJ had a heartfelt message that brought mostly everyone to tears, then performed the traditional breaking of a Champagne bottle on the boat's hull to christen it. I also asked each of my sisters and nephews to record a short message that we could insert into the final version of the video, which they graciously did.

A Christmas surprise

Monique, TJ and I flew to Chicago a few days before Christmas, and Pam, Chris and Miles flew from Atlanta and met us at O'Hare airport. We rented an SUV and raced to surprise my family, who were all gathered at Mom's house, waiting on the video call that we used as cover, to get everyone together. Monique told Fran that we were coming, so she was able to keep the group in one place until we arrived. Of course, we had to make a quick pit-stop in Blue Island, Illinois, to pick up TJ's favorite pizza from Beggar's. My heart was beating fast during the drive, as I was anxious to see Mom and the family. We arrived in the parking lot and made our way to the elevator, and up to the sixth floor, then walked toward Mom's apartment. TJ was in the lead as usual when it was time to see his family. He knocked on the door, then waited for a response. We all spread out on either side of the door, hoping to avoid being seen through the security peep hole by the person answering it.

We could hear someone inside asking other people who would be visiting this late in the evening. Because Fran knew it was us, she came to the door, trying to act surprised by the knock as well. The door opened and we rushed in, smiling and cheering, wishing everyone a Merry Christmas. My eyes searched the room from left to right, looking for Mom. At first, I didn't see her, so I moved inside a little more to get a better view of the entire room. Her reclining chair was empty, which is where she usually sat. As I got a wider range of view, I noticed a frail lady sitting on the right side, with reading glasses on, smiling at me as only my Mom could. My heart dropped, and I immediately felt an overwhelming sense of sadness and pain. My mind raced, trying to understand what happened in the last five weeks since I had seen her last. She was so thin. I walked over to her with my eyes staying focused on her, then leaned over to hug and kiss her. I remember noticing how my hands could feel the bones in her arms and shoulders because she had lost so much weight. I don't remember talking to or hugging anyone else, although I'm sure I did, but I do recall sitting next to Mom on the couch holding her small hand in mine, not wanting to let go. As usual, I had to show strength for others because that's what us men are supposed to do. Besides, I operate very well in stressful situations, constantly searching my mind for solutions, opposed to focusing on the problem.

In this case, I shifted my focus to appreciating the time we had together. No matter how frail Mom was, she was alive, we could speak with each other. I could physically touch her, and she could touch me, and that's all that mattered. Eventually my internal sadness subsided as my face surely reflected a more engaged demeanor. Mom was so happy to see all of us, she said. She told me she was sad that Christmas in PR would not happen this year, but if we were together, that's all that matters.

Early the next morning, which was Christmas Eve, I woke up extra early in my hotel room, not really feeling rested. Without waking Monique, I sat up and quietly cried openly for the first time since my Dad died back in 2006. I felt so helpless. I had an empty feeling in my stomach and a little nausea. "What happened?" I remember thinking repeatedly. How could Mom have such a dramatic change in health over such a short amount of time? During our calls, my sisters had told me that she had lost some weight, but she was still going to the mall to get out of the house and be among people. They pushed her in a wheelchair, while Kaelyn walked along side and entertained her. Even Mom told me she felt OK when we spoke every day, sometimes saying she wanted some lightweight dumbbells so she could tone her arm muscles. I replayed the sound of her quiet voice from last night, hoping to burn it into my memory so I could one day down the road summon the sound when I would need it most.

Once Monique and TJ awoke, we got dressed and ready to leave the hotel. Our plan for the day was to go to Pam and Tom's house to celebrate Christmas Eve with them. They were always very supportive, and we loved spending time with them. After a couple hours at Pam's house, laughing and catching up, more people started to show up, including Monique's aunts, uncles and cousins. This was as good a time as any to share our surprise with Mom, so Monique gathered everyone in the living room. Mom and Monique's uncle Cedric, who was using a walking cane at the time, sat front and center on the couch. Tom slipped the DVD into the player and pressed play. The short movie started playing, chronicling the first days of the boat settling into its new home in the marina. There were photos and videos of the refit, showing Captain Bill and others working hard to get it ready to live up to its namesake's high quality and standards. A few minutes later, the video of Captain Bill performing the renaming ceremony played, followed by the taped greetings from family and friends. Near the end of the video, the portion played that showed the photos and videos of the finished product, Lady Dee in all her glory, proudly displaying Mom's name. Everybody at Pam's house cheered loudly and clapped and some cried. Mom's thin, wan face was filled with pride, surprise and humility. The closing song began to play as the names of the people who helped do the refit scrolled down the screen. I chose the song "Three Times a Lady" by the Commodores. As I looked at Mom, everyone was kissing and hugging her, while the lyrics from Lionel Richie blared from the speakers, saying how thankful we were for the times you've given me that are there, in my mind. I knew this could be the end of the rainbow, and if it was, that Mom was three times a lady and that I'd love her forever. The words fit the power of the moment. I felt a sense of relief for the first time over the past eight months, anticipating mom's reaction when seeing a boat named after her. She was pleased. Even though she couldn't be there in person, she still got to see it on video. Although the video lasted only 20 minutes, a lifetime of gratitude and love went into this moment. I was able to do one more thing to show Mom how much I appreciated everything she had done for me since my birth.

We stayed at Pam and Tom's house until the wee hours of the morning, much past the time my sisters took Mom home to rest. It was good to spend quality time with them as well. I remember feeling that Monique needed to visit Chicago more often and spend time with family.

The next day was Christmas, and Mom and I got some one-on-one time together. Mom and I are alike in so many ways, and even now, she was concerned about everyone except herself. Mom walked over to the old-fashioned metal file cabinet sitting in the corner of her bedroom. She opened the top drawer and flipped between the section dividers from front to back until she located two folders. The first folder contained some random bills that she wanted to get paid but didn't have energy enough to deal with. I told her that I would take care of them, but not now, let's enjoy our time together. The second folder contained her life insurance policy. I had nothing to say at first, because if I would have opened my mouth to speak at that moment, I would have broken down in tears. I pretended to read the documents, allowing my eyes to move up and down the page, left and right, just long enough for me to compose myself. Mom must have known that it was a painful conversation to have because she broke the silence and told me she just wanted me to know where it was, just in case I would need it later. I told Mom that I remembered that she had made me the beneficiary and thanked her for letting me know where it was. I still could not believe we were having this conversation when she looked perfectly healthy last month. We made our way back out to the living room to join the rest of the family, Mom leading the way, pushing her walker with the green tennis balls positioned on each leg to make it easier to push. All of us sat and talked for hours about everything and about nothing. We watched movies and enjoyed Kaelyn doing all the things babies do at that age. What a great time.

The call no one wants to get

Monday morning arrived and our flight was leaving early, so we left the hotel at 5:30a.m.. Chris, Pam and Miles had already departed for Atlanta. The flight time is approximately four hours, which put our landing at 2:00p.m. into San Juan local time. It was good to be back at home, in the 80-degree weather. The ride was quiet, each of us glancing out the windows at the mountains and palm trees. I texted the family as usual, letting them know we landed safely and asking them to let me know how Mom's doctor's appointment was that afternoon. We reached home, and my phone rang; it was Fran. I was excited to see her name on the caller ID and anxious to hear the update, hoping for good news. Fran wanted to know if we were home yet and where TJ and Monique were.

"They're upstairs. How did the doctor's visit go?" I said. Fran replied, "call Monique downstairs." I yelled upstairs, asking Monique to come down and told Fran I had done so. Fran then said that the doctor admitted Mom to the hospital and told the family that she had less than 24 hours to live. Everything inside and outside of me stopped, instantly. My mind locked up, my heart sank, my stomach turned, my eyes focused straight ahead but not processing anything, and I could not speak. I remember Monique walking out the door onto the terrace where I was. She approached me from my left side, moving forward until we were side by side. I didn't speak, I passed her my cell phone with my left hand and walked over to the outdoor couch and laid down, still in shock. I didn't hear anything else from Monique, I only recall laying there, lost, confused and helpless. I don't remember how much time passed or how it happened, but I woke up later, in my bed, and it was dark outside. TJ came into our bedroom a few seconds later and gently tapped me on my right arm. I thought maybe I was dreaming about the whole situation because I was in bed, in the dark and didn't remember getting in the bed.

Monique came into the room as well and told me that she had been communicating with Fran. I asked TJ if he knew Grandma was in the hospital and he said that he did and he also told me to have faith, in a very confident manner. Now I realized I wasn't dreaming. I wanted to get up, make some calls and get a better understanding of what was happening. I called Fran and she explained that Mom's kidneys had failed and her organs were not functioning properly. I asked what had happened since yesterday when we were all sitting in her living room laughing and talking. She said the doctor was coming back to the room soon and she would call me so I could speak with him directly. I needed to speak with Mom so I asked Fran if she could talk. Fran gave the phone to Mom and she sounded fine, no different than yesterday. I pushed through all the worry and other feelings I had, so we could have an upbeat conversation. Mom asked me if Fran told me what the doctor said and I told her yes, she did. I asked how she was feeling, and she replied "Fine." Mom told me that it was not up to the doctor how much time she had, it was up to her father, meaning God. We ended the conversation in an upbeat way, holding on to every bit of hope that we could find. I called my uncle Benji and explained to him what was happening and told him I needed to go to be with Mom right away. He was going with me, he said, and agreed that we should coordinate our flight schedules. Monique and Benji worked hard to find flights on such a short notice. Adding to the challenge was the fact that most major airlines that fly out of PR only had one non-stop flight each day, and those time slots had already passed. Monique was finally able to book me on a flight for 4:00a.m. the next day, leaving PR, making a connecting flight in Charleston, South Carolina, then arriving at O'Hare by 11:00a.m. Chicago time. Benji was booked as well.

A short time later, Fran called back. The doctor was in the room to check on Mom and to provide updates and she wanted me to be on speakerphone to hear the details for myself. Monique was sitting next to me on the couch, so I put my phone on speaker as well so she could hear. The update was the same as earlier in the day. The doctor then asked to speak with me alone, so he brought Fran's phone into the hallway, just outside of Mom's room. He told me that I needed to get to the hospital right away if I wanted to spend her last few hours together. I explained that I had a flight for the next morning, and that was the only option I had. He didn't seem to understand this and kept asking if there was any other way to get there sooner. I was annoyed that he would think I was not doing everything I could to be with my mom. I had to take deep breaths several times while on the phone with him in order to not say something I'd regret. He finally said that she was not going to make it through the night and there was nothing he could do for her at this time except to make her comfortable. It felt like a sharp knife was being pushed into my heart, very slowly and deliberately. Again, I was searching for every possible solution: Could I charter a plane, was there a no-brand airline that had a flight leaving that night, could the doctor do anything he had not thought of that would keep Mom alive? After the call, Monique and I sat there, quietly, trying to digest what we had heard. Luckily, TJ and his friend George were upstairs, so we could spare him from the reality for the moment.

I don't remember how, but Benji and I ended up at the airport together, waiting on our flight to depart. I texted Fran and Maritza before the plane departed, letting them know not to call or text me, no matter what, and that I would see them at the hospital soon. I didn't want to know anything else, I wanted to hold on to all hope and faith that I would get to spend at least a few minutes speaking with Mom. I had been on long, intercontinental flights before, but this was the longest flight of my life. Each moment felt like a year. I wanted to be with Mom. I sat in my seat on the right side of the plane, staring out of the window the entire flight, even when it was dark. I have the ability during tough times to lay out the best-case scenarios and worst-case scenarios and prepare myself for either, in order to manage my emotions and to see a path forward. I consciously chose not to do this for this life event. I was pushing out every thought I could about what was happening. Instead, I forced my mind to start concentrating on the tasks I had to complete in order to get to the hospital. I visualized myself walking off the plane, taking a shuttle to the rental car area, making sure I got the I-Pass for tollbooths. I planned which route I would take to drive to the hospital, considered whether to park in the parking lot or use the valet service instead to save time. When would I turn on my cell phone, before or after I got to the hospital? Did I let my employees know I was in Chicago and direct them not to call me?

This process worked for me. After two early-morning flights, my uncle and I were pulling up to the hospital. We stopped at the valet booth, grabbed the ticket from the young man and made our way up to the floor where Mom's room was. We exited the elevator and walked over to the nearby information desk. I told them Mom's name and they gave me her room number. On this floor, because it is an area where end-of-life patients are cared for, there is no need for guest passes, nor do they limit the number of visitors a patient could have. The person told us how to get to the room. We turned to our right side as we left the desk, then went past a small seating area, then made a left turn into a wide corridor. I looked at the numbers above the rooms closest to us. On my right side were the even numbers, so I knew it would ultimately be on our right. We walked down the hall without speaking to each other or anyone we passed. We slowly approached the doorway to the room just before Mom's. My heart started beating faster and faster, and I felt nauseous all over again. We moved toward Mom's room, my uncle using his right hand to gently push me in front, so I could enter the room first. From the doorway, I could see several family members on the left side and a few more directly ahead.

As they saw me, they gently put their heads down and kind of straightened up their stance a little. Everyone knows how special the bond between my mom and me is, and I could not imagine what they were thinking or feeling when they saw me. Off to the right side, farther inside the room, I could see the very tip of the hospital bed, with Mom's feet pointed up, with the blankets on top. As I walked further into the room, I could see others on my right side, out of the corner of my eyes. I did not look to the right, nor did I look at my mom at all. Instead, I approached and hugged and kissed my cousin Melissa, aunts and other family members that were lined up around the room. I made my way from left, then straight ahead to hug more people, then finally turned my head and body to the right, my eyes searched for Mom's face. There she was, smiling at me. Maritza and Fran were standing on the other side of the bed, smiling as well. I leaned over to hug and kiss Mom. I rubbed her smooth, silky gray hair, kissed her again on the forehead and held her right hand, telling myself I would never leave her side again.

In Mom's typically selfless fashion, she asked what I was doing there. I joked and told her I left something at her house and had to fly back to pick it up. She smiled and told me to stop playing. Then, she asked where Monique and TJ were. I explained that they would be coming to see her in a few days. Mom was also very happy to see my uncle. We spent the entire day in Mom's room, entertaining a constant stream of visitors. I had the opportunity to meet with the doctor that I had spoken to the night before. He said that Mom was lucky to have lived through the night and that we should not get our hopes up too high because her condition had not changed. This was the beginning of the push by the hospital to get Mom checked out, because their job was essentially over. If I had had the time and energy to being annoyed by them, I probably would have, but we were all focused solely on Mom.

Monique and TJ arrived in Chicago a couple of days later. When they came to Mom's room and made that right-hand turn to be within her viewing area, she lit up with joy. TJ went to Grandma and gave her a big hug and kiss, smiling from ear to ear. Monique did the same. The days were filled with talking with Mom, family and friends and meeting with doctors and health care providers. There was an important decision we had to make, which was whether to have Mom moved to an assisted living facility for hospice or have her moved back home to receive in-home hospice services. Also, the doctors wanted us to decide whether we would agree to a "Do Not Resuscitate" or DNR. They explained that if she went into cardiac arrest and did not have a DNR on record, they would be required to do whatever they could to try to save her life, including chest compressions. The problem was, Mom was so frail that a chest compression could lead to a broken rib, which would be very painful for her. None of us wanted to make this decision, so we told the doctor we would revisit the decision soon. The immediate family, including my sisters and nephews, knew we had to decide on hospice, so we asked Benji and our dear friend Lola to join us in a separate meeting room to discuss it. Lola had provided care for her late husband Oliver, who passed several years before of cancer at home, so she had intimate knowledge with this situation.

We interviewed a few representatives from various hospice facilities at the hospital. After they left, we talked among ourselves and listened to Lola and Uncle provide some very good insight. The only question we kept coming back to was, "How does it benefit Mom?" Whatever adjustments we had to make in our lives didn't matter right then, nor did how much would or wouldn't be covered by insurance. Our decision was that Mom would go back and be in the comfort of her home. We informed the doctor of our decision, and they began to work on discharge papers. The doctor told us that while we were meeting with hospice providers, Mom signed her own DNR request form. This took all of us by shock. Why didn't she ask our opinion, and why did she sign it when all of us were out of the room? None of us questioned Mom about her decision when we got back to the room. I leaned over and kissed Mom on her forehead as I did every time I came back into the room, even if I was just going to the restroom. I held her hand and smiled, and she smiled back. I knew in my heart that she signed the DNR so none of us would have to make that very difficult decision. She did not want that for us. This is who Mom is, always thinking of others. Mom's smile back at me confirmed what I was feeling in my heart.

The last night Mom was in the hospital—and after the hospice provider had delivered the medical supplies and equipment to her house—we sat in the room listening to Mom's favorite music. Monique, Fran and Maritza were on

Mom's left side; TJ, Cousin Melissa and I were on her right. We had a small Bluetooth speaker playing songs I had never heard of and others I had. Most were from church and some from the commercial space, but the one that stood out more than any other was "Happy" by Pharrell Williams. Yep, this song summed up Mom's life and spirit. She was not worried, she was not overwhelmed, she always knew she'd be just fine, and she remained happy. Mom whispered the words of the songs while tapping to the beat with her left hand, gently going up and down into Monique's left hand, displaying to everyone in the room what true faith and peace are.

Monique and TJ flew back to PR so they could prepare for his classes to resume. The three of us sat and talked about where I was needed most, which was with Mom. It wasn't a discussion, it was more like, "OK, we'll see you soon, and be sure to call as often as possible." They are the best support system in the world.

At Mom's house, we worked out a schedule so there was always someone home with her. Luis and Mom lived together, which helped a lot. Fran was in the process of starting her business, which provided flexibility. Maritza's works hours were from 9 to 5, therefore she could come by afterward. Gabe and I went to the office each morning and arrived at home by early evening. The gap was during the morning hours. It was a big responsibility for Fran to manage on her own, so we hired a nurse, who was also a family friend, to come to Mom's house each day from 7a.m. till 3p.m. We moved her regular bed over toward the balcony to make room for the hospital bed. This would be my bed each night, only a few feet from Mom. Neither she nor I would not have it any other way.

Despite what was happening in my personal life, I still had other worldly responsibilities such as a business to run, customers to service, employees to manage and bills to pay. If I could have, I would have snapped my fingers and made all that go away. I had a hard time working with business partners who were only concerned about sales commissions and customers who only cared about their public profiles.

> *Despite what was happening in my personal life, I still had other worldly responsibilities such as a business to run, customers to service, employees to manage and bills to pay.*

There was one incident that, looking back, was the genesis of the change I would eventually make in the future. While I was sitting in the hospital room watching Mom sleep, I received a call on my work cell phone from a business partner. I told them I'd call back in a few minutes. I left the room, took the elevator down to a floor when there was a large lobby, with couches, work tables and enough seating to be able to have a quiet moment on the phone. I called the partner back, and we spoke for a few minutes. This company has annual revenues in the tens of billions of dollars, and we always enjoyed doing deals together. The young lady asked me if I could push through some orders right away, before the end of the business day on December 31st. I informed her that we had not even received the orders from them yet, so there was nothing to process. I also told her that even when we eventually receive the new orders from them, we would have to coordinate with suppliers and complete others tasks that were out of our control, so there was no way we could get all of this done by the end of the business day today. I had known this lady for nearly six years at this point so I felt comfortable telling her that I was with my mom, who has terminal cancer, and I would have limited access to email for the next few days. Her reply still has the piercing sound of indifference today that it did then. She said, "OK, then call me when you all have processed the orders today." I ended the call and did not waste another second answering any other business call while my mom was awake. I had witnessed people using "business" as a shield to deflect human feelings and empathy when people needed it the most. Instead of being understanding, they care more about their bonus check and meeting quotas. The business industry has no soul. Right then, each moment was dedicated to Mom, and the heartless business world that I was a part of instantly lost me forever, but I would not realize how much until several years later.

My mom's sleep pattern was just like that of a newborn baby. She napped, then had a burst of energy, then napped again then wanted to stay awake all night. Mom always said that people are born babies, live as adults for a while, then turn back into babies. This is true. Fran and Diane, the friend and nurse we hired, bathed Mom every day and put on the baby nighttime lotion that we used to use on TJ. She smelled so good, just like a baby. After getting washed up each day, she would use her walker to come to the living room and sit in her reclining chair. This is the same recliner my dad had from their last house, and I'm sure she thought of him like I did, whenever she sat in. Monique's mom Pam bought Mom these really cool, low-cut socks that came in different bright colors. Mom would have them on every day, no matter what, and she would always tell everyone that Pam bought them for her.

There was a mystery that has still has not been solved regarding Mom's clothes. One day, after Fran and Diane got Mom dressed, she was sitting in the living room, reading her Bible. At some point during the day, we noticed she had a shirt with the name Puerto Rico spelled out in big letters across the front. We asked where she got the shirt and she simply smiled. We asked Fran since she had dressed Mom and she told us she didn't put that shirt on Mom. She should remember because it was only a few hours earlier. There was never an explanation: Mom couldn't get up, go to her room and change shirts by herself, then walk back out to the living room without someone noticing.

As much as I treasured this time together as a family and with Mom, it was mentally and physically grueling for all of us. None of us really slept more than a couple of hours each day. When we did sleep, it wasn't deep; we could be woken up by the slightest sound, like Mom shifting in her bed. Every day, when the hospice nurse arrived, they checked Mom's vitals and gave us the exact same update each time: she has 24 hours to live. We heard this every day. I was sick of hearing it; each time I heard those words, it instantly took my mind back to standing outside in PR, when Fran first gave us the update from the doctor's visit. A solemn feeling overcame me; I knew that I was here with Mom not for a vacation, but to provide emotional support and love during her last days.

Words and wishes

I enjoyed the conversations Mom and I had each day. I learned so much about life, strength and faith just by watching her. I never heard my Mom say she was hurting or in pain. She never said she was sick, nor did she complain about anything. There were plenty of things she could have said were unfair, but never did. She never questioned why cancer was in her body. There was one thing, however, that she did contemplate a few times during our conversations. Mom was concerned about Maritza, Kaelyn and TJ. She asked me twice during my stay to take care of Maritza. She didn't mean in the sense that Maritza couldn't handle herself; Mom meant emotionally. Because Maritza was the baby of the family, each of us at one point in time was responsible for watching over her as a child. Although she is a very capable and responsible adult, she is still my baby sister and always will be. I feel Mom wanted me to ensure that Maritza would have the support she needed emotionally for the future without her parents. The same was true when Mom mentioned Kaelyn. Mom told me to continue to be active in Gabe's life and give him as much support as he needed to raise a young child. Regarding TJ, Mom's wish was simple: don't let him forget her.

I dreaded any call from family members during this time while I was away from Mom's house. One afternoon, I was on my way to Mom's house from the office. As I pulled into the parking lot, Fran called me saying Mom was asking for me. I let her know I was in the parking lot and would be upstairs in a few seconds. Once I made it inside, I went straight to Mom's room. I asked her if she was stalking me and she smiled. She reached out for my hand as I kissed her on the forehead. Every time we spoke lately, I would tell her that she was the most beautiful woman in the world. I'd also ask her to not tell Monique so I wouldn't get in trouble. This day, Mom seemed to think that I was heading back home soon and asked me when I was leaving. I told her that I did not have any plans to go and would be with her if she needed me. She of course asked if Monique and TJ were OK with this and I replied that yes, they were.

Early the next morning, while sleeping in my Mom's bed, I felt something leaning on my left arm. I woke to my mom laying in the bed with me, with her arms holding me like a young child. At some point during the night, she had gotten out of her hospital bed and, while walking toward the bed I was in, dislodged her catheter. I awoke her right away and told her we needed to get her back to her bed, which we did. I then called Fran to let her know Mom's catheter was out. Diane was already on her way to Mom's house and would be able to take care of it. Once Fran and Diane arrived, they got everything back in order. My heart was beating fast because I didn't know whether this was or wasn't an urgent situation.

It was clear that both Mom and I felt the strong need and desire to be as physically close as possible. We'd sit in her bed and she would lean on my shoulder, and we would rock, like I was putting her to sleep. Sometimes we just sat and didn't say anything.

As each day passed, the hospice workers reminded us that Mom only had a short time left. Sick of hearing it, each of us kindly told them separately not to mention that again. One of the nurses was extremely nice, and we had the chance to speak while she was tending to Mom. I asked her to explain why everyone kept mentioning 24 hours. She said that when a person is near death, there are certain physical signs that can be seen on their body. For example, a person's toes start to curl, like they are trying to grip something. The hands do the same. The ear lobes also begin to curl under. The body pulls every resource possible from the extremities and uses them to preserve heart and brain functions. She then showed me how this was happening to Mom. First, she uncovered Mom's legs and pointed at her toes, then she lifted one of Mom's hands and we noticed how they were curled somewhat. As much as I wanted to understand, I didn't want to see these signs on my mom.

The primary nurse sat us down as a family and told us that we needed to begin making plans so that when Mom passed, we would be prepared. I didn't want to hear this, either. These conversations made the experience grueling. A sense of finality filled my mind, as I wondered to myself if this was our last 24 hours together. It didn't make sense, because Mom was still awake, talking and smiling. We reluctantly called Leak & Sons Funeral home, the same company that took good care of Dad, and made an appointment for the next day. Spencer Leak, Jr. sent out one of his best funeral directors to Mom's house, where we would have one of the most surreal meetings of my life. We sat at a small table where I could look down the short hallway to Mom's bedroom and see her lying in bed. We always kept Mom's bedroom door open, but this time, a few minutes into the meeting, I went to close it. I still don't know how I feel today about the fact we were planning Mom's funeral while she was still alive and alert. I provided no input in the planning process except to tell my family that whatever they wanted I was OK with. I couldn't help to select a color for Mom's casket, nor decide what flowers she would appreciate at her funeral. I felt like I was betraying my faith and Mom's faith by conceding that she would not be with us soon. The conversation was happening as if she was already gone. This was a painful, gut-wrenching experience I never want to have again, ever.

A couple of days later, Mom got a little fidgety and uncomfortable for a single day. She was lying in bed and pulling at her clothes, as if someone was tugging on her arms and she was trying to pull herself away from them. While Mom was doing this, we asked if she was OK and to describe what was happening. Her eyes were open, and she seemed to be gazing at something very specific but not within her physical room. Her eyes moved left to right, tracking something that had caught her attention. Afterward, she was back to her usual self. I asked again if everything was OK and she said yes and nodded in the affirmative. To break the tension of her experience, I said "Mom, did you see Dad a few minutes ago?" She said no. I told her that if she saw him, tell him you are busy, and you'll have to see him later. This made her smile. That's the way she and I roll, buddies forever.

I recognized this experience from Lola's description of going through it with Oliver. Monique's cousin Doug in Atlanta also witnessed it years ago when her aunt was in her last days of life. Doug describes it as a person going through purgatory. Lola said the same thing. They said it is the person walking through a gauntlet of souls, grabbing at them from both sides, and they are pushing the souls away and yanking back on their clothes hoping to prevent from being pulled in either direction. This is exactly what it looks like. Soon, Mom was back to her calm self.

> *Time seemed to move differently. On Saturday, from early afternoon to late into the evening, family and friends from all over participated in a parade of love for Mom.*

Time seemed to move differently. On Saturday, from early afternoon to late into the evening, family and friends from all over participated in a parade of love for Mom. Some of Mom's friends came by that I had not seen since I was in high school. It felt like a party, but an uncoordinated one. People brought food; some came to visit for a few minutes while others stayed for several hours. We did what we could to keep the noise level down, but it didn't help much. She was happy to see everyone but too weak to get out of bed and speak much. Her soft, peaceful voice greeted everyone that entered her room to see her.

Sunday rolled around, and the party feeling gave way to a solemn quiet. Cousin Melissa spent the night downstairs at Maritza's apartment, and we spent the day talking and watching children's movies with Kaelyn. Tracey left in the late evening hours, at approximately 11:00p.m. Maritza, Luis, Gabe, Melissa and our friend David were having a really good conversation about raising children and the meaning of life. I was sitting on a couch, facing the front door, with the hallway to Mom's room straight ahead and to the right. Maritza and Melissa were on the couch on my left side, facing the wall where Luis's room is. The hospice nurse came walking from the hallway quickly, with a concerned look on her face. Her mouth was open, and she glanced the room looking for me. I told her many times, if anything was wrong, anything at all, come get me no matter what I was doing. When she spotted me, I was already getting up to go to her because I knew her look was an urgent one. I followed her back into the room, and Luis, Gabe and David followed while Maritza and Melissa stayed in the living room.

The nurse moved to the left side of Mom's bed, and I stood on the right side. She explained that Mom's breathing had gotten very sporadic, and these may be her last moments. I gently picked up Mom's right hand and placed it in my left palm, then placed my right hand over the top of her hand and leaned in a little closer. I had never felt so nervous. I didn't know what I was anticipating, I just stared at her face. Mom's rate of breathing was down to about one breath per minute, each one seeming more like a gulp of air than a smooth in and out motion. I glanced at the hospice nurse, and our eyes met; she looked as nervous as I felt.

I was waiting for Mom's next breath, which would never come. The hospice nurse checked for a pulse, but there wasn't one. We waited another minute or so, hoping for the slightest signs of life, but there weren't any. The nurse looked at me and said, "She's gone." I felt instant horror and grabbed the person nearest to me, which was David, hugged him and leaned my head on his should and cried like a baby for a while. I eventually turned back toward Mom to get another look: her eyes were still open, gazing into nowhere. I moved my right hand over her head and gently closed her eyes. I thought back to my childhood and was very conscious of the fact that she was the first person to ever hold my hand as a newborn, and I would return the honor of being the last person to hold hers. She gave me life, and I painfully witnessed the end of hers.

The only thoughts that brought me a tiny bit of peace was that she knew I kept my promise to stay with her until she didn't need me anymore. That she had probably reconnected already with Dad was another thought that provided a little comfort. I went out to the living room and saw that Melissa and Maritza were sitting right next to each other, probably knowing that Mom had passed. When I made eye contact with Maritza, I couldn't do anything but cry again. I could not form the words in my mouth to say Mom was gone, so I just went and sat on the couch next Maritza and leaned on her shoulder.

Traumatic events have always forced my mind to block out certain memories. The same was true this time. At some point, Jerry appeared in the room with us, hugging and kissing everyone as he usually does. I don't know who called him or how long it was that he came over after Mom passed; I was just relieved to see my brother. I don't recall much else from that early morning on January 19, 2015, except someone from the funeral home taking Mom away and Jerry escorting him to ensure she was not alone, just like he had done after Dad died. The difference this time was that I knew not to try to go with Mom because Jerry would not have allowed me to, to protect me from myself.

My sisters and I have discussed whether it was less painful to have someone we love to pass unexpectedly or to have knowledge that someone's disease was terminal and have had time to share with them during their last portion of life. My feeling is that the loss is just as great in both circumstances. The pain is different for each but then doubly hard when I realize that the people who gave me life, knew me best and saw me first, are now both gone. I felt lonely and didn't know what to do except to put my emotions aside, push through the pain and tuck the grieving process away until I could fully confront it.

Between work, family and everyone I shared an ecosystem with, there were hundreds of people depending on me. As much as my mom's passing had had a devastating impact on me, life outside my feelings continued. I don't remember much after the morning Mom passed; I know there was a funeral but can't recall the details surrounding it. I remember eventually being back at home in PR and still receiving bills in the mail, so I had to quickly snap back into my businessman role, with little time or concern about my own well-being.

The sweetness of memory

I pause when I see photos of my parents together at a young age. I see the hope and determination in my dad's eyes as he is surely thinking about the enormous responsibility of taking care of his family. I recognize the smile and joy on Mom's face, after having given birth to three children, all of whom are healthy and productive members of society. I can imagine the thoughts they had, wondering how their children would view them later. Would they be forgiven for the mistakes they made as parents and humans? Would their children know they gave everything and more, to provide

Would their children know they gave everything and more, to provide a stable, nurturing life?

a stable, nurturing life? Will we acknowledge the deep sacrifices they made for us to participate in sports, music lessons, scouting and private education? Would we always remember them?

I give them both a A+++. There are no people I hold in higher regard than my parents. I know what they gave up for me; I recognized it while they were alive. Both knew how special they were to me because my words and actions reflected it to them. Many of the dreams they deferred while raising me, they were able to realize later in life when they didn't expect it. I look back to when we visited model homes on the weekends, houses that they dreamed of one day owning. The first home I built was by the same developer they visited many times, in the same subdivision they dreamed of living in. Both got to spend time in the home of their dreams. I purchased my first boat because of the good feeling I had as a young boy visiting boat show rooms with Dad. His dream of owning a boat became mine. There are countless other examples of how my parents influenced every aspect of my life, then and now. While I'm alive, everyone I meet will experience the kindness, positive energy and joy my parents embodied through my actions and words. Their spirits live through me. I live to tell their stories.

THE GIFT OF PAIN:
My mom's faith lives on

I miss Mom every day. She left me a gift, and to this day, I have leaned on it each day, some more than others. A word with as few as five letters represents part of my inner being. When everything is crazy, whether I have money or not, whether my current circumstances are favorable, I always have FAITH.

This gift was presented to me in the most beautiful package I have ever seen. It was 5 feet, five inches in height, beautiful mocha wrapping that had the feel of smooth velvet and produced the most tranquil and soothing sound. The faith that was contained in the vessel that was mom has given me the strength to endure life's challenges. Her faith was forged over 68 years, had been through success and failure, love and heartbreak and emerged victorious over struggle. It witnessed miracles and never allowed her to get sad or worry that things would get better, because she could look back at all the examples of its truth. I know that no matter how difficult my days and challenges may be, the faith I have tells me that I will be fine. I believe this to my core.

My faith sustains me when my eyes fail me.

You must realize that there is better for you in your life. There is peace during tough times and there is good that can come after bad. There is prosperity after loss, and you deserve all these wonderful gifts. First, you must believe it with your head, then your heart, then you will begin to live it.

Faith can be strengthened like a muscle. The more you use it, the more you depend on it, the more you realize how strong it is. Start small and each day, challenge yourself to believe and have faith in something meaningful. Each person's results will be different, but the results you get are directly proportional and specifically geared toward your needs.

11: HURRICANE MARIA

In July 2017, we had just gotten back from travels to Kenya and other locations in the States. TJ was starting school soon, so all of us were trying to get back to some sort of normal sleep schedule. This is typically the time of the year when everyone in PR is gearing up for our version of the "winter," so it includes end-of-summer parties, shopping for school supplies and preparing for hurricane season, which is in effect from July through November.

When we initially purchased our home in PR, we wanted to add as much storm-proofing as we could. We added rolling shutters to each door and window and kept a few more food supplies and flashlights on hand than we did in our home in Chicago. I never felt we were fully prepared for any storm, but at least we had taken some proactive steps just in case.

Monique was in Chicago visiting her parents in early September when our friend and boat captain Javier called me. Javier knows everything about boats, the seas and the weather. He also knows I don't watch local news and very little national news, so he wanted to make me aware of some weather that was coming our way. From years of experience, Javier can tell how likely it is for a storm to have an impact on PR, based on where it originally forms after leaving Africa. He told me that a storm he was tracking could be upgraded from a system, to a storm number, then ultimately to a named storm. Named storms are what gets Javier's attention.

Named storms that may impact PR start a chain reaction of events for individuals, businesses and government agencies. The storm in question remained on a trajectory that could impact us, so Javier told me to start our preparations. The most pressing thing was to get the boats into a safe position. Each year, we enroll in an emergency haul-out program at our home marina. This means when there is a named storm, the marina will only haul out boats that are on that list, on a first-come, first-served basis. The marina assigned us a day and time for the haul-out, and Javier and I met at the dock to move the boat. Watching a 65-foot yacht being hoisted out of the water by a crane, then slowly moved nearly three city blocks through a shipyard, then lowered onto stilts and wooden blocks is a nail-biting experience. The smaller 23-foot Boston Whaler was taken down from dry-stack and moved to the same area of the marina. Meanwhile, Captain Bill was preparing Lady Dee, which would stay at her slip during the storm, by removing sails, doubling up on dock lines and ensuring all hatches and canvas were secure.

This is a process we went through each year during hurricane season as a precaution. Javier explained to me years ago that the safest place for a boat during a storm is on dry land. If it gets blown over while on stilts, the boat's damage will be limited to cosmetic work. If it is in the water at a dock or slip during a storm, the wind could push it to or away from the dock, and it could sink. Saltwater destroys the interior of a boat.

Once the boats were secure, we went on with our normal days. Each year, usually in the second week of September, we always get a tropical storm or tropical depression, so we didn't panic or overthink the possibility of it getting much worse than projected. Plus, Javier told me that the projected path would take the storm north of PR, out to sea, so we would not experience a direct hit. We were in contact with Monique each day, and she wanted to make sure we were safe and that we had everything we needed. TJ wasn't alarmed; he figured he would have a day out of school, but the Internet may be out so his video game time would be gone.

To finish our pre-storm preparations, TJ and I went to the grocery store to get a few items and made sure the Jeep was filled with gas. People were out, moving around as they usually do, and the gas stations had lines just a little longer than normal, mostly with people filling up the red five-gallon gas cans. Javier called and told me that the storm was now classified as Hurricane Irma. He also mentioned that it was heading to the British Virgins Islands (BVI) and would surely make landfall. Both of us were concerned because we have friends in the BVI. I called our friend Ella and checked in on her, asking if they were prepared and to get an update on their local weather forecast. Ella is a lifelong resident of Tortola and told me they would be all right, and this storm would pass like all the others over the years. This gave me confidence that our friends were mentally prepared, just in case.

On September 7, 2017, Irma did a drive-by on PR. Our side, which is on the island's east coast, was barely damaged from the storm's outer bands. The winds were moderate, and the rainfall lasted a day or two. We lost power for two days, which meant no TV or internet. I felt relieved because this was the biggest hurricane to "graze" PR since we had been living here, and it did not make landfall. It wasn't until I spoke with Monique, who saw the reality of the storm on TV in Chicago, that I learned that the BVIs were devastated and in fact, the northern part of Puerto Rico had sustained damage from the outer bands as well. During all of this, TJ mentioned to Monique during a phone call that there was another storm that had formed and headed toward PR.

There was flooding, trees were down, and homes were destroyed. I called to check on family and friends to see how they were doing and to my relief, everyone was safe. My thoughts now turned to our friends in the BVI. I called Ella but didn't get through. I checked my cell phone for news updates from Tortola and saw some of the photos of the damage to the very places we had visited only a few months earlier. Homes were flattened, cars were overturned, boats were tossed around like toys and debris was strewn all over the place. My heart sank. I didn't like the feeling of calling a friend and not getting confirmation that they were all right.

Helping out as a community

Monique arrived home, and we quickly began working on a plan to help others locally and abroad. I called Javier and shared our desire to take supplies on the boat over to the BVIs. He agreed and began working on getting the Riviera boat back into the water. Meanwhile, Bill was on the same page and was already asked to captain another boat from PR to BVI to take over supplies. Bill made many runs over the next couple of weeks, sailing those 80 miles each way to provide relief. I asked Jerry to fly down so he could make the trip with us to the BVI and he agreed without hesitation; that's my brother.

Monique, TJ and I purchased supplies such as tarps, gas cans, first aid kits, flashlights and batteries, cases of bottled water, military Meals Ready to Eat (MREs) and much more. We had a whole garage full of aid. The locals in our neighborhood were also donating as much as they could to relief efforts. There was a 53-foot tractor-trailer staged in our neighborhood and a team of workers ready to receive supplies from the locals. We took clothes from our closets and donated them. I felt a sense of global community at this time from people who were dealing with their own issues but also saw that others in a different country who had greater needs and were willing to sacrifice for them. Within a week, our community had put on a massive display of support for the people in the BVI. Bill said there was an almost constant caravan of boats making the trip between PR and the BVIs each day. Javier had finally gotten a slot to have the Riviera "splashed" back into the water so we could prepare it for the journey over. I was also finally able to reach Ella. She said that the island was destroyed, they didn't have running water, and that electricity and roofs were gone from the houses. I told her that we would be coming over soon and asked what her immediate needs were. There was a shortage of portable generators and gas was also depleted, so if we could provide these, it would help greatly, Ella mentioned.

I received another call from Javier on Friday, September 15th. Javier and I have spent several hundred hours together on the ocean, and we know each other well. I could hear in his voice that there was something he didn't like and wanted to share with me. I was outside a local store, walking toward the entrance at the time and figured I needed to stop and listen carefully. Javier said he was tracking another storm that had formed a few days before, and he didn't like the location in Africa where it had started.

If a storm comes from the Cape Peninsula of Africa, it will usually follow a certain path west and maintain that trajectory. If one originates on the west coast of Africa, the path will be different. Wherever this new storm originated from, the path that it was now on would bring it directly toward PR. Although the storm was sitting more southerly than normal, this gave it the ability to make a northwestern turn at some point and hit us head on from the east. Javier said he recommended that we haul the Riviera back out of the water. Javier understands hauling this boat out costs me nearly $5,000 each time. This would be the second haul-out in two weeks. I told Javier that I trusted him and his judgment and to go ahead and get the boat back on dry land. The painful part of this decision for me was that it meant we wouldn't be able to get the supplies we had to our friends and neighbors in Tortola. This was the same storm TJ had mentioned to Monique several days ago.

The weekend of September 16th was different. The locals were taking more precautions than they did when Irma was heading our way. I remember going to the grocery store on Sunday and finding that the shelves were nearly empty. The canned goods were all but gone, and I didn't see any bottled water, eggs, bread, rice or milk. I went to a local hardware store to pick up pre-made sandbags and some heavy-duty plastic liners. Each gas station I passed had long lines of cars, and the people already at the pumps were filling gas cans. Unlike in the days before Irma, people were more somber. They weren't the upbeat, jovial souls that I was used to.

On Tuesday, September 19th, I kept my appointment at the Jeep dealer for the regularly scheduled maintenance and oil change. It was a ghost town, and I was the only customer at the dealership for service. On my way home, the realization that this storm may be bad set in. Once home, I called Javier to get the latest update. He said that the storm was going to hit us directly for sure, based on its current path, which was coming upward from the neighboring island of St. Croix. He went over a list of things to do and not to do. He advised that no matter what I hear or see, do not go outside until the storm is over. He asked if we had enough diesel for the generator, did we have enough bottled water, were our cell phones fully charged? I have never heard this note of caution in Javier's voice. I remember taking a few deep breaths during the short conversation, my body determined to resolve itself to the reality that this storm could do some real damage. Afterward, I called uncle Benji and other family members on the island. They were all familiar with big storms and had been through other major ones in the past. They also took time to go through a checklist of things with me since this was our first big one. Staying indoors no matter what was a common theme.

There was a lot to do to prepare for the evening that was to come. Monique, TJ and I went outside and moved all the outdoor furniture to the large rectangular terrace at the back of the house. It has four large rolling shutters that, when closed, create a secure, enclosed room. We walked through the front and back yards and garden area, removing anything that could be picked up by the wind and shot out like a projectile, including coconuts and flowerpots. We went to each upstairs balcony and made sure all patio furniture was moved inside the house and checked each floor drain to ensure nothing was blocking them so water could flow properly. Packing the vehicles, barbeque grill and other items in the garage was challenge because of all the relief supplies we had for Tortola already in there.

Once we were confident the outside was secure, we decided that the closet in the master bedroom would be our safe room if things got really bad. We brought one case of bottled water, a few flashlights, extra batteries, folding beach chairs and cell phone chargers into the closet as part of our emergency kit. A neighbor and I placed the sandbags against the outside of the bedroom's French balcony doors.

By early afternoon, we had done everything we could to prepare for the incoming storm. I walked out to the garden area, looked at our home and absorbed the view. It felt like when I parked my car at a grocery store and walked toward the building. I always look back at my car as if I would never see it again. That was how I felt today. Monique told me months later that she did the very same thing.

Our home is in an area that is designated a tsunami zone. We can see the ocean from our backyard, just under a mile away. On a normal day, I can look out toward the ocean and see rain clouds coming toward us. On this afternoon, I was able to see the dark clouds slowly moving our way, but probably 20 miles away, just southeast of the island of Vieques, which is clearly visible from our home.

While standing in the backyard, we heard the storm siren for the first time since living in Puerto Rico. It was loud and immediately instilled a sense of realization that the danger was approaching. We looked at each other soberly. TJ was inside, gaming with his friends, soaking up all the Internet he could. I made more calls, connecting to Maritza, Fran and Jerry. I also called a couple of managers at the office in Chicago and told them I may not have power and Internet for a couple of days, but I would call most likely on Friday. I spent a few hours sitting out back, staring at the palm trees, ocean and sky, not worried about the future, just staying in the moment.

I'd been through a couple of storms at this point, lesser in magnitude, and had never experienced the "quiet before the storm." That sounds like something a person who has never actually lived through a storm would say. There is a storm before a storm, not quiet. With hurricanes, there are a few days of advance warning before they hit. There is also a lot of preparation to do the days and hours leading up to their arrival. The weather is surely not calm either. All afternoon, there were rain showers, cloudy skies, then clear skies, then cloudy ones all over again. The temperature was hot, then a strong breeze would come, bringing chilly air. My mind was in preparation mode, continually replaying checklists to ensure I did everything I was advised to do by Javier and others. I told Monique and TJ that I was going to bed and to let me know if they needed anything. I went to each room of the house and pressed the buttons on the remote control to lower the rolling storm shutters into place. There was nothing left to do except wait. I laid there in bed, reading an e-book on my tablet, until I eventually fell asleep.

In the early morning hours of September 20, 2017, a little past 1:00a.m., Hurricane Maria introduced herself to my beloved Puerto Rico. The rain and winds had begun the previous night, but now, I could hear the howling, whistling sounds of air coursing through every tiny hole and crevice outside. I continue lying in bed as the power abruptly shut off. About 10 seconds later, the quick beeping sound from the alarm control panel could be heard, indicating the generator had kicked on and that we were now on borrowed time until the diesel ran out. I could not hear the engine of the generator running as I usually can, due to the pulsing rain beating against the windows and doors. TJ was in the bed with me, then he got up and went to his room to continue to sleep. Monique came and got in the bed, but not to sleep, just to pass the time, hoping for the best. The winds picked up even faster, and gusts slammed against the rolling shutters on our bedroom balcony; it sounded like someone swinging and hitting it with a baseball bat as hard as they could. The sound was jarring, sudden and deliberate. Monique got out of bed and went to the safe place we decided on, which was our closet, the only room in our house without windows.

I sat up in bed and put my gym shoes on as if I was getting ready to run a race. It was time to make my rounds to double check to see if any shutter had been damaged. I started upstairs, moving towards TJ's room, hoping all along that everything was still secure. I turned on the lights in each room to see if water was leaking from window seals or from under balcony doors. I made my way downstairs to the main level, stopping on the last step and slowing peeking toward the back of the house to avoid being hit by any flying debris if a shutter had in fact given way. I continued through the kitchen, the back set of French doors, the front door and so on, checking to ensure that each window and door was still secure.

At the front door, I looked out of the small, narrow windowpane on the left side. I couldn't see anything. It was pitch black, and the window had such a constant bashing of water against it, it was like looking into salty ocean water without goggles. I went back upstairs to check on Monique.

In the closet, she was sitting in a folding beach chair with pajamas and gym shoes on, resting her head on a pillow with her eyes were wide open. I knew she was nervous, so I reassured her by saying everything in the house was holding up and we were fine.

I pulled the door back toward me to close it. As I did, I first saw the French doors moving in and out a little, then I could faintly hear metal hitting metal around the door frame. I walked over to the doors and grabbed the handle and could now feel how much tension was on them. I'm strong and these doors were pulling my hands like we were in an arm-wrestling match. I grabbed the handle with both hands, trying to stop them from moving even more. We were only in the first several minutes of the storm, I thought. How are these doors moving when they are deadbolted and covered with 300-pound storm shutters reinforced by sandbags? I knew then that this was going to be a long night.

I took some bungee cords from the utility closet and took them back to the bedroom. I tied one of the cords to the handle of the balcony door, then to the frame of the bed. I tied the second cord to the same handle and the other end to the bed post. I thought this would keep the doors from flapping so much. I laid across the bed again with my eyes open, trying to let my mind settle. Monique came out of the closet to see how everything was going and noticed the cords that I had tied to the doors. We sat there, listening to the winds and rain get even louder, then she walked to TJ's room to check on him.

I felt the storm getting progressively more intense; there was no pause or break in the pounding we were taking. I felt a movement from the bed, then a few seconds later, another one. I sat up quickly and as my weight shifted, the bed moved about five-six inches toward the balcony doors. I jumped up and ran over to the doors and the bed slid across the room and beat me to the door, wedging itself against the door frame. The doors were now flopping faster and faster. I grabbed the handle with both hands, leaning back to try and stop the shaking. During the struggle, I felt a pool of water rush into my shoes. The floor was beginning to flood. I held the handles without a long-term plan in mind. I couldn't hold them forever, but in the moment, I didn't know what else to do. Poof - the handle ripped off the frame, and the doors slammed back toward the shutters. I stepped back, in a pool of water, with a door handle in my hand. Maria was not even here yet; this was just a text message from her letting us know she was on the way.

I grabbed a flashlight so I could see how much water was inside. There was a puddle a couple of feet wide, so I walked down the hallway to the closet and grabbed a few beach towels. I called for Monique and asked her to come to our room. While I was mopping, Monique came in and saw the water and said we needed to move to another room. We went to Mom's former room, where TJ was asleep on the floor, cuddled up on the area rug.

I soon went to check each room again. As I stood in the living room at the center of the house, I was able to hear how loud the storm was. The noise was the loudest banging, pounding, metallic grinding I had ever heard, and it was coming from every direction with pure and mounting intensity. It reminded me of sitting on an airplane, going through rough turbulence. This was life for the next several hours. Maria was relentless, unwavering in her attempt to get inside. There was a battle inside the house, us trying to keep the storm out and the storm trying to get in.

Despite all this, I wasn't afraid. I clearly understood the gravity and seriousness of our situation. I took nothing for granted, not for a single second, but I knew that if I showed one bit of doubt or concern or uncertainty, it would terrify my family. Taking a deep breath, I went back upstairs to the master bedroom. By now, the water had spread across the entire room. I opened the bathroom door and it was full; the closet was also filled with water. I knew that I needed to open certain interior doors and close other doors during the storm, depending on where the winds were hitting hardest. I did this to relieve pressure in those areas so there wouldn't be a blowout of any of the doors. I left the bathroom door open now, to relieve pressure but closed the master room main door. I opened the door to a hallway bathroom and closed TJ's door.

I went to check on everyone. Monique was sitting on the couch quietly, 2,200 miles from Chicago's South Side, here on this island because of me. I felt responsibility for putting my family square center in the eye of a hurricane. I felt resolve and determination to protect them no matter what I had to do.

Then I smelled smoke. The smell intensified as I walked toward my bedroom. When I opened the door and shone my flashlight into the room, I could only see cloudy smoke. I ran to the laundry room, opened the circuit breaker box and started flipping switches to the off position as fast as possible. Water was now spilling into the hallway from the master bedroom. While I was flipping switches, TJ called out that the shutters were failing.

My heart was now beating fast. As I came down the stairs, I could see that the dining and living room shutters were still intact. In the family room, though, I could see lightning flashes through the windows above the couch. Through the French doors leading out to the patio, I could see that the bottom half of an 8-foot-tall by 12-foot-wide shutter was gone, completely missing. I came face to face with Maria, the deadly beast of a storm. I saw wind and debris flying so densely that it looked like a cloud. It felt like looking into the window of a washing machine filled with suds from the detergent, flying faster than anything I could imagine. I stayed put, glancing to the right a few more feet into the kitchen to see if the shutters on that side were holding, and they were. I pulled my head back and stayed in place. I took a deep breath and had to prepare my mind for the possibility that Maria would come inside the house and make herself at home.

TJ came downstairs and stood behind me, leaning his entire body against my back with his hands on my shoulders. He wanted to see what I saw. I told him to stay behind me as we stepped down to the main floor and slowly took one step into the open area. His eyes teared up and he said, "It's hard to see this." I pushed him back as I slowly stepped backward, shielding him against any debris that could fly through the now-unprotected windows. I wanted to start putting anything away that was exposed on the countertops so it would not become a projectile inside the house—but there was too much stuff and no time.

I went back to Mom's room with Monique and TJ. We rested for a short time, listening to the pounding. The howling wind and rain were literally stripping the paint off the house. Then we heard an extremely loud sound on the roof for the first time. It sounded like someone was dropping a thousand bowling balls on the roof. It sounded like the concrete roof was going to cave in. Then, the sound got louder, and I could hear a rolling noise up there, as if a small car was being dragged across the roof. Next, we heard an even louder crash on the right side of the house. This was when Monique lost it. She began to cry and rock back and forth, asking God what was happening. I was sitting on her right side and pulled her body toward me with my left arm and held her tight. I told her it was going to be OK. Monique was searching her mind for a Bible verse that could comfort her. Nothing came to mind under the pressure of the moment, but she knew Mom must have a bible somewhere in the room, so she got up from the couch and looked in each dresser drawer. Sure enough, in the top drawer, was Mom's Bible. She opened the Bible and there was a handwritten set of notes written by Mom, on a piece of paper. There were seven Bible verses that Mom listed that she had previously included in the church's bulletin the last time they attended church together in November 2014. The first one was Luke 6:48, NLT version:

> *It is like a person building a house who digs deep*
> *and lays the foundation on solid rock. When the*
> *floodwaters rise and break against that house,*
> *it stands firm because it is well built.*

Coincidence or blessing? I know it was a blessing.

We noticed that now the floor of Mom's room was flooding, so we grabbed more towels to place near the balcony door. I saw water in the hallway as well now. At this point, I decided to get everyone up and moving. I had to get a plan together to get their minds off the horror of our present moment. Back downstairs, I saw that all four of the shutters on the back patio had been ripped to shreds. Each shutter weights approximately 700-800 pounds. It takes four men to hold them in place when they are being installed. Now they were torn like loose-leaf paper and dangling on the hinges from Maria's devastating winds. My heart sank as I looked at a wall of windows in the family room and kitchen, all completely exposed to a massive storm. I saw the storm even clearer now, whirling and twirling, pickup up everything in its path like leaves on the ground, pounding and surging against every surface that got in its way. All the furniture that we stored within the confines of the shutters was plastered against the wall where the windows were.

I had no time to waste worrying about something I couldn't control. I quickly moved back upstairs and laid out the plan. Monique and TJ would be positioned in the hallway, TJ at the entrance to the master bedroom and Monique at the end of the hallway corner, right at the 45-degree angle. I positioned myself in the hallway bathroom. Before we took our places, we had one final thing to do: open the master bedroom door. When TJ did, a tsunami of water flowed out toward the laundry room, along the hallway and down the stairs, like a waterfall that never ends. The water ran down to the first level and entered each room below except the dining room.

Water was now everywhere; the house was flooding, and fast. We set up a relay system: TJ quickly began sweeping the deep water toward Monique at the end of the hall, where she would push it along toward me in the bathroom. With a huge industrial-size dustpan, I scooped as much water as possible and shoveled it into the open shower door and onto the shower floor towards the drain. We continued pushing water for hours as the noise continued to beat the heck out of our house.

All night, the rains and winds continued to intensify; they did not let up. It felt like the storm was personally coming for us. My focus was singular—we had to focus on ourselves and the present and nothing else. I had to get my family through to the other side, no matter how long it took. We had been awake for about 21 or 22 hours at this point, working pretty much nonstop preparing for and living within the storm.

After we had gotten as much water out as possible, TJ went to his room to rest, and Monique and I went to the guest room next to his. We sat in the bed and didn't say much. My mind was trained on the game plan that would follow after our rest break. We had lots of water to remove, we didn't know if the downstairs area was destroyed and we didn't know how much longer Maria would be imposing her will on us. Maybe 30-45 minutes later, we noticed the loud noises had stopped, almost instantly. It was surreal, like a dream. There was silence like I had not heard in years. We looked at each other and smiled. Monique asked if it was over, but I didn't have an answer for her. A feeling of relief set in and a small weight had been lifted.

We left the room and saw TJ was sound asleep in his bed before making our way downstairs. My heart was beating fast, in anticipation of what we were going to see. As we made the left turn toward the family room, we looked out and saw outside faintly, just enough, to know the strong winds had died down. It was still dark, and only a tiny bit of rain was falling. I took a deep breath and said a personal prayer of thanks that my family was safe. I felt that whatever damage we sustained could be dealt with later as long as my wife and son were alive and well.

We went back upstairs to the master bedroom. It was a mess: There was water all over the place, the door handle ripped off, the bed had been shoved over toward the doors. Exhausted, I walked back to the guest room and laid on the bed again. Monique and I agreed that this was a storm that we would never forget, and we were glad it was over. We were happy but still knew we had a lot of cleaning to do.

After a short time, I heard the rain start to pick up, hitting against the shutters in the room. Shortly after, a gust of wind slammed against the house, jolting the shutters sharply. I was confused because the storm had passed and these things shouldn't be still happening, right? We found out later, of course, that the quiet, peaceful lull was the eye of the storm passing over our house.

Now, Maria's beautiful backside had its turn. Everything started all over again and lasted for several more hours. The house was being battered, but this time it was less able to handle the beating. The rear shutters were gone, and the water found the perfect access points to enter whenever it wanted to. We were mentally spent, exhausted. I had resolved that that best thing to do was for all of us to stay upstairs, between TJ's room and the guest room. Both were positioned at the front of the house, the opposite side of the clear path of destruction from the ocean that Maria was using to kill everything in her path.

Picking up the pieces

We waited in the guest room until the winds and rain were consistently low. The three of us walked downstairs hours later and glanced out toward the backyard. We could see that the sun was now out, the rain was nothing more than the usual Caribbean daily shower and the winds had died down significantly as well. The only safe place to exit the house without having to open a storm shutter was the front door. Before opening the front security gate, we looked out and saw the devastation right away. The heavy Spanish-style roof titles were spread out in a million pieces, covering every inch of the driveway. I couldn't take a single step without my feet landing on a piece of them. The entire street in front of our house was flooded, which was strange, because our home sits at the end of a cul-de-sac at the bottom of a hill, so water naturally drains. We made our way out to the street, moving slowly through the minefield of debris.

We turned back to look at our house and gasped at the destruction. The roof tiles were gone, and leaves from palm trees, bushes and other vegetation were plastered to the front of the house like wallpaper. Light fixtures were crushed like someone had beat them with a hammer. Glancing up the street to our right, we saw more devastation. What once was a windy road filled with beautiful flamboyan tree branches extending across to form a shaded canopy was now a barren street with no signs of natural vegetation. It was like someone had pulled every leaf off every tree in sight. Some of our neighbors were undertaking the same painstaking experiment in humility, looking back at their homes wondering how they would recover.

I was glad the storm was over, for the second time. Now came the overwhelming feeling of where to start. There was so much devastation that I didn't know where to begin cleaning. TJ and I went upstairs into the master bedroom and grabbed the remote control for the roll-up shutter. Once it was in the up position, we had to use a set of pliers to turn the handle on the balcony doors and open them. We pushed the door open slowly as the weight of the waterlogged sandbags formed a blockade of sorts. The water came streaming into the bedroom out into the hallway and down the stairs. I could hear what sounded like a waterfall behind me from all the water that was rushing in, hitting each step until it reached the main level. We focused on getting to the two main drains and unclogging them as fast as possible. We repeated this on every balcony and throughout the house, working on removing water for hours.

Now I wanted to go outside and see if any of our neighbors were hurt and needed immediate assistance. We went into the garage and loaded into the Jeep. TJ brought our satellite phone with him. I slowly pulled out of the driveway, driving gingerly over the broken roof tiles covering our entire driveway. Once out on the street, we had to navigate downed trees, metal, plastic and roof tiles all over the road. Our neighbors were out doing the same, making connections to each other.

My neighbor Jose saw that we had a satellite phone, which Monique was using trying to call her mother. He said that there was a family a couple of blocks away whose house was destroyed and asked if we could go with him so the wife could call her husband in the States to let him know she was alive. This would be the first of hundreds of similar calls we experienced. As we approached the neighbor's home, it didn't look bad from the outside. We exited the Jeep and greeted everyone, asking if they were OK. The owner explained that the windows had shattered because they didn't have storm shutters. She walked us into the back door, and it looked like terror. The furniture was thrown all over, lamps knocked down, just stuff everywhere. She explained that her family had to hurry into a safe room when the first windows blew out. They stayed there, huddled up for hours.

Devastation and destruction were all around. I thought that our island would never be the same. The work to restore what had been just 48 hours ago overwhelmed me. I saw snapped palm trees, a destroyed hotel, a car rental booth at the marina that had been wiped out. Boats were on their sides, half in the water and half out. Some of the boats looked as if someone picked them up, raised them about 30 feet into the air, then let them fall back to the earth. We had seen enough for the day.

We made our way back to our house to begin the cleaning phase. It took a full day to get most of the water out of the house. The next morning, I woke up early, put my shoes on and got my mind together to deal with the back of the house. This was what faced the ocean and sustained the brunt of Maria's fury. It was utter chaos. The walls were scarred and sliced, paint blasted off the surfaces of the ceiling and almost all the patio furniture we stored was gone. Amid the destruction, I noticed something that still amazes me today. Maria had lifted 700-pound storm shutters and tossed them like LEGO blocks, but the two small remote controls for the ceiling fans were still sitting in their cradles on the wall.

I looked toward the ocean. What used to be a lush, deeply green landscape was now a dull shade of brown. The scene reminded me of a movie that depicted the aftermath of areas that have been decimated by napalm bombs. Not knowing where to start, I found in amazement that the speaker system for the backyard was untouched. We have six speakers around the perimeter of the pool that create a surround sound effect. All of them were still connected. I walked over to the gazebo to see if the stereo receiver located in the closet was OK and it was. I plugged it in, powered on the music player and played my favorite playlist. The first song on the list was "Happy," by Pharrell Williams, the same song we played at Mom's side during her hospital visit and at her funeral. My heart instantly filled up with thanks to God. Mom had given me a sign that everything would be just fine. A few seconds later, Monique came walking out the patio doors, clapping her hands and singing along to Mom's favorite song. We smiled at each other and started to pick up the pieces, one at a time.

The aftermath

We were living on an island where none of the essentials were working: no electrical power, no running water, no cell phone service, no Internet, no banks, no gas stations, no grocery stores, no pharmacies, no police, no fire department, hospitals running on generators if open at all, no traffic lights, no airport, no shipping ports, no access to cash, credit cards or ATM terminals, nothing. The only resource the 3.5 million people on the island had was themselves. Expressways were impassable, roads were blocked, streets were flooded, and a vulnerable group of people was lacking medicine, food and water.

Even in this reality, the people of Puerto Rico were kind, helpful to one another, with smiles on their faces and thankful to be alive. We witnessed the best of humanity during this period. I drove several hours and checked on my friends and family and found them alive.

Each day, people came to our house and ask to make a call on our satellite phone. TJ had already designated himself as the main user and knew certain spots out back where the signal was the strongest. We were able to witness several joyful calls as friends and neighbors reached loved ones who had worried greatly.

Our community set up an information dissemination and collection process. Each day, the security guards at the main entrance to the community would pass out flyers, detailing things that we needed to be aware of. There was a need for volunteers to assist in many ways, and we quickly decided we had to participate. The homeowners association purchased thousands of gallons of drinkable water that were delivered in large tanker trucks. Our job was to go to the water distribution point, fill containers that community members would bring to collect water and limit quantities to a certain number of gallons per family.

It was time to check on the boats. During the long drive to the marina, we saw the devastation firsthand and got a bigger picture of how the other parts of the island had been affected, which saddened us more the farther we traveled from home. When we arrived at the marina, there was a line of cars double parked at the main entrance. While waiting to get in, Antonio Vecino motored up on the golf cart he uses to make his way around the marina each day. It was so good to see him, and he was equally happy to see us. Antonio leaned toward me and asked if I had seen Lady Dee. I told him no. He looked me in the eyes and shook his head from left to right, giving me the "it's not good" look. I took a deep breath and tried to prepare my mind for whatever that meant. Antonio told us to get on his cart. He said something to the security guard in Spanish that I didn't recognize, and we were allowed to enter without a security escort, all four of us.

As we drove through the marina, Antonio didn't take us to the slip where Lady Dee was docked; he drove us toward the opposite side, where his shop was located. We cleared one additional security checkpoint and drove through the dry-stack area. We were now driving straight to the haul-out area, when TJ tapped on my left shoulder and pointed straight ahead. I saw something that I could not have imagined. Lady Dee was half in and half out of the water. Maria had yanked her from the double line-cleats that held her to the dock, then spun her around and hurled her more than 150 yards away, bouncing up and down until she landed on the tip of the haul-out dock. The corner of the concrete structure was impaled into her hull. Lady Dee sat there at nearly a 45-degree angle, with a massive hole in the bottom. This was a tough sight to see: After all the work and the months and months of making her special enough to bear Mom's name, now she lay helpless,

This was a tough sight to see: After all the work and the months and months of making her special enough to bear Mom's name, now she lay helpless, wounded and in need of immediate attention.

wounded and in need of immediate attention. Even though it's only a material item, so much love and attention to detail went into the project.

Antonio, who had initially said the boat should be sunk when he first saw it, considered it to be his boat as well. He promised to make Lady Dee beautiful again: his masterpiece was damaged, and he wanted to make it right. As Monique, TJ and I stood there taking it all in, Antonio went to find the Riviera on the other side of the marina to see if it had sustained any damage. About 15 minutes later, he returned and said that the boat was fine, no major damage. This was a bit of good news for all of us. All over, I saw dozens of boats tossed around like toys, some on the docks, some shoved against others. Altogether, there were more than 36 boats that sank, right there at their docks, and dozens more that had sustained major damage.

The most pressing concern I had each day was the generator. A full tank of diesel only lasts about five days, and there was no place I could find any to refill it. To problem-solve, I asked Javier if we could siphon diesel from the Riviera boat and fill gas cans with it. In addition to helping me siphon, he gave me 30 gallons of regular gas that he had stored at his house. He knew I was driving a lot helping others and donated the last of his supply.

Coming home with fresh diesel is like bringing a winning lottery ticket home to show the family. It was our lifeline for the next three days or so. I felt a sense of accomplishment, worth and purpose. I am the leader of my family, which means I can't make excuses or be tired or have doubt and ever consider giving up. When Monique and TJ wake up each morning, they are counting on me to provide a stable life, and this was a test for sure.

With a functioning generator and reliable water supply, our house become an oasis of sorts. A friend named Martha came by each day and brought her 84-year-old mother. Martha's mom needed a breathing treatment each day with a machine that required electrical power. Others came by and took warm showers; some people came by to get food. Whatever we had, we shared with anyone in need. There was one family who came from a completely different town, asking to use our sat phone. Their relatives were neighbors of ours. I had never heard so many grown people crying in my entire life as when people made calls to loved ones on our phone.

Our good friends Rudy and Vilma came by our house the next day to make some calls and check in with us. Rudy told Monique and me that he thought he was going to have a heart attack that night. Now that the storm had passed, his concerns moved from surviving a storm to surviving life. As a realtor, he was concerned that he may not have any business for the next two years. He questioned how he would continue to take care of Vilma and their four boys. I could see the stress on his face, and I could relate to that deep feeling of uncertainty. I grabbed a cold beer from the fridge and popped in the DVD of the Lady Dee tribute for my mom, who he knew well. Rudy sat inside, under the AC, with a brewskie and Vilma enjoyed the pool. This is what we had to offer during that time.

This experience also gave me the idea that we needed to do this for more people. I told Monique and TJ that we should have a pool party and cook for our friends and neighbors. We planned it for the next week and went by people's homes and invited them over. Connecting with people took me back to my childhood. I rode my bike or walked to friends' houses that could be a mile or two away, not knowing if they were home. TJ experienced this firsthand now. He rode his bike several miles, hoping to catch his friends at home. People were outside, doing whatever salvage work they could and avoiding the sweltering temperatures inside the house. Despite the strain, there was a sense of peace that came over us at night. Because no one could call, there weren't social media notifications beeping on our phones, nor the 24-hour news cycle plastered on a TV screen. As dusk settled in, so did my family, enjoying nightly conversation and the occasional card game.

A little more than a week after the largest storm to hit Puerto Rico in more than 50 years, we hosted a pool party. Monique cooked chicken, salmon and hot dogs on the grill, our friend made a huge pot of rice and beans and fresh plantains, and we had fresh salad, cold water, cold beer and even ice cream for the kids. Salsa music blasted from the outdoor speakers, kids swam in the pool, adults sat in the jacuzzi while others watched DVD movies and sat out back and talked. We had been blessed to be prepared for the storm season, and it was our responsibility and desire to share with anyone we could. For those several hours, I think all of us could forget about the events of last week and let go of worrying about the tough times ahead. We simply lived in the moment and appreciated what we had in front of us, which was life, friends and family.

Two weeks after the storm, while TJ was out at his friend's house and Monique and I were at home on the back patio, the doorbell rang. Our friends Ray and Tonya were at the front gate with sober, sad faces. Ray said that he was sorry for our loss and hugged me. My heart sank, wondering who he could be talking about. Who had died? It was Rudy, Vilma's husband.

Immediately I got Monique. Ray told Monique that Rudy had passed, and she sat down on the couch with Tonya in silence, not wanting to believe it either. He said that there was a black bow on Rudy's real estate office door with a note. We needed to find Vilma to be with her during this time, and I knew I had to get to my uncle's house as well, because they were best friends. I asked if he knew where Vilma lives and if he would go with me to find her, which he agreed to do.

Ray and Tonya followed us to Rudy's office. We wanted to see the black bow and handwritten notice. We left, trying to find Vilma's house, in the dark, without streetlights. When we eventually arrived, Vilma was standing next to Rudy Jr., and her other sons were sitting in the driveway with their friends. We later found out that Rudy passed on the evening that he shared a special dinner together with Vilma and their four sons.

Rudy's loss was devastating for the family as well as the rest of us. He had been a part of our lives since the first days we'd lived in Puerto Rico. I would see Rudy walking the trails around the neighborhood early in the morning and from a distance, I could tell it was him from his height, square shoulders and signature swagger. Rudy taught Monique early on how to embrace the tropical workday. He'd have a table and chair setup in front of his office, sipping on a glass of wine at noon while talking on his cell phone. Monique always commented how cool that was and she would be glad when she could do the same.

This was the aftermath of Maria. So many things happened as a result of the storm. Rats displaced by the storm defecate and urinate in open areas, leaving behind a bacterium called leptospirosis. People can be sickened by picking up contaminated debris from their yards. I also saw people desperate for water collecting dirty water from a stream running down the side of the mountain. People were hurting in a major way. The workers that we had known for years at the local stores, restaurants and shops for example, lost their homes and businesses in one night. They woke up one day with no home, no job, no insurance and no means to rebuild. This happened to more people than we could imagine.

Helping hands helping others

Monique and some ladies from church connected and initiated a formal strategy for community assistance. Between the church, the community and our garage, these wonderful angels went out in the hardest-hit areas on our side of the island to deliver supplies. A community leader named Mrs. Margarita had already solidified her place in heaven, right there at the top spot, because of her good deeds. Every Tuesday, the ladies would come to our house to put together supply kits and take them directly to the people who needed them. It gave them purpose, a sense of community, pride and pleasure to help others. Each of these ladies had lost so much personally, especially Vilma, but they gathered, packed gift bags, joined in a group prayer and set out to help others.

What they witnessed was heartbreaking. Monique described finding a lady sitting in a chair in the middle of a small house. The raindrops were falling on her because the roof was totally gone. She had no family to move in with, and her neighbors were in the same situation she was in. Everything she owned was there, in dressers, drawers and closets, soaked in water, mildewing more and more each day. With all that, she still smiled and thanked God for the gift of life.

The needs of our community changed over the weeks. The first few weeks, the ladies had given away flashlights, batteries, plastic tarps, water and food items. Later, people needed medicine, ladies needed feminine products, elderly people needed bandages replaced and soap to wash up with. We distributed MREs to a neighboring community to sustain them. TJ and I could not have been prouder of Monique and the ladies. They are angels, and I've often told Monique that this was surely the best work she has ever done. The work continues today.

Our insurance broker came to our house a couple of weeks after the storm. He brought an underwriter from the insurance company that holds our policy to take photos and review the damage done to our home and property. During this conversation, he mentioned that each of the three towns on our side of the island-Ceiba to the north, Humacao, which is our city, and Yabucoa to the south-all clocked wind gusts or more than 226 miles per hour during the storm. He also confirmed that several tornadoes had touched down near the hotel where we previously witnessed the damage. I was told that filing a claim was one thing, but getting approved and paid would be a very long process. We had structural problems that could not wait another week and decided to begin rebuilding, in hopes the insurance company would live up to its responsibilities.

I went to find the owner of a construction company that we used in the past for roof work. I found George out with his crew near his house and asked him to come by my house so we could get a quote and start rebuilding. We had a construction crew at our house from October 2017 through late June 2018, nearly every day. Looking at our house, we could see the obvious damage, but a construction expert could show us the things that were structural, not cosmetic that an untrained eye would miss. We had a lot to do. One advantage we had was electricity. Other homeowners that needed to rebuild didn't have power, so the construction crews couldn't use power tools and had to wait to start those projects. This put us first in line.

This was a noisy time. The generator engine constantly hummed amid the deafening drilling noises, breaking of concrete and sawing of metal that rang in my ears all day every day it seemed. My nerves were strained. Two weeks or so went by before I could call my office in Chicago. The call was brief, to let them know I was alive and to keep things running. There were rumors around our neighborhood that we may be able to get cell service near San Juan. All around us, "normal" life was still limited by gas, supply availability, and long lines of desperate and exhausted residents.

This was what life was like for several months. Grocery store, gas station and bank lines got shorter and shorter over time. We

This was what life was like for several months.

adapted to the new normal and made the best out of every situation. Each person that I speak to who was here during the storm and stayed after has unique stories of survival, destruction and most important, hope and faith. Each of them also has an emotional scar that will be a continual reminder of that day in September that changed so many people's lives. For me, Rudy was the biggest loss, a special person who would still be here if it were not for Maria. I also experience post-traumatic stress every time I hear our generator start or stop. The sound of the generator running for months was more than just a machine; it represented the link to a semi-stable life for my family and a base of operation to support our community. Our generator ran all day and night except for times we would proactively shut it down to prevent damage to its components.

One Sunday evening, however, as we were sitting out back, I could hear an unusual noise coming from it. The engine was revving high, then low, then high again, then there was a clanking sound like a metal pipe being hit against a light pole. I walked to the generator and opened the large cover door and looked inside. To my untrained eye, everything looked fine. A few moments later, it powered down. I tried to manually start it without success. It reminded me of trying to start a car sitting out in the cold air back in Chicago after the battery had died. Instantly, all the thoughts of what this meant flooded my head: The fridge would lose cold air, the alarm system would not work, garage doors and storm shutters would not work, we wouldn't have a stove and the construction crew would have to stop, mid-work.

Desperate to solve this problem, I drove to my friend Anthony's house. He is an electrician. He followed me back to try to diagnose the problem but could not. Next, I went searching for a technician from any generator company that may be out in the neighborhood. I was lucky to find our regular technician. He said we needed parts, which were in short supply. The next day, Anthony and I drove to a huge warehouse facility and purchased a 7500-kilowatt generator that would be our backup for the next week until the main one was repaired. Even today, several years later, the sound and smells of a generator are enough to take me right back to the aftermath of Hurricane Maria and this time of rebuilding.

I also encountered a traumatic reaction one day when George, a few of his workers and Anthony the electrician were standing in our backyard, discussing how to re-route a power line under some concrete. We were talking and joking when the storm siren blared from an area near the ocean. All of us froze. I scanned the ocean for dark clouds. George dropped his head as if to say, not again. My heart was pounding. I felt that all too familiar sick pain in my stomach as I wondered how we would go through another storm when everything was still in shambles. Without TV, radio or a cell phone to check the Internet, we could not confirm if it was real or a test of the emergency broadcast system. We sat there, stunned, for what seemed like a lifetime but was probably only 3-4 minutes. No storm came through, so I could only conclude it was a test. All the workers left to go home to be with their families. I tucked this trauma away with everything else from my past, into a little box in my heart that seems to grow every year in size.

After the storm, a blessing arrived from Mom. Though she had been gone for some time, she knows how to show up right when we need her. While doing a complete house cleaning, TJ found a letter from Mom. It was in an unopened envelope, under his bed in a corner. She must have placed it on his bed and it somehow fell behind it without him knowing. The letter was dated November 2014, the last time she was at our home. The spirit of the letter was about what to do in her absence, and it was written in Spanish. TJ understood every word, but he had to translate parts of it for me. As he read it, my eyes teared up as I could hear Mom saying the words. It was exactly how she talked to me and how she talked to him. It was not only a physical representation of her life but a spiritual reminder that she is still with us and that we have an angel protecting us during everything we experience in life. I scanned the letter to preserve the words and framed it for TJ to hang in his room.

After the storm, a blessing arrived from Mom.

The aftermath of Maria would have a lasting impact on our island and its people. Our power was finally restored in the middle of December 2017, more than three months after the storm. Others had to wait until May 2018. There were still blue FEMA tarps on people's homes years later, and the death toll is in the thousands. Knowing what I know now and having experienced the eye of this storm, if another category 5 storm followed the exact path as Maria and was projected to have the same impact and level of destruction, I would remain in my home, on this island and ride it out.

During and after disasters, families and communities need strong people to be present to help put things back together. There was a group of Americans that came to Puerto Rico to take advantage of a tax break under a provision called Act 20 and Act 22. The majority of them came to the island to avoid paying taxes, legally of course, but not for the love of the island, nor the love of the people, nor to embrace the culture. The day after Maria hit, as we drove around seeing if anyone needed assistance, all they talked about was leaving. They scattered back to the comfort of the mainland where the AC units were working, the electricity was available at the touch of a button and the lattes were flowing freely. When the island needed them the most, they abandoned my people, my neighbors, my island.

Many came back to the island after they heard the power was back on. To me, though, it was clear: They had run from the first hint of adversity. The storm only lasted for a day or two, but the aftermath continues. Communities must be anchored by people that care and are vested in their well-being. I would sit through the sounds, winds, destruction, flooding and aftermath again, to ensure when it was over, I could go find my family and help them recover. I would find Mrs. Margarita and help her distribute supplies to needy families. I would be there to give hope to others that we could rebuild together. I would cook and give our last egg to those in need and stand at the side of all my family, friends and neighbors.

12: EXIT WOUNDS

When a bullet enters an object, the hole it creates is roughly the same size as the diameter of the bullet. When the bullet exits that same object in a different location, the hole is usually much larger and way more devastating. This is the exit wound.

When starting a business, one of the first things to consider is the kind of exit you will want. Founders should ask themselves: Am I growing a business to sell it for a huge financial gain years later? Am I starting the business to pass it on to a relative? Am I starting a business to keep it until I die? All these endings are referred to as "exits" in the business world.

I've already shared my business's beginning. When its ending wasn't one of these positive ones mentioned above, I could only describe the damage as an exit wound: a tragic, earth-shaking, end-of-the-world, financially ruinous blast to my company. It was the kind of wound that anyone on the outside would say, "We are not sure he will make it after this." Do I die on the table or barely survive and have long-term scars and years of recovery?

Business is not easy. It is extremely difficult to run a successful company for an extended period of time and continue to be profitable and growing. For 29 of my 49 years on earth, I had employees, payroll, creditors, suppliers and successes. As I look back, it's hard to remember life before

> *It is extremely difficult to run a successful company for an extended period of time and continue to be profitable and growing.*

I was in business. The one constant over all these years is change. Each day, week, month and year, there was something in my business that required us to shift and adjust. Some were small, such as hiring a new employee, and some were more dramatic, such as winning a new contract and putting systems in place to manage its terms and conditions. For example, here was a typical day for me:

- Wake up at 4:00a.m.
- Lie in bed and read the national and local newspapers for Chicago and surrounding areas. I had to know everything that was happening in politics, education, business, international tariffs, mergers and acquisitions, taxes, etc. because they had an impact on my business.
- Shower, get dressed and be in the office by 7:15a.m.
- Check emails that came in after 7:00p.m. the night before through this morning and reply to each of them. On average, I would process 125-150 emails each day.
- Go through and complete each task on my calendar for the day, an average of 30-35 things.
- Start making calls at 8:00a.m.

- Connect with our Illinois and New York sales team via a video call to discuss progress from the previous day. We considered these our "cadence" calls, where everyone got on the same step.
- Work with our proposal team to respond to request for proposals.
- Work with our marketing team to review and approve ad buys.
- Join calls with customers and vendors to track progress on various projects.
- Initiate new calls with prospective customers and partners.
- Meet with our operations team regarding payroll, accounts receivable and payable, and human resource matters.
- Attend an off-site meeting with a prospective customer.
- Attend networking receptions for elected officials.
- Attend speaker events where one of our largest customers was discussing their three-five-year plans.
- Have an end-of-day meeting with our management team to review the activities for the day and prepare for the next day.

The average day would end at approximately 7:00p.m. I'd spend time with Monique and TJ, then read a book or work-related information that I need to be prepared for tomorrow. This was the roller coaster ride for 29 years.

Of course, business doesn't start out this way. The early days were exciting, and I was very energetic because everything I was doing was new. I had a "let's conquer the world" mindset and work ethic, which pushed me through the times when I was exhausted. Over time, my primary business focus had to evolve from what I intended it to be at the beginning. When I first started the company, I had no idea that we would participate in such vastly different projects years later. This is also the beauty of having my own company: I could be as agile as I wanted or needed to be in order to develop services and solutions for our customers' needs. Agility is key to longevity: Look at all the huge global corporations that have expanded into new markets as the world changes. Electric companies that made light bulbs also make engines for airplanes. Computer companies now stream content for internet viewers and car manufacturers now make robots.

Any business shift creates change in the company's culture and internal operations. We went through many growth spurts over the years, some of which were painful while others were easier to manage. These changes can also be initiated by internal factors such as growth and planning for future needs, or by external factors that are out of our control. This is why I had to be aware of current events across the world, because any number of them could be good news or bad news for my company. This is one of the things that business owners stress over a lot: the things we can't control.

The year 2019 started out as another typical year in business. We typically get a lot of new orders in the first part of the year because many of our customers' fiscal years start

January 1st. We were still in the midst of transitioning from a previous location, a project that took about three months to complete, from buildout to moving of equipment and furniture to be fully operational in the new facility. I had high hopes: We had just ended a year with the highest-ever revenue and steady margins. We also had several existing contracts in place that were going to provide some special projects throughout the year, giving us an opportunity to make more investments in people and equipment to grow the company. We had a really talented group of young people, and I was excited about cultivating and developing their skills even further.

To help manage this fast-moving environment, I asked Mike to rejoin the team after a break of about two years. His departure likely had to do with burnout: Our contracts had very demanding requirements and each day brought a new fire to extinguish. When Mike agreed to return, I was thankful. We were 100% in sync with what we needed to do to move the company forward and to manage our growth opportunities. We had video calls a few times each week with the teams, including them in every update we received from our customers. It was important that everyone understand how business is done, what the terms and conditions were for each engagement, what our customers' expectations of us were and what reporting and post-service delivery deliverables we were responsible for.

In early March 2019, one of our customers informed us about a large project that was scheduled to start in September 2019. We started planning for this engagement as well.

This project was a multimillion-dollar engagement that had many moving parts and would take a couple of months to complete. Mike and I again met with our operations and technical service teams to map out our strategy. Even though we had a lot of warehouse space, we needed to increase our capacity to manage the new project as well as our existing workload. We therefore made a big investment in infrastructure, including shelving, moving equipment, vehicles and software to manage the growth. These were changes that also required additional training for all team members. We spent numerous hours on development calls with our software providers as well as other service providers for asset management systems. On the operational side of the house, we had to lay out a plan for our customer, identifying the staff that we would dedicate to the new project. We had to increase our insurance coverage so that every piece of customer equipment that was held in our facility would be covered against theft and loss. Even though there were other services we delivered as a company, such as annual software and solution renewals, equipment purchases and much more, these areas didn't require as much physical labor as the deployment work we were prepping for.

This year was an election year for local officials. I always paid close attention to elections, because a lot of our work as a company touches public sector customers such as schools, government agencies and municipalities. This election was unique because it ended in a run-off, which basically means that because there was no clear-cut winner on the main election night, a special election, or runoff, would have to occur. The run-off election resulted in a complete upset to the establishment. An outsider had won, and the political landscape shifted in ways not many could imagine—not all for the best. The challenge is that whenever a new person is elected to an office that controls purse strings, at a certain point, they make changes that impact everyone and every business in very different ways. This time was no different.

Dripping instead of flowing

Though we were always busy, September is when things really begin to pick up every year. Executives are back to work after their August vacations and government budget years begin. Many of our customers spend a great deal at this time and expect current and future orders to be processed immediately. Because our company worked as a Tier 2 provider, or subcontractor, to many large corporations, we lacked influence on scheduling of projects, order issuance and many other factors. Essentially, we go when our customer tells us to go.

That September, I noticed that some of our usual annual renewal orders were not coming in. I reached out personally to our customer to get a status update. They were having contractual issues that could not be disclosed, but they were aware that orders for our company were being affected, as well as other partners across the country. October rolled around, bringing more of the same: The orders we were expecting were not coming through, and our partner could not give us a date on when they would.

At the same time, our team was still attending in-person meetings and conference calls about the large deployment project that we were gearing up for. The customer kept telling us that the orders would be placed soon. This is the life we had grown accustomed to. It's like in the Army, where there is a common theme that everyone knows, which is "hurry up and wait."

As a result of the delays, we were burning through cash fast. Our main sources of revenue were dripping instead of flowing. We have a decent-sized team of workers and many suppliers, subcontractors and other obligations that still must be paid whether or not our customers are having procurement or contractual challenges. In early November, I was still in touch each week with our customers, asking for status updates. They could only provide limited information because of contract terms, but essentially, they were still trying to get things freed up for themselves, which in turn would free up our orders as well as those for partners throughout the country.

These days were sheer terror. Our phones were ringing off the hook, and email was blowing up from our "downstream" vendors that were waiting us on to process their orders. We couldn't issue purchase orders to providers if we hadn't received them from our customer. We had vendors that we couldn't pay because our cash flow was nearly non-existent. Every dollar that came in had been allocated to keeping the company going, to payroll and other obligations. I had excluded myself from payroll a long time ago to limit the burden on the company. Every night and day, I fervently prayed that the orders we so desperately needed would hit the next day. We had been through times in the past where our customer orders were slowed down and held up for various reasons, including the same ones we were dealing with today. The difference was that we were much smaller as a company then—and much more profitable.

Each day brought new hope and ultimately renewed pain: no orders, but many incoming calls from vendors. The only person at the office I could speak to about this situation was Mike. One day after a meeting with our tech team, Mike and I were sitting in the conference room. I received a call on my cell phone from a vendor who was as nasty as anyone could imagine. For some people, there is no rationalizing with them nor is there any hope that their humanity could mitigate their actions and emotions. I was on the receiving end of a vicious and hateful attack, all for the almighty dollar. After I ended the call, Mike looked at me and asked if I was OK. I closed the conference room door and shared my worries. I explained the difficulty of the holding pattern on these large engagements and how we were burning through every dollar that came in, trying to hold on. I told him I was not sure what to do but holding out hope was my only plan at this point. I felt relief to be able to talk to someone at work about the situation. Mike said he could see the stress on my face and knew that I must have been dealing with something pretty significant. We didn't leave the office until after 10p.m. that night, trying to work out ideas on the whiteboard to get out of this situation.

Monique and TJ also noticed the zombie that I had become. I was there, but not really there. I would be in the office by 7a.m. and not back home to 7p.m. or 8p.m. I sat while the family ate dinner, not hungry most of the time, and when I ate, I was just chewing to be chewing. I'd go to bed at 8:30p.m., feeling drained, hopeless and my mind exhausted from trying to come up with solutions. I woke up each night between 12:30a.m. and 2a.m., shocked out of my light sleep at the terror of what was happening with my business. It felt like someone hit me in the head with a bat, every night. I would sit up straight within seconds, look around to try to figure out where I was. I would turn and move toward the edge of the bed, leaning over and placing both hands on my face and both elbows on my knees. I had every nightmare, from losing the business, to vendors hiding outside the office and running up and shooting me as I left, to losing all my family's possessions, including our home.

Nothing shook these feelings. I tried: I prayed, I put on headphones and blasted music, I listened to church music, I watched videos on the internet of happy things, but nothing worked. I tried to read books and news articles but found my mind elsewhere instead of the words on the screen. I stayed there in bed, waiting on the sun to rise so I could go to the office and try something new. The problem was our company had grown to a point that we had a lot of overhead. It was required to service the contracts we were on, but because we were subcontractors, we had zero control of the engagements on those deals. There was nothing I could do. There was nothing our company could do.

I quickly learned that no one cared about what I was going through; they only cared about themselves in business. I was now seeing this firsthand, not as a third-party spectator. Mike called often—every hour it seemed. Having been through difficulties in his life, he knew the lonely feeling that settles in during such times.

A wake-up call

Monique was visiting her parents for a few days in Chicago during this time and knew I was stressed. One night in particular, at about 2:00a.m., I felt a very aggressive feeling: My heart was beating so hard and deep that I couldn't move. I was lying on my left side, where Monique usually was. I whispered her name, not remembering she wasn't there. I whispered again and moved my left hand to try to reach for her, but she was gone. I was too afraid to make any sudden movements because I felt like it would push my body past a certain point and my heart would stop. I could feel a sharp poking sensation that made me squint my eyes in pain. I could only take deep breaths, slowly exhaling. I felt that if I moved at all, even breathing any harder than I was doing, my heart would pop. I couldn't reach for my phone, sitting only a few inches from me to the right on my nightstand. I didn't have the strength to yell out to my son, nor did I want him to see me like this, especially if I was having a heart attack. I lay there in bed, thinking that this was the end. It was peaceful, like when I saw my mom pass. The only thoughts I had were of family and friends—and that I didn't want my son to find me dead when he got up to get ready for school.

I must have fallen back to sleep, because I remember the alarm clock on my phone buzzing at 6:25a.m. I know I didn't have a bad dream; it was real. I looked around to be sure I was home, not in heaven. I walked quickly to TJ's room and opened his door. I walked inside, leaned over and gave him the biggest hug and kiss ever. I quietly said a prayer thanking God that I was still here for him.

I called Mike earlier than I usually do and told him about my early morning "wake-up" call. Again, he could relate to this from personal experience. He told me that he had a status call on the big project and would hope to have some updates and possibly good news and would call me back right after.

I continued my daily routine, calling every business owner I knew, trying to get perspective and guidance. The interesting thing is, they were dealing with similar situations. Even though none of us had heard of COVID-19 at this point, nor did we ever imagine a pandemic, there was something already happening in the business world that was having an impact similar to the shutdowns of 2020. Government and corporate spending were way down. I was calling people for guidance, and the conversation turned to them asking me for guidance. None of the people I knew were sleeping at night either. They were laying off workers and had not been paying themselves for months, just like I was. I didn't feel comforted by these conversations. Instead, I felt even more stressed at the thought that the issues our company was facing were more widespread and impacted far more businesses than I initially thought. Every hour or so, I would have to get up and walk outside the office a few minutes.

I was in a deep haze, seeing only cloudy outlines of things I could clearly see days and weeks before. I walked more slowly than usual, each step more deliberate. My mind would not allow me to have visions beyond one or two days, not the usual months and years like I used to. I was truly a zombie, not smiling, operating on very little sleep, with the loss of my long-term outlook. I was feeling alone.

When Mike and I spoke again later that evening, he was in the office by himself. He had awful news: The project we were counting on had been pushed off until summer 2020, if then. I sat in silence, shaking my head, thinking that this was the end. I told Mike that I would call him tomorrow and he responded that he knew I needed to process the news and he would talk with me later.

I stood up from my desk and walked over to the couch in my office. I sat down, leaned back and stared out of the window. In this quiet, I thought about the fact that we were in a position that we didn't create, nor could we control. I thought about my family, my employees and partners. As I gazed into the abyss, I had a vision, not a dream as I was fully awake with my eyes open. The vision was my funeral. Monique and TJ were at the burial, TJ seated to her right. He was crying uncontrollably, so loudly that I could hear his heart beating. I saw Jerry and Mike, standing to Monique's left, leaning down slightly as she stared straight ahead at my casket, saying that they wished I would have let it all go.

I had this same vision the next day, as clear as day.

With just shy of 29 years in business and having spoken with more attorneys and our accounting firm, the dominant guidance was to close the company. I took the rest of the day to digest this thought and needed to get my family's input. I told Monique and TJ about what my advisors had recommended and asked what their opinions were. Monique said whatever I decided to do, she was with me 100%. She said we would do whatever we needed to move forward. TJ's advice was sage beyond his years: He took his right hand and made the up-and-down roller coaster motion, telling me that life is full of ups and downs, this is just one of them. He said that I should close the business sooner than later, to avoid getting into a deeper hole.

My daily, even hourly prayers had gone from asking for new orders, which never came, to thanking God for this experience. I was more thankful now for each day, knowing this experience was meant for my own good. I didn't know what lessons or blessings would come from this, but I was thankful for what did NOT happen, which was my sudden death.

The next day, I called my attorney back, let him know what my decision was, and he proceeded to dissolve the corporation. The week of Thanksgiving 2019, I had to let all my employees go and begin the most painful business journey I have ever been on to close my business. My attorney braced me for the fallout, including possible lawsuits or that our bank would come after our business—and me personally. He warned me that they would try to tarnish my reputation and make all sorts of accusations against me. He and others said this is the way it is; it's the way people are. Money is the most important thing to them, and they will do anything they can do get it. I told him that all that mattered was my life and that I was present for my family, and I'd deal with those things when they occurred.

I spent the next several months not knowing what to do each day. It was surreal, like I had awoken in another time, in another world. Nothing was normal. I experienced every possible emotion that I ever felt about business. I went from never wanting to say the word business again, to going to my office each day without checking email or answering the phone, per my attorney's counsel. There was still work I had to do, but it was geared toward the "wind down," as it is called when you close a company.

I thought I'd never sleep a full night again. In the night, my mind still raced, as my concerns moved to the suppliers and vendors and bank obligations that the company could not honor. I felt absolutely horrible. I had always lived a respectable life, and my word was my bond. My attorneys tried to provide some comfort in the process, asking me this question: Over the past 29 years, have any of your suppliers, customers and vendors gone out of business, meaning your company lost money? Yes, I replied, many times. Did your company survive, they asked? Yes, we did. What makes you so special that the world is going to end just because your company is no longer operating, they asked? I paused and reluctantly said, "We are not that special." This helped me to put the situation into a better frame. I had a similar conversation with our accounting firm owner. The owner explained during this conversation that she had a business failure many years ago and told me how bad it was. She also told me that I would get through it, and this is part of the risk we accept as business owners. We go out and take chances that others run from. The bigger the leap of faith, the more likely we are to fail. I understood all of this and knew it to be true, but that didn't keep me from having the real feelings I was dealing with.

The first time I slept the entire night since October was just before Christmas 2019. Friends of ours who have a condo here in PR were in town. We had been introduced to them by Ray and Tonya. They were having a small get-together at their place, but I didn't feel like leaving home. I was still dealing with trauma. Bruce insisted we stop by to say hello. I wanted to see them but didn't want to get dressed up and go outside. Bruce finally said they would stop by our house on their way to a relative's house. I was pleased with his determination and looking forward to spending time with them.

Out back, Ray, Bruce and I sat together, while the ladies were nearby sipping sangrias. Ray and Bruce have so much life experience to share. I could listen to them forever, soaking it all up, even while feeling half-man, half-zombie.

Hearing his story was a turning point for me. Slowly but surely, I was able to return to a positive space.

During this night, Bruce asked how business was going, and I gave him the update, blow by blow. He asked if I was getting any sleep and whether I could focus during the day. The questions went on until finally he said, "I'm going to slap you upside your head." Then he began to tell Ray and me his story, one that in some ways was worse than mine. I sat up a little straighter. With all that Bruce had endured, here he was able to talk about it without having a nervous breakdown. I felt hope for the first time. Hearing his story was a turning point for me. Slowly but surely, I was able to return to a positive space. I started to feel more upbeat and less solemn. Bruce was an angel that evening, coming to deliver a message of hope to me. I thank God for him and Ray and their willingness to be open and vulnerable with me.

Here is how I am coming to terms with what happened: There was a devastating train crash, a horrible explosion, an unexplainable accident, but I survived it. The exit wound is there, but it's healing slowly. And I am alive.

GAIN FROM PAIN:
I can do this

I learned many lessons from this experience. The power of the thoughts and feelings I had several years before closing the business became clear to me months after. Since Mom passed and Hurricane Maria blew through my life, my feelings on business had changed. They were no longer positive. I was going through the motions as I continued to try to build and grow the company, but my heart was no longer in it. It had become **difficult to separate the push to do better from the reality of the** *company. At some level, I felt guilty. Had my negative thoughts and feelings created the energy in the universe that I no longer wanted the company? I am very aware of the strength of the human mind and how it can manifest things for better or worse.*

Through this experience, I relearned the lesson of positivity, how powerful it is to appreciate everyone and everything you have, lest it be taken away.

Closing the business and all the subsequent drama, legal and other processes that follow are new to me. The pain is not. Even when this has hurt, I feel the power of being able to move beyond fear and pain. No pain compares to the loss of Mom and Dad, including the effects of the hurricane and the loss of my business. This pain is different. I'm equipped for it. Life has prepared me for this, only because I viewed prior experiences as lessons and held on to these lessons as tools for the future. Imagine if I had not lost material possessions during the hurricane; how would I manage losing material things after closing a business? While it is tough and no one wants to endure difficult times, I know I am strong enough to make it to the other side. I will come out better. I know this because I have faith that has been tested and tempered and proven true and resilient throughout the tests my life has brought.

I also know that in the greatest moment of stress—my wake-up call—I recognized what I needed to do for those who depend on me—and I did it.

13: THE GIFTS

Count your blessings

I've told you my story, from the family bonds of my childhood and the discoveries of my early adulthood to the hunger that drove me to build a business from nothing. I've shared the joy of my relationship with my parents and my good fortune in forging the life I was meant to live. I've also taken you through some of the most painful periods of my life, from the loss of my beloved father and mother to the devastation of Hurricane Maria and the difficult end to my business—and a large part of my identity and definition of success.

In some ways, my story is the story of any of us: Understand and follow your dreams, but don't forget to fortify yourself for the ups and downs of life. In other ways, though, my story is ripe for telling in 2020. Many of us—millions, in fact—have had the hardest year of our lives because of the COVID-19 pandemic. We've had

> *In some ways, my story is the story of any of us: Understand and follow your dreams, but don't forget to fortify yourself for the ups and downs of life.*

to change how we live, work, learn and socialize, often overnight. Without resilience, strength and faith, it can feel impossible to go on.

Yet the gift of pain can be ours, during and after this time. This is why I believe that telling my story can be a beacon of purpose during and after this difficult period.

I believe you can achieve every goal you set for yourself. I believe you can be the best person you were created to be. I offer you the lessons I have learned from personal experiences and those I have learned from people who have imparted wisdom into my heart.

The greatest success stories I've ever heard highlight the great distance the person traveled in the course of becoming what it is they were meant to be. It's in this period that we learn our greatest lessons and develop our greatest strengths. In my case, I began life in the most average way possible. Dad had only completed the third grade in school, Mom had a low-paying job as an administrative assistant, we had very limited money, and all our friends and neighbors were in similar positions. On my road to success, there were no handouts. We didn't win the lottery, and nothing shortened the time I had to spend on the road that needed to be traveled in order to receive my gifts.

This fact alone should give anyone reading this book immense hope and optimism. I know that if I was able to do it, you surely can. You have unique talents and abilities that, when presented to the world, will change your life forever. How, you ask? How do I, being in the position I am in today, get to the point I want to be in life? You look at the amount of money you have today and don't see how you can buy the new car, new house, pay the tuition, let alone save any money. "How can I start a business? I don't have the experience, and the banks won't loan me money," you say. "I can't lose weight because my work schedule doesn't allow me to have a consistent exercise schedule," you believe. "I can't do that, because my situation is different than everyone else's," you think.

But you can. What worked for me can work for you. The success formula is actually quite simple:

1. Understand and utilize fear.

2. Harness the power of positive thoughts and feelings.

3. Recognize the gifts that can only come from pain.

Let me explain.

1. Face your fears.

What is fear? At its most basic level, fear is simply a thought, a mental reaction to real or perceived threat. You may hear about something that someone else experienced and believe that you will end up with the same negative outcome they had. Or you may believe a story that your mind has created, and your body ultimately bought into, about an event that may possibly, but not surely, occur one day in the future.

Ask yourself: How many times have you feared something, and it never came to pass? Or, you did experience it, but the anticipation was worse than the reality? If you push past your fear, you will move beyond the paralysis it causes in your life.

I'll give you an example. Over the years, I've taken many people out on the ocean for a boat ride. We would stop and hook onto a mooring, say 100 yards from the beach. The water depth was typically between 15 and 25 feet. I encouraged everyone to get in the water so they could at least say they had the experience of swimming in the ocean. I helped get their life vests on and tightened the straps. I made sure their goggles were properly fitted and free of fog. Every time, the person would be ready, standing near the edge of the swim platform, frozen. The same questions came out of each of their mouths: Are there sharks in the water? How deep is the water, do the fish bite, are you coming in with me, is the water cold, what if I drown, how do I get back on the boat and how do I breathe when I get in the water? Every time, I would turn them toward me, with their back toward the ocean. I would say, "Look at my eyes. Do you trust me?" I would tell them that if I allowed my young son to get in the water, then it was safe. Then I'd ask again, "Do you trust me?" As soon as they said yes, I pushed them into the water. I then stepped toward the edge of the swim platform to observe. I waited for them to stop yelling and flopping around. Then I'd say, "Hey, stop fighting, take deep breaths and look at me. You are floating in a life vest with your head completely out of the water. "Take deep breaths." After a few seconds, they always calmed down and relaxed. I would then tell them to slowly lean their heads forward and put their goggles beneath the surface and tell me what they see. One-hundred percent of the time, they would follow my instructions, then soon after, raise their heads very fast and start hollering, "I see fish!" Letting go of fear led them to discovering new things in the water such as beautiful coral reefs, sea turtles, stingrays and even an occasional dolphin.

We solved one problem only to have to deal with the next one: I couldn't convince them to get back on the boat. They would talk about this adventure for hours, days and years. By moving past fear, voluntarily or involuntarily, they were able to experience an entirely new world. They saw things they had never seen before. They reaped the rewards that were on the other side of fear. Each person was very thankful for being pushed and has since pushed others to move past their fear.

This example may be specific but is true in every aspect of life. You might say, I've tried to work through my fear, but I have not been able to. I understand this is true for many people. The answer is to get someone to help you do so. The best athletes in the world have coaches. The most successful business and political leaders have coaches, advisors and counselors for this very reason. Don't use this as an excuse to potentially miss out on the best parts of your life.

Fear does not only make an appearance to alert you to bad things; it is an equal opportunity messenger that delivers a message that complacency is a safer place than success. Have you ever thought about starting a business, writing a book, changing jobs or moving past unfulfilling relationships, only to have your mind tell you that you will be leaving others behind, which will create pain for you and them? Has your mind convinced you that by striving to move forward, you will have to transform into a different person and people will view you differently? Does your mind have a love affair with the notion that money is the root of all evil, therefore convincing you not to pursue a more financially prosperous life?

When you have any of these or other similar thoughts, immediately move forward. While you can't prevent the thoughts from forming, you can quickly isolate and minimize the impact they have on your spirit. If you want to relocate to a different city and are excited about the possibilities the move will bring, but your mind starts to ask questions such as how, when, can I afford it and will I find new friends, then start looking for properties immediately. Do a search on places you want to live, the type of neighborhood you desire to live in and the weather that is most desirable to you. Do not give your mind the opportunity to talk you out of your dream. Once you start taking action, you'll find that the doubt and fear will go away. Your mind is now forced to focus on what is in front of it, which are photos of beautiful homes and the positive feelings your heart is now experiencing.

Do not give your mind the opportunity to talk you out of your dream.

Do you want to write a book? Don't think about whether it will sell, how vulnerable you will be by sharing your feelings or anything else. Pick up a pen and paper, open your computer or tablet and start writing. Motion creates emotion. Your mind will follow your heart, and your heart, if concentrating on what is possible, will bring you joy.

2. Think positive thoughts.

In order to achieve everything you want, you must change the way you think, speak and act. Every word you speak is a brick being laid onto the pathway to your tomorrow. If you speak hopelessness, fear, anger, doubt and any other word or phrase that lacks positivity, your path will be made of fragile ground that easily crumbles under the weight of the smallest pressure. Your surroundings will seem to mirror the way you described them as being. If you speak with confidence, hope, resolve and gratitude, your path will be made of material strong enough not only to support you but all the people you want to bring along on the journey with you.

Each time I experience difficulty in life, I always remember the phrase, "This too shall pass." It has always been true. Each day, start with thanks for what you have, beginning with life. Be thankful for the smallest things, such as being able to breathe, being able to call a friend or family member to say good morning. Gratitude makes you happier and more centered. Success is more about mindset than anything else. There is always someone in life in a much worse position than you. I think about this as well when challenging situations come my way. I think to myself that as bad as this may be, someone has it worse than me. I immediately feel better, because of the gratitude I feel and the confidence I have, forged through experience, that I can get through it.

Give your dreams and desires the attention and focus they deserve. Eliminate words and phrases such as "I can't,

I don't have, I can't afford, I don't know how, I wish I could, I'm broke, nothing good ever happens to me, I have bad luck and that will never happen to me."

Replace them with words and phrases such as "I can, I have everything I need, I will be the best, I will achieve my goals, I have good friends and family, I appreciate my job and I can make the money I need."

By doing this, you will begin to feel optimism, hope and passion. You will also notice as you look around that you have much more than most people across the world.

Cultivate your sphere of control and influence. Turn off the television, disconnect from social media, stay off the internet and block out all the outside sources that deliver the messages they want you to digest as opposed to what your heart needs. Does anyone else know what makes you happy inside, besides you? Are your hopes and dreams important to you? Do you want to have peace in your life? Turn off everything. If you spend only two hours each day watching TV and on social media, that equals 728 hours per year. The more sobering fact is that you spend more than 30 days per year allowing news outlets and social media personalities to pour toxic content into your mind and spirit. I imagine the average person spends way more time than this having their minds altered by what is important to others as opposed to what is important to you.

Once, I was no different than you. I digested so much news in the past, feeling that I needed to keep up with current affairs. I felt it was important to my business survival as well as crucial to being aware of global issues and concerns.

I remember waking up in the morning and turning on the news channels while getting ready for work. Although I couldn't see everything happening on the screen, I could hear the reports. Once I left home, there was always a sense of concern in the air, not optimism. There was an ever-present cloud, threatening to rain on me, be it in the form of partisan politics, rampant crime or a failing economy. This was what my mind focused on because this is what I allowed to enter my mind. Fast-forward to recent years. I made the conscious decision to stop watching the news for a few days to focus on a project I was involved in. My daily routine was the same, but I felt more optimistic. My feelings were consistent, not constantly fluctuating between sad and happy. The world continued to exist, even though I did not have specific details about current events. My focus increased significantly, and I had an overall better demeanor. Once the project was completed, I turned on the news the next morning as I had done for years. I noticed almost immediately that I felt anxious and concerned. I was not confident of the future and overall I became more pessimistic. The only change was what I had allowed in my mind that day, in the form of unwanted and undesirable information from the television.

I cannot stress how important it is for you to stop other people from feeding you things that are unhealthy. Spending time on social media, looking at photos posted by "influencers" standing in front of their rented cars and rented homes is no different than watching negative stories on the news. Your mind will convince you that somewhere in your life, you are not worthy. It will whisper that you will never accomplish your dreams. You see other people who are your age and younger living their best life while you are still trying to figure out what your purpose is. None of these thoughts you experience are true. They are a way for your mind to process the images you are allowing it to see and trying to somehow associate them with you. Turn it off.

I listen to music, I listen to podcasts and I watch television. I now use these as vehicles to deliver positive, upbeat, encouraging and informative messages to my mind and spirit. I choose the content and influences that I desire instead of allowing others to dictate what I should consume.

You will see immediate results.

3. Unwrap the gift of pain.

Another reason people don't live their best lives is because of pain. They fear it. But pain is part of every life. If you are a good person and things have happened that caused you pain, small or great, you can get past it.

I think back to how I first leaned to overcome fear and deal with pain in my childhood. Fear is an instinct, of course, but you can strengthen your response. My parents pushed me so much early on that I didn't have the opportunity to consider whether I should be afraid or not about anything I was encountering.

Even today, I would jump into any body of water in the ocean, board any helicopter or airplane that can fly, walk among wild animals and spend countless hours in the dark mountains along the Appalachian Trail by myself.

Is there danger in any of these environments? Of course, but I understand that on the other side of the fear lie unbelievable rewards. That's what I choose to focus on. Fear is temporary and will go away as soon as I walk toward the goal.

Many people are fearful about starting a business, writing a book, giving a speech and exploring unfamiliar parts of the world. Here's a dirty little secret about business: You have more control of your future and financial stability in your own business than you ever will working for someone else. Why? Because you can see the pitfalls and challenges ahead when you are in business; you can't when you are an employee. The last person to see the layoff coming is the person being laid off from a job. If you are a business owner and you see hazards up ahead, you at least can try to avoid them. You can work day and night to adjust your business model to adapt to changing times. You can bring on unpaid interns to assist during difficult times until you can afford to pay them. Now tell me, are you more afraid of knowing in advance you'll face challenges or going to work tomorrow morning not knowing that you will be let go? I'd never want someone else to determine my fate.

The longer you sit and think about the risks of acting, the more stories your mind will create to talk you out of moving forward. My mind is constantly processing the things I see, hear, smell, taste and feel. I've learned to silence my thoughts. How many times have you had a great idea, then the longer you thought about it, your mind convinced you that it was a bad idea? Your mind said you didn't have enough money to do it, nobody would believe in you and many other things that made you ultimately give up. You convince yourself that it is easier to just stay at the same place you live today than to move across country. You think, "Starting a business is hard, and I might make less money than I make at my job today. Plus, I would be working way more hours than I do now. What was I thinking?" The fear that is created when your mind presents the worst-case scenarios to you each second of each day can be overwhelming. You try to think of "safe places" in your head to avoid the fearful ones. These places are graveyards filled with the unfulfilled treasures of imagination, creation, greatness and progress. How many dreams have been buried before they ever had a chance to be brought to life by one of us? I am not the smartest nor the hardest-working person I know. What I do know for sure, however, is that I will take a chance and try when others won't. I've learned to move past fear, take my chances and work toward the goals I have. If I fail, I fail.

Embrace your fear and prove it wrong. The more times in life you act despite those thoughts, the more your brain gets used to the idea that it no longer controls you. When this happens, your brain will take your lead and shift its energy to figuring out how to do the positive things your heart desires.

You can gain an extraordinary gift in life is when you can experience pain, eventually come to grips with it, and even identify and receive the blessings of the experience. No one wants to experience loss in any form, whether the loss is a loved one, or business, finances or a relationship. When you have experienced all of these, "You see how the pain differs in each. If you live long enough, you will experience many episodes of pain.

During my still-young life, I've seen and experienced many painful moments that have turned into memories that will last forever. Fear may be in your mind, but you feel pain in your physical body, including your heart. You can't simply tell your body not to feel the pain and it will go away; that's not how it works. Pain is real and lasts, and the life of pain **differs**. The pain of losing material things may last only a few hours or days, until you replace what was taken or destroyed. The pain from the loss of loved ones will never go away, although it may become a little less potent as the years go by.

My earliest experience with true pain in my heart was when my dad died. As a child, this was exactly what I prayed would not happen. I prayed that my parents would live forever. I couldn't imagine burying a parent. The pain was intense and unlike any other I had ever felt. The earthly compass that I referred to so often, which had guided me toward manhood and fatherhood, was gone. The immediate sense of loss made my whole inner world turn upside-down. I still can't think about Dad too long without tears forming in my eyes, but I now use the power of pain for good, not sorrow. I know that his job on earth was done. He raised his children, got to see the birth of his grandchildren, and it was time for him to sit under that Georgia peach tree in heaven and watch us from there. Changing my vision of Dad from what is was the day of his death to him being the first angel in heaven that I can call by name was so powerful. I turned to the pain and said, "You will not hold me back. You will not stop me from living the best life I can." Those tears I cry are not because I'm sad; they are because of the immense love I feel when I think about him. I can feel the power of his spirit more than I could when he was here on earth with me. He is still my compass in many ways; as I think about how to navigate situations today, I consider what he would suggest. I turned my pain into motivation to be the best father I could.

Even when the toughest of times confront you, life continues all around you. I had to choose whether to ball up in a corner and feel sorry for myself because of my pain or to honor my father. My workdays were fueled by determination to be half the man my father was. Because of this conversion from pain to motivation, my company's revenue doubled within three years. Death is not the end of life unless it is you who has died.

The pain that came along with my mom's cancer diagnosis—and the two years of living with cancer and her ultimate death from it—was the longest period of sustained pain I had experienced. I had something already that would help me with this process though. The pain of my dad's death gave me the strength to handle my mother's in a different way. I had tools that I could now use for this next difficult period.

Even while sitting with Mom for those three weeks prior to her passing, I was developing tools that I would need soon for situations that I could have never predicted. I was conscious enough to know this at the time, so I observed every little detail I could when I was with Mom: every facial expression, every body movement, every spiritual sign, I made a note of and tucked it into my heart. I did not want Mom to go but, like after my dad's passing, I knew her job here on earth was complete.

My mother gave me—and everyone who visited her those last days of her life—the most informative gift I have received to this point in life. My view of the world had forever shifted: Mom showed me that life came down to a few simple things: Her faith in God, her family and her friends. She didn't care about anything else at that time. It was peaceful sitting on the side of her bed as she leaned on my shoulder. Nothing mattered but the moment we were sharing. Mom allowed us to witness her transition from the natural world to the spiritual world. I saw the physical and spiritual changing each day, and it was subtle, not violent. It was like a caterpillar becoming a butterfly. Mom showed us a level of grace, peace, elegance and faith that I had never witnessed in my entire life. One night while sitting in Mom's room, the day before she passed, I remember saying to myself that I was not afraid of death. It had been demystified right in front of my eyes. There was no pain in me at this point. I was extremely sad after she passed, but the pain that I had a few days ago had blossomed into an enormous amount of positive energy and hope. I knew that my second angel, Mom, would be teaming up with Dad and push through even more blessings for me and family.

Again, life continued all around me, and there was no pause button that I could press to deal with the loss. We turned the upcoming summer into a rebirth instead of a memorial. Monique had one of the biggest business successes with her Overflow event in San Juan. Following this, we had our family back at our house to hold our annual summer reunion. One night, we lit and released Kongming "sky lanterns" in the mountains near our house and watched them drift over the Caribbean Sea in her honor.

Here was another opportunity to use the pain for energy. The company grew again and had its best year ever until that point. You can recover from every painful situation. It may take longer than you want, but I promise, it can happen.

If you've ever heard a pastor or preacher use a metaphor for difficult times in life, they usually call it a storm. They also like to refer to the terrain of the earth, such as valleys, mountains, streams, rivers and so many other. Well, these analogies are usually accurate. When Hurricane Maria visited us, we were prepared in so many ways. I had been through so many ups and downs over the years, managing emotions, experiencing unfathomable loss, that when the little storm hit, I had no fear. My emotional toolbox was full. I had gathered so many tools over all the years of dealing with adverse situations. Some of these tools you never want to use again. Others you dust off and use more frequently. It's interesting that my friends tell me, even today, that they never worried about us during the storm and the aftermath. They said that they knew that if anyone could survive a horrendous tragedy it would be me and everyone around me. They were saying that I'm the ultimate survivalist. What they point out is that over all the years, they have witnessed how I dealt with difficult times and came out better than I went it. I believe this with 100% certainty as well. Because of my ability to transform my fear and pain into gifts and use those gifts to move forward, I find that I perform extremely well under pressure. The most important tool I have is my faith in God. With the spiritual and worldly lessons and blessings, how can I not push through difficult times?

Less than two short years after Maria devastated us, my business crashed and burned after posting record revenues from the previous year. From this tragedy, I have been able to witness more gifts than I can ever imagine. I continue to say each day that this too shall pass. As I look in my rear-view mirror sometimes, I can see the many breadcrumbs along the path that lead me to the lessons I learned as a child. Nothing has happened to me—none of these deeply painful events. They happened to others I care about, they happened to my home, they happened to my business.

I'm still standing.

I reject the thinking that somehow all bad things happen to me. That would create a negative energy in the universe, something that I refuse to do. All the experiences I've had have given me tools for the future, insights, lessons, and inspiration. Closing my business could be considered a failure by some, but I view it differently. If I would not have taken a chance and pushed past the fear and prospect of pain, I would have never started a business. The gifts that came from the profits of the business are immeasurable. We employed hundreds of young, talented people over the years. We helped people obtain apartments and homes through the income they made from the company. Children in a small Kenyan town in Africa now have the only technology center available to them in the entire region. Thirty-seven children have been formally educated because of the charitable giving our company did in Kenya.

There are so many gifts and blessings that were realized because I took a leap of faith and took a chance. This is no failure; it is a success. In the Army, we had days of physical training that were named "muscle failure" days. This meant we would be pushed beyond what our minds told us our bodies could achieve. If I felt like the most I could do was 75 push ups, they would push me to do 80 or 85. I learned to push hard and fail, get back up, push even harder, then fail again. Dust off my face, spit the mud from my teeth and try even harder. When I could no longer move because my arms were shaking from muscle failure, then I could stop. Until then, I had to keep moving. I learned that failing meant I first had to try. I had to take a stance. I had to take a leap of faith. I had to push myself beyond anything I thought my physical and mental being would allow. I never viewed failure from that point on as anything but confirmation that I was attempting to do great things.

I will never stop or be satisfied until I no longer breathe the air that fills my lungs. After the slow singing and last family member has left my graveside, will I stop fighting to be the best I can be and achieving every goal I strive for. Failure only serves to show me which way doesn't work, so I can get back up and try a different path.

I am sharing a few of the tough times I've experienced in life and how I was able to move past them over time. I have met some extraordinary people from across the world. There are some common traits among them. Traveling has been one of the best teachers of life's lessons, as I was able to see how others live and what makes them happy. You can also get an understanding of what success looks like to them. At its core, life is really about family and friends and the experiences we share along this journey with them. I believe in God, and faith and trust are the most important factors in my life by far. You may or may not believe in a higher power, and that's OK.

The most precious gifts I've ever received came from the potential for the greatest amount of pain. One was Monique carrying our son TJ for nine months, then enduring the pain of childbirth. We were born into an environment of pain. The second was witnessing my mom's last breath and death. These are two times in our lives when we cannot escape pain, birth and death, but we can still thrive after each.

The happiest faces I've ever seen were from the people that have the least in material possessions and creature comforts. Their joy each day is rooted in the time they spend talking with each other, enjoying meals together and seeing their children and grandchildren grow.

The most successful people I've had the privilege of spending time with also share some common traits. They never give up, and they believe in whatever it is they are working toward. If you blend simplicity, the ability to push past pain and a strong belief system, you can accomplish the most amazing

If you blend simplicity, the ability to push past pain and a strong belief system, you can accomplish the most amazing things.

things. I have a belief that if another man can do something,

I can as well. This simply means that there are no super-humans born with unrealistic skills and talents. Everything you need to succeed in life is already within you. You can become extraordinary, by going the "extra" step while others are simply doing the "ordinary." Think about what holds you back from doing the things you really want to do. Is there pain associated with moving past those things in order to live the life you want? Now, consider the pain of one day running out of time and realizing that you didn't achieve the goals you once had in life. Which is more painful?

The blade of a steel sword is forged by heating it up to very high temperatures, usually upwards of 1600 degrees Fahrenheit. Diamonds are formed by heat and pressure as well. Our character, as humans, is also created and formed by the tough experiences we endure during life. Each time you experienced pain in the past, it added a level of perseverance to your being. Each time you overcame fear in the past, you gained an added sense of confidence to your mind. Every challenge you failed at gave you courage. You have more strength inside of you than you can imagine. Consider what you have already been through. Life has already provided many opportunities for you to overcome fear, pain and other difficulties, and you're still here, still standing. Celebrate those victories. The lessons we have learned are cumulative and have prepared us for the next time a challenging event will occur. It will be difficult, but you will get through it for sure. You can do anything you want, and your past is all the evidence you need to know this to be true. When thoughts of failure and disappointment periodically creep into your mind, remind yourself that you learned valuable lessons from them in the past. Realize that failing at something is not bad; not attempting to do something is.

We get a new opportunity each morning to create the life we want. Nothing can stop you but yourself if you follow your heart, never quit and don't run from anything that will ultimately make you stronger, including pain.

Your birth created extreme pain for your mother. There is a reason you are here, beyond what you may already realize. Through someone else's pain, you came into existence and have the ability to reward others with the talents and gifts you have been endowed with. Step from behind the clouds of fear and pain, and let the world see you shine.

ACKNOWLEDGEMENTS

Monique – I could have never imagined the love, support, friendship and experiences we would realize since first meeting in 1991. I openly express to the world that you are my better half. We are figuring out life together, and because of you, I have become a better person. My heart is protected by you, my mind is challenged by you and my love has grown because of you.

TJ – When I see your face, nothing else matters. Each time you smile, my hopes and dreams of being the best dad possible comes into focus, hoping that I served you well. One day you will have your own family, and my hope is that you will look back at our time together and know that I did my best with the tools I had to be a great father. You are the best part of me. Please carry my flame after I am reunited with Grandma and Grandpa.